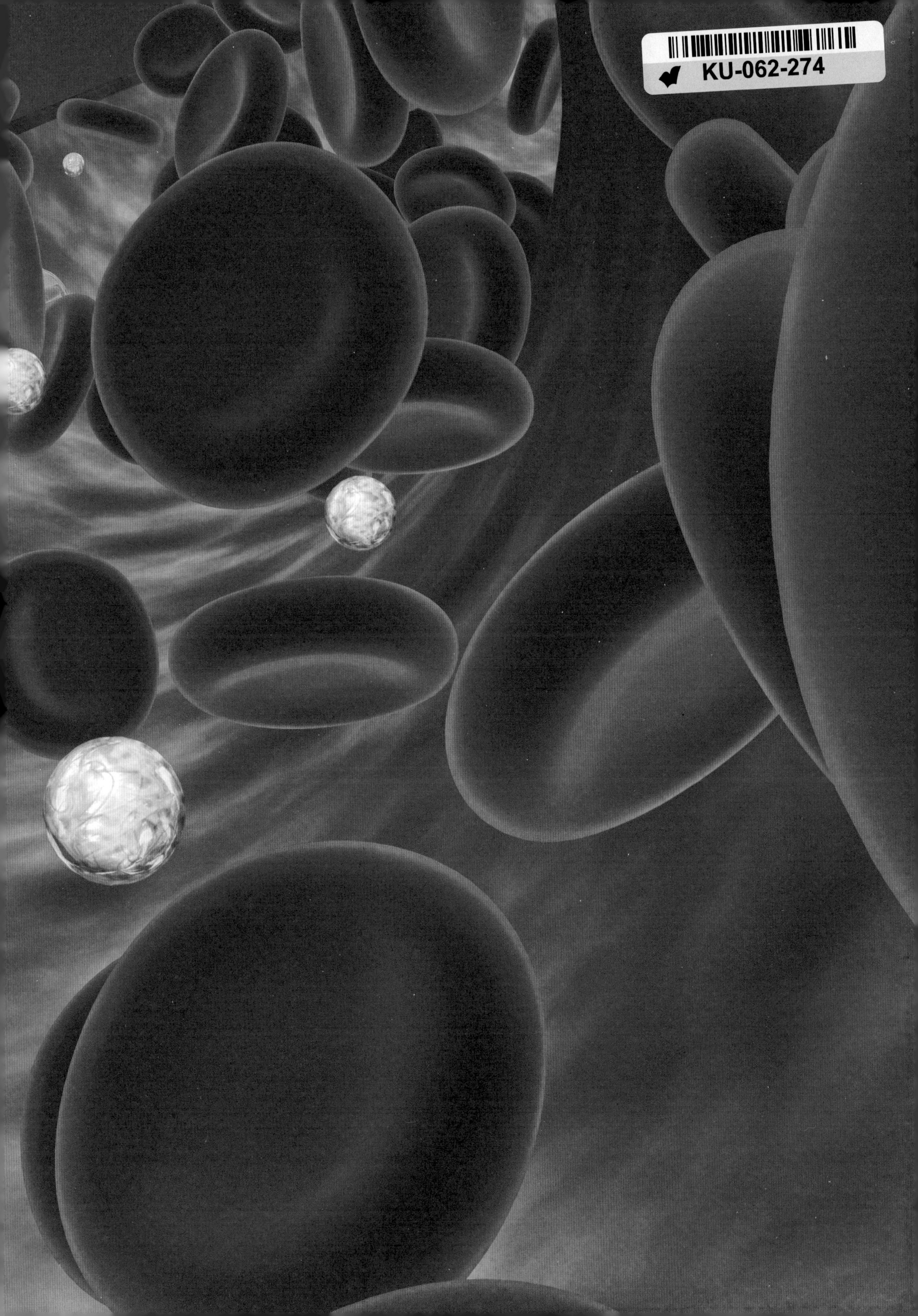

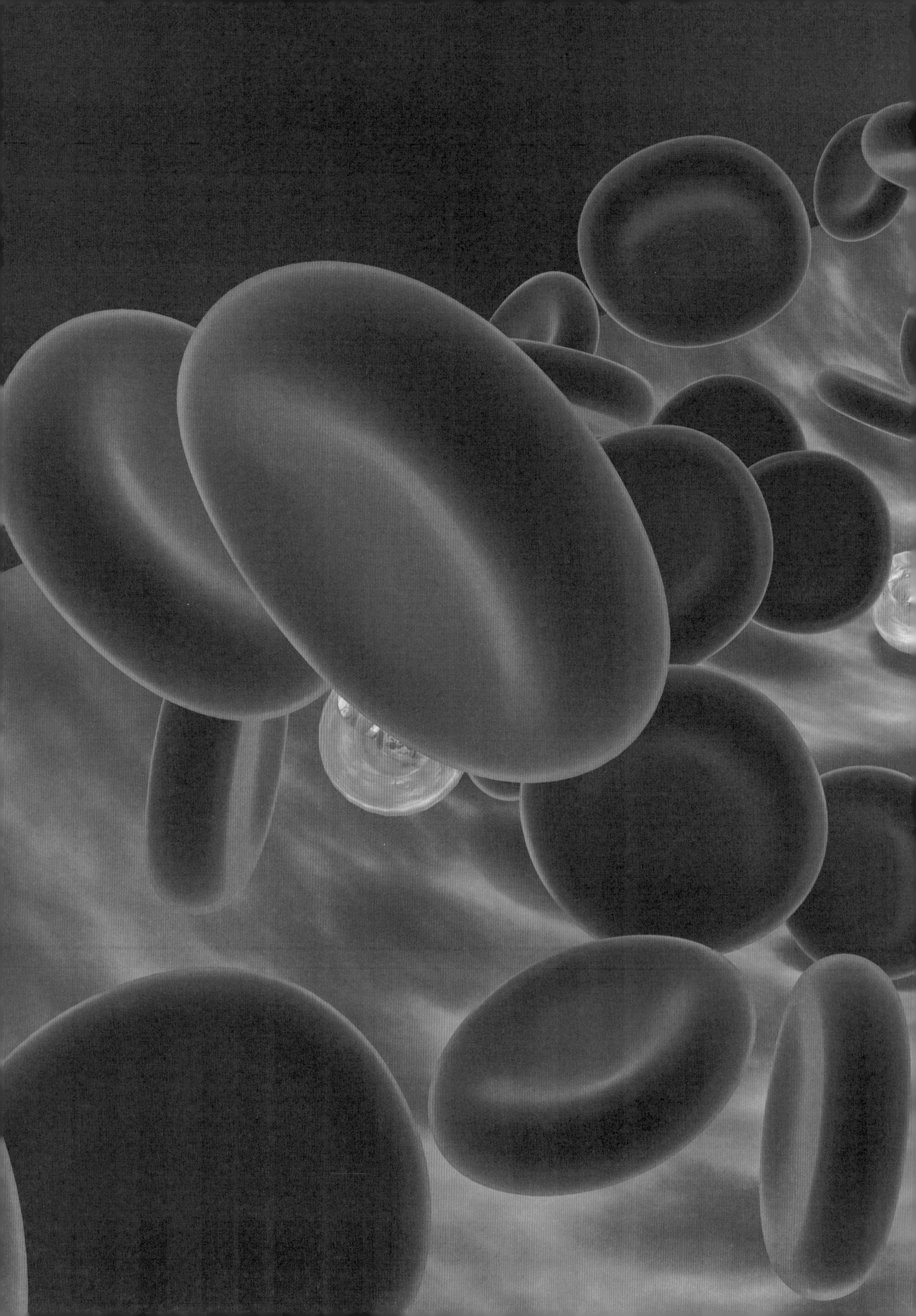

The Ultimate Guide
BODY

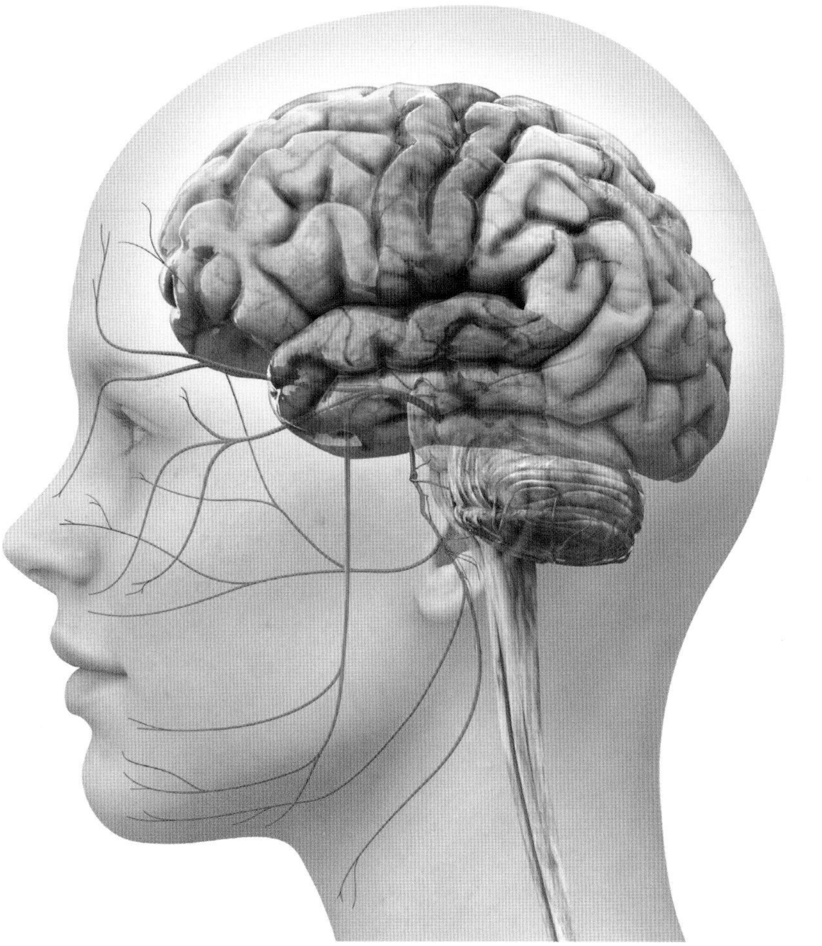

Miles Kelly

First published in 2016 by
Miles Kelly Publishing Ltd
Harding's Barn, Bardfield End Green,
Thaxted, Essex, CM6 3PX, UK

2 4 6 8 10 9 7 5 3 1

Authors Eleanor Clarke BSc MB ChB MD, John Farndon, Dr Kristina Routh MB ChB

Publishing Director Belinda Gallagher
Creative Director Jo Cowan
Editorial Director Rosie Neave
Senior Editor Sarah Parkin
Cover Designer Simon Lee
Design Manager Joe Jones
Image Manager Liberty Newton
Indexer Marie Lorimer
Production Elizabeth Collins, Caroline Kelly
Reprographics Stephan Davis, Jennifer Cozens, Thom Allaway

ISBN 978-1-78209-989-5

Printed in China

British Library Cataloguing-in-Publication Data
A catalogue record for this book is available from the British Library

Made with paper from a sustainable forest

www.mileskelly.net

ACKNOWLEDGEMENTS

The publishers would like to thank Tim Loughhead for the artworks he has contributed to this book.

All other artworks are from the Miles Kelly Artwork Bank

The publishers would like to thank the following sources for the use of their photographs:

Key: t = top, b = bottom, c = centre, l = left, r = right, m = main

Front cover Deposit Photos/Glowimages.com, circle (& pocket) BioMedical

Main pages

Dreamstime.com 10(tl) Mykola Velychko, (bc) Fragles; 44(b) Cb34inc; 45(c) Elena Schweitzer; 51(t) Axelkock, (b) Galina Barskaya; 55(tl) & (br) Jelen80

Fotolia.com 35(t) chrisharvey; 43(b) NiDerLander; 45(t) Celso Pupo, (b) Elena Schweitzer

iStockphoto.com 22(t) Enjoylife2; 31(t) David Marchal; 38(t) cdascher; 46(t) hartcreations

Shutterstock.com 3 & 59(b) Africa Studio; (rt 4–17) Sebastian Kaulitzki; 4(l)BlueRingMedia; 7(tr) BlueRingMedia; 11(t) Galina Barskaya, (bc) Harm Kruyshaar; 12(c) Ilike; 15(t) Air Images, (b) aastock; 16(t) Andresr, (b) Valua Vitaly; 17(tl) wavebreakmedia, (br) Maridav; (rt 18–27) BioMedical; 23(tl) Mopic; 26(b) Pete Saloutos; 27(tc) Alila Medical Media; (rt 28–39) zimowa; 29(b) Mega Pixel; 30(t) Sebastian Kaulitzki; 34(t), (b) Alila Medical Media; 35(b) Alila Medical Media; 36(br) Galina Barskaya; (rt 40–49) Vlue; 42(b) Nerthuz; 43(t) ifong; 44(t) Sergieiev; 47(t) decade3d – anatomy online, (b) Gordon Bell; 48(tr) Markus Mainka; 49(t) Hans Christiansson, (b) Tefi; (rt 50–62) Tatiana Makotra; 50(tr) CLIPAREA l Custom media; 52(tr) Lisa F. Young; 54(br) CroMary; 58(bl) FamVeld; 62(t) hartphotography, (b) michaeljung

Science Photo Library 13(c) Jacopin/BSIP; 14(tr) Clouds Hill Imaging LTD; 20(bl) Sputnik; 21(tr) Zephyr; 22(bl) Medical RF.com; 23(br) Steve Gschmeissner; 27(br) Ami Images; 29(t) Mikkel Juul Jensen; 30(bl) & 31(b) Sebastian Kaulitzki; 37(b) Jacopin; 60(tr) Kateryna Kon

Acetate feature pages

Head 8(tr) tmcphotos/Shutterstock.com; acetate (tr) Alfred Pasieka/Science Photo Library, (br) Dave Roberts/Science Photo Library; 9(tr) Medical Body Scans/Science Photo Library, (br) Alexilusmedical/ Shutterstock.com

Chest 24(tr) Wallenrock/Shutterstock.com, (br) V. Yakobchuk/Fotolia.com; acetate (cr) BlueRingMedia/Shutterstock.com, (br) Du Cane Medical Imaging LTD/Science Photo Library; 25(tr) Alila Medical Media/ Shutterstock.com, (bc) Pavel L Photo and Video/Shutterstock.com

Muscles and bones 32(tr) Vector Goddess/ Shutterstock.com, (bc) Creations/Shutterstock. com; acetate (bc) Jacob Lund/Shutterstock. com, (br) Monkey Business Images/ Shutterstock.com; 33(tr) Medical Images, Universal Images Group/Science Photo Library, (bc) Puwadol Jaturawutthichai/ Shutterstock.com

Abdomen 40(b) Asklepios Medical Atlas/ Science Photo Library, (tr) mimagephotography/ Shutterstock.com, (br) Carol and Mike Werner/Science Photo Library; acetate (br) Monica Schroeder/Science Photo Library; 41(br) Picsfive/Shutterstock.com

Pregnancy 56(tc) Mega Pixel/Shutterstock. com, (tr) nevodka/Shutterstock.com; acetate (bl) koya979/Shutterstock.com, (br) Hans-Ulrich Osterwalder/Science Photo Library; 57(bl) Bernard Benoit/Science Photo Library, (br) Shippee/dreamstime.com

All other photographs are from: Corel, digitalSTOCK, digitalvision, Fotolia, iStock/Getty, PhotoDisc

Every effort has been made to acknowledge the source and copyright holder of each picture.

Miles Kelly Publishing apologizes for any unintentional errors or omissions.

Contents

NERVES & SENSES

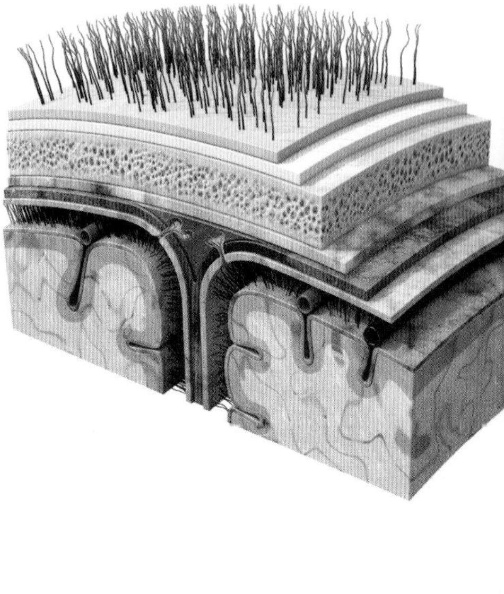

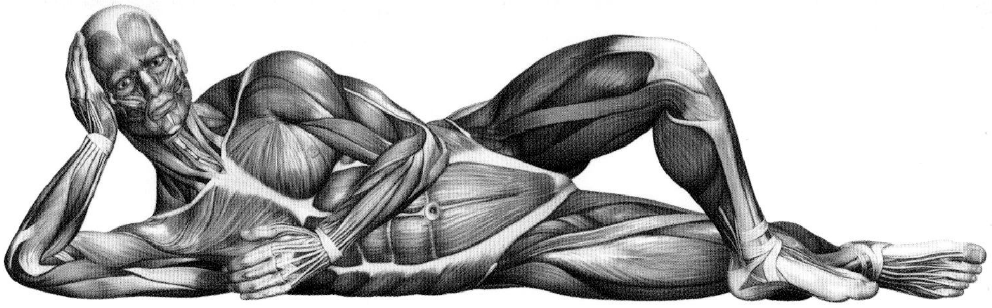

HEART & LUNGS

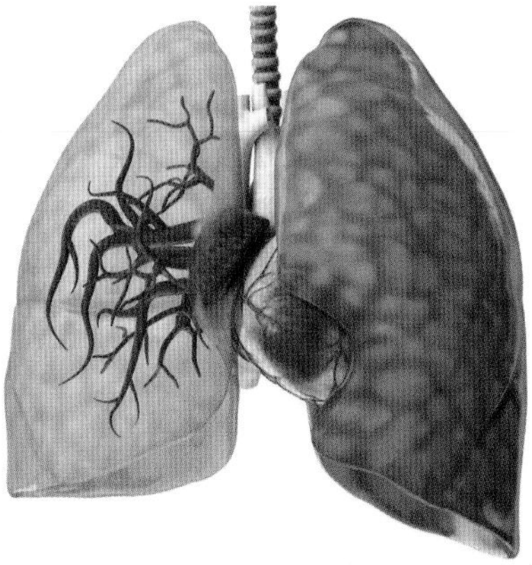

TISSUES, MUSCLES & BONES

DIGESTION & NUTRITION

HORMONES, DEVELOPMENT & IMMUNITY

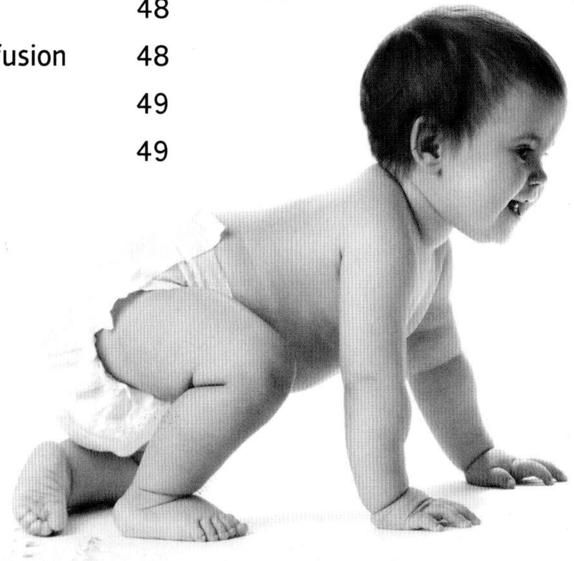

The nervous system

DID YOU KNOW?

The longest and largest nerve is the sciatic nerve, which is as wide as your thumb.

- **The nervous system** is the body's control and communication system, made up of nerves, the spinal cord and the brain. Nerves carry instant messages from the brain to every organ and muscle – and send back a constant stream of data to the brain about what is going on both inside and outside the body.

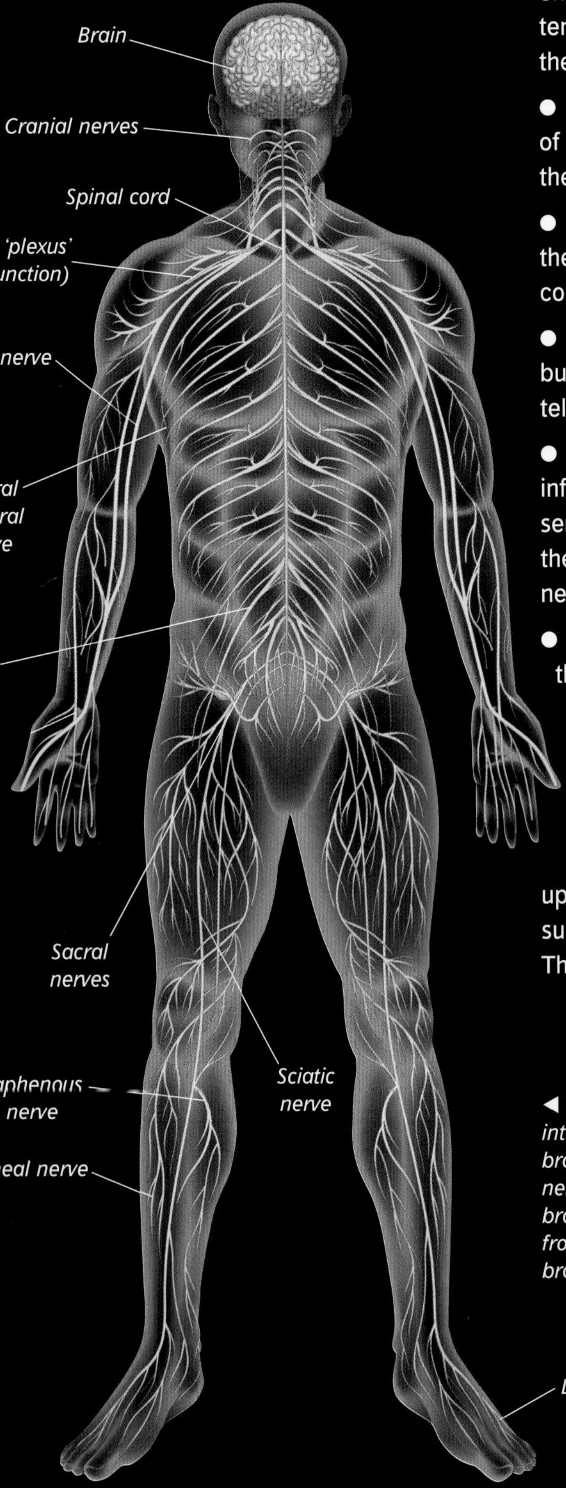
Brain
Cranial nerves
Spinal cord
Brachial 'plexus' (nerve junction)
Ulnar nerve
Lateral pectoral nerve
Lumbar nerves
Radial nerve
Sacral nerves
Saphenous nerve
Sciatic nerve
Peroneal nerve
Lateral plantar nerve

- **The central nervous system** (CNS) is the brain and spinal cord.
- **The CNS** maintains all bodily functions that keep you alive, and can adjust according to the environment you are in. For example, it controls body temperature, appetite and breathing. The CNS is also the source of thoughts, emotions and memories.
- **The peripheral nervous system** (PNS) is made up of the nerves that branch out in pairs from the CNS to the rest of the body.
- **The PNS** are the 12 cranial nerves in the head, and the 31 pairs of spinal nerves that branch off the spinal cord.
- **The nerves of the PNS** are made up of long bundles of nerve fibres, arranged like the wires in a telephone cable.
- **Nerves that contain only fibres** that send information to the brain from the body are called sensory nerves. Nerves that only send signals from the brain to the body are called motor nerves. Mixed nerves contain both types of fibre.
- **The autonomic nervous system** (ANS) is the body's third nervous system. It controls all internal body processes, such as breathing, automatically, without you even being aware of it.
- **The ANS** is split into two complementary (balancing) parts – the sympathetic and the parasympathetic. The sympathetic system speeds up body processes when they need to be more active, such as when the body is exercising or under stress. The parasympathetic slows them down.

◀ The nervous system is an incredibly intricate network of nerves linking the brain to every part of the body. The nerves of the peripheral nervous system branch out to every limb and body part from the central nervous system (the brain and spinal cord).

Nerve cells

- **Nerves are made of cells** called neurons that link up like beads on a string.
- **Neurons are spider-shaped cells**. They have a cell body (the power house), a number of slender projections (dendrites) from the cell body that receive signals, and a long tail-like projection called an axon, which can be up to 1 m long.
- **The axon** ends in club-shaped swellings called axon terminals that transmit the nerve impulse to other nerve cells by linking with the cell body or the dendrites.
- **Neurons cannot multiply** like other body cells, so they cannot be replaced if they are damaged. However, neurons have a long life and can live for over 100 years.
- **Neurons need** a plentiful supply of oxygen and glucose to keep working.
- **The outer skin** (membrane) of a neuron is electrically active. A nerve signal is a series of electrical pulses each lasting about 0.001 sec that passes along the axon to another nerve cell.
- **With myelin**, nerve signals travel at 100 m/sec. Without myelin the signals travel at 1–2 m/sec.

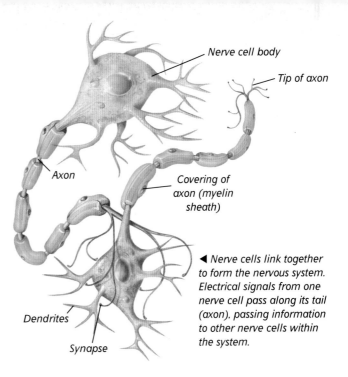

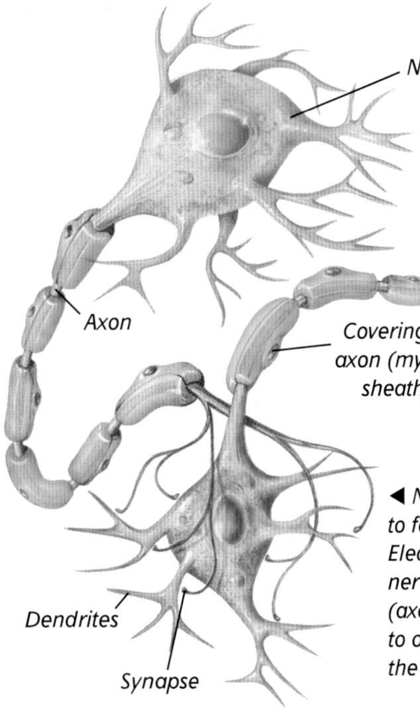
Nerve cell body
Tip of axon
Axon
Covering of axon (myelin sheath)
Dendrites
Synapse

◀ *Nerve cells link together to form the nervous system. Electrical signals from one nerve cell pass along its tail (axon), passing information to other nerve cells within the system.*

- **The axons of long-distance nerves** are insulated by a sheath of a fatty substance called myelin. This stops the electrical signal from weakening as it travels.
- **The electrical pulse** of a nerve cell firing is created by the movement of electrically charged body salts (sodium and potassium) in and out of the nerve cell.

Synapses

- **Synapses are the gaps** between nerve cells.
- **When a nerve signal** goes from one nerve cell to another, it must be transmitted (sent) across the synapse by neurotransmitters.
- **Neurotransmitters are chemicals** used to relay, amplify (increase) and alter electrical signals between a neuron and another cell.
- **Droplets of neurotransmitter** are released into the synapse whenever a nerve signal arrives.
- **As the neurotransmitter droplets** lock onto the receiving nerve's receptors, they fire the signal onwards.
- **Each receptor site** on a nerve-ending only reacts to certain neurotransmitters.

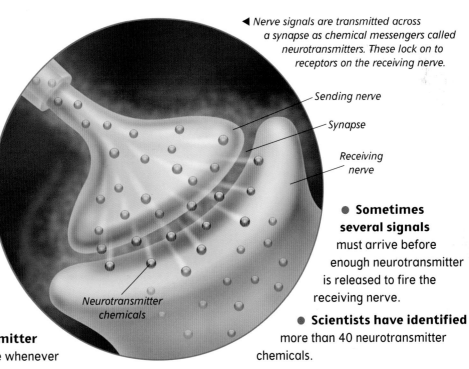

◀ *Nerve signals are transmitted across a synapse as chemical messengers called neurotransmitters. These lock on to receptors on the receiving nerve.*

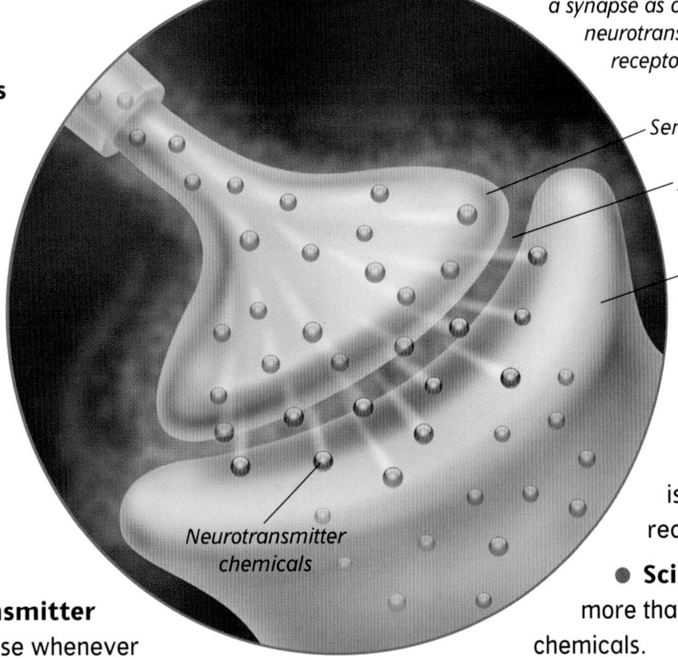
Sending nerve
Synapse
Receiving nerve
Neurotransmitter chemicals

- **Sometimes several signals** must arrive before enough neurotransmitter is released to fire the receiving nerve.
- **Scientists have identified** more than 40 neurotransmitter chemicals.
- **Dopamine** is a neurotransmitter that works in the parts of the brain that control movement and learning.
- **Serotonin** is a neurotransmitter that is linked to sleeping and waking up, and also to your mood.

The brain

● **The brain** is a delicate organ made up of more than 100 billion nerve cells (neurons). It is protected by the skull, three membrane (skin-like) layers (meninges) and a pool of clear fluid called cerebrospinal fluid (CSF).

● **The CSF** bathes the outside of the brain and circulates through a series of cavities inside the brain called ventricles. It also bathes and protects the spinal cord.

● **Each neuron** is connected to as many as 25,000 other neurons – so the brain has many trillions of different pathways for nerve signals.

● **In an adult**, the brain makes up about 2 percent of the weight of the body.

● **About 0.85 l of blood** shoots through your brain every minute. The brain may be as little as 2 percent of your body weight, but it demands 15 percent of your blood supply.

● **The human brain** is far bigger in relation to the body than the brains of most other animals.

● **The cerebral cortex** is the outside of the upper part of the brain.

● **The brain** is divided into two halves (hemispheres). The right hemisphere controls the left side of the body and the left hemisphere controls the right side of the body.

● **Underneath the hemispheres** lie the parts of the brain that control automatic bodily functions, such as breathing, swallowing and sleep. The parts of the brain involved in these activities include the brainstem, midbrain (at the top of the brainstem), thalamus and hypothalamus.

● **The cerebellum** mainly controls body co-ordination and balance. It lies at the back of the skull under the cerebral hemispheres.

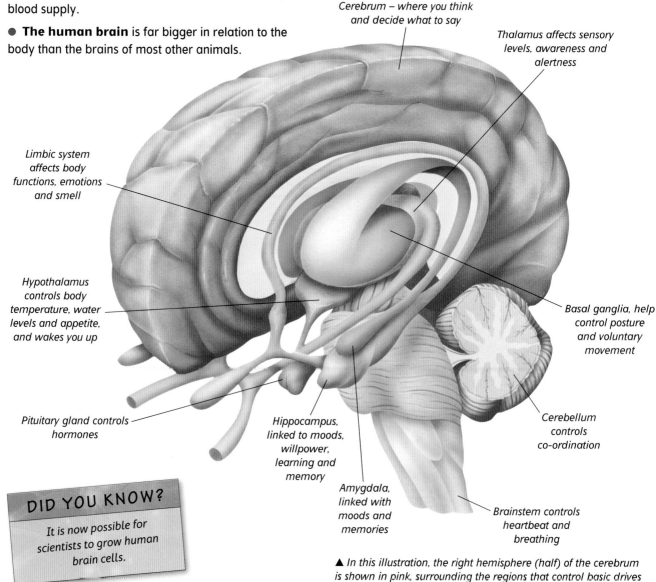

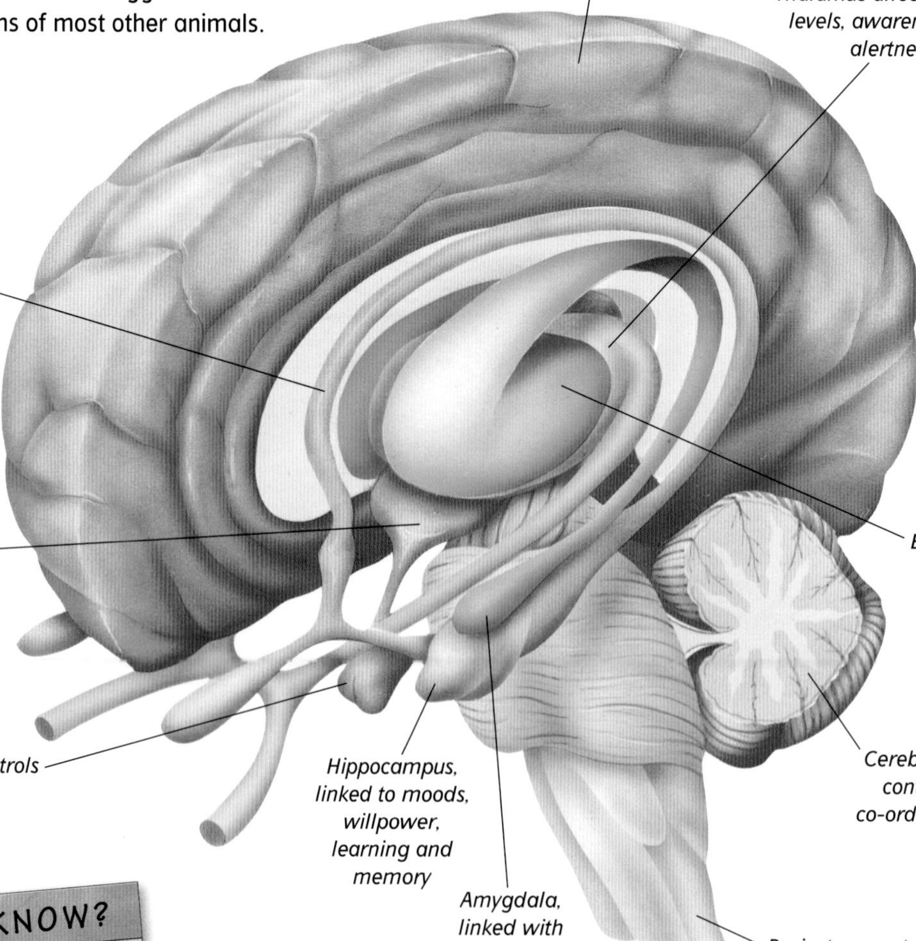
Cerebrum – where you think and decide what to say
Thalamus affects sensory levels, awareness and alertness
Limbic system affects body functions, emotions and smell
Hypothalamus controls body temperature, water levels and appetite, and wakes you up
Basal ganglia, help control posture and voluntary movement
Pituitary gland controls hormones
Hippocampus, linked to moods, willpower, learning and memory
Cerebellum controls co-ordination
Amygdala, linked with moods and memories
Brainstem controls heartbeat and breathing

▲ *In this illustration, the right hemisphere (half) of the cerebrum is shown in pink, surrounding the regions that control basic drives such as hunger, thirst and emotion.*

DID YOU KNOW?

It is now possible for scientists to grow human brain cells.

The cerebral cortex

- **A cortex** is the outer layer of any organ.
- **The name of the brain's cortex** is the cerebral cortex. It consists of a layer of nerve cells around the brain, also known as 'grey matter'.
- **The cerebral cortex** is where many signals from the senses are registered in the brain. It is also where conscious thoughts happen.
- **The visual cortex** is the place where all the things you see are registered in the brain.
- **The somatosensory cortex** is the place where a touch on any part of the body is registered, and each part of the body is represented in the somatosensory cortex.
- **The motor cortex** sends out signals telling body muscles to move.
- **The prefrontal cortex** is the most complicated cortical area because it is linked to your personality, reasoning ability, imagination, behaviour and your ability to learn complex things.
- **A human's cerebral cortex** is four times as big as that of a chimpanzee, about 20 times as big as a monkey's, and about 300 times as big as a rat's.

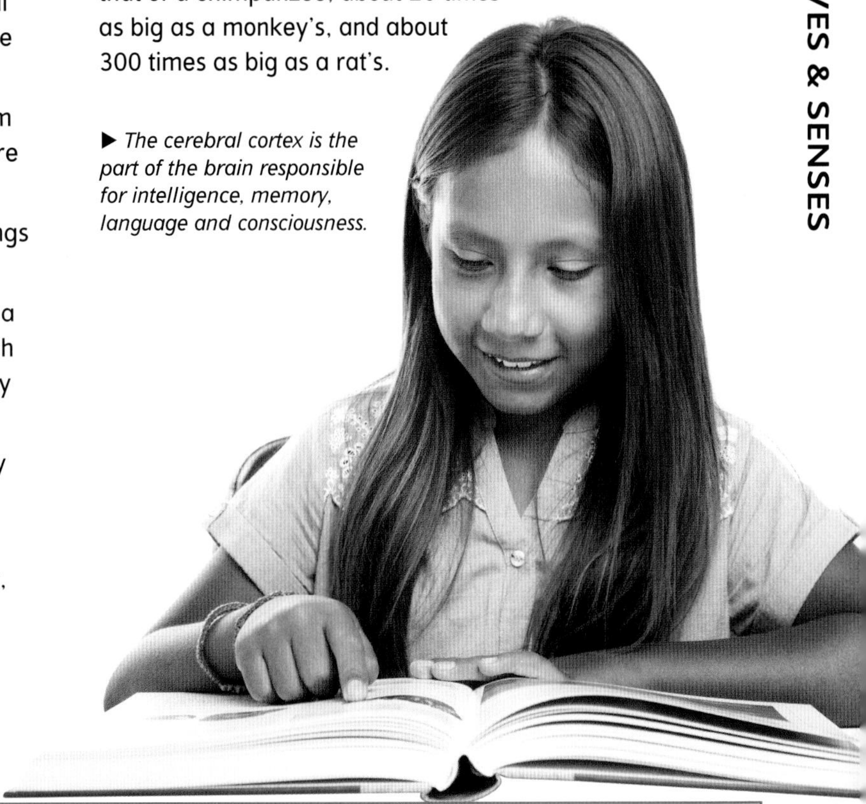

▶ *The cerebral cortex is the part of the brain responsible for intelligence, memory, language and consciousness.*

The spinal cord

- **The spinal cord** is the bundle of nerves that runs down a tunnel in the middle of the backbone, and is the route for all nerve signals travelling between the brain and the body.
- **The spinal cord** can work independently of the brain, sending out responses to the muscles directly. This is called a reflex response.
- **The outside** of the spinal cord is made up of the long tails (axons) of nerve cells and is called white matter. The inside is made up of the main nerve bodies and is called grey matter.
- **The spinal cord** is about 43 cm long and 1 cm thick. It stops growing when you are about five years old.

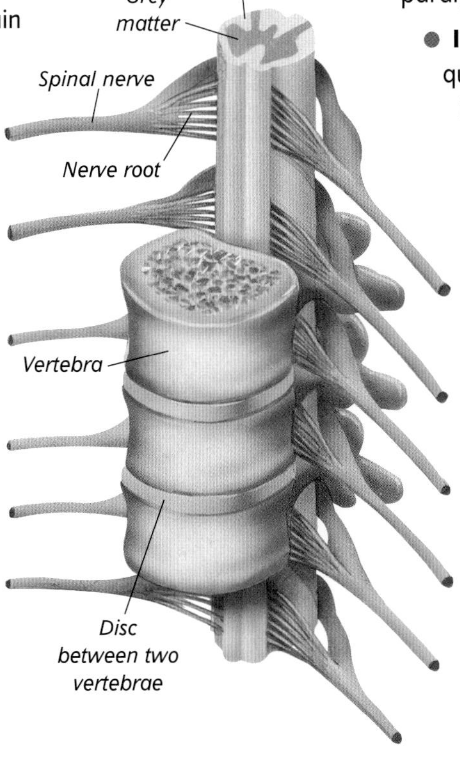
White matter
Grey matter
Spinal nerve
Nerve root
Vertebra
Disc between two vertebrae

- **Damage to the spinal cord** can cause paralysis.
- **Injuries below the neck** can cause paraplegia – paralysis below the waist.
- **Injuries to the neck** can cause quadraplegia – paralysis below the neck including both arms and legs.
- **Descending pathways** are groups of nerves that carry nerve signals down the spinal cord – typically signals from the brain for muscles to move.
- **Ascending pathways** are groups of nerves that carry nerve signals up the spinal cord – typically signals from the skin and internal body sensors going to the brain.

◀ *The spinal cord is encased in a tunnel in the backbone at the back of each vertebra. Nerves branch off to the body in pairs either side.*

Inside the head

Your head contains many delicate, soft structures that are necessary or important for a healthy life. These are surrounded and supported by protective layers of tissue and bone to help prevent them from getting damaged.

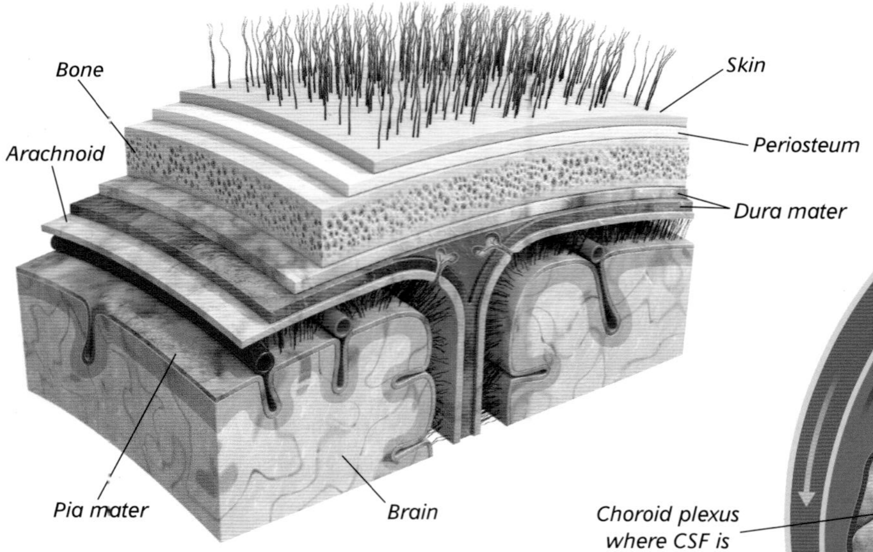
Bone
Arachnoid
Pia mater
Brain
Skin
Periosteum
Dura mater

▲ PROTECTIVE LAYERS
Your brain is well protected by layers of membrane, fluid, bone and skin.

The skin of the scalp covers the bony skull, which forms a protective cage for the brain and supports the other soft structures inside the head. Inside the skull the brain is surrounded and protected by three layers of membrane called the meninges. The innermost is the pia mater, then comes the arachnoid and then the dura mater. The illness meningitis is an infection of these meninges.

The brain is bathed by a clear, colourless liquid called cerebrospinal fluid (CSF). This is produced within spaces inside the brain called ventricles, and its main job is to act as a cushion, or shock absorber, for the brain and spinal cord.

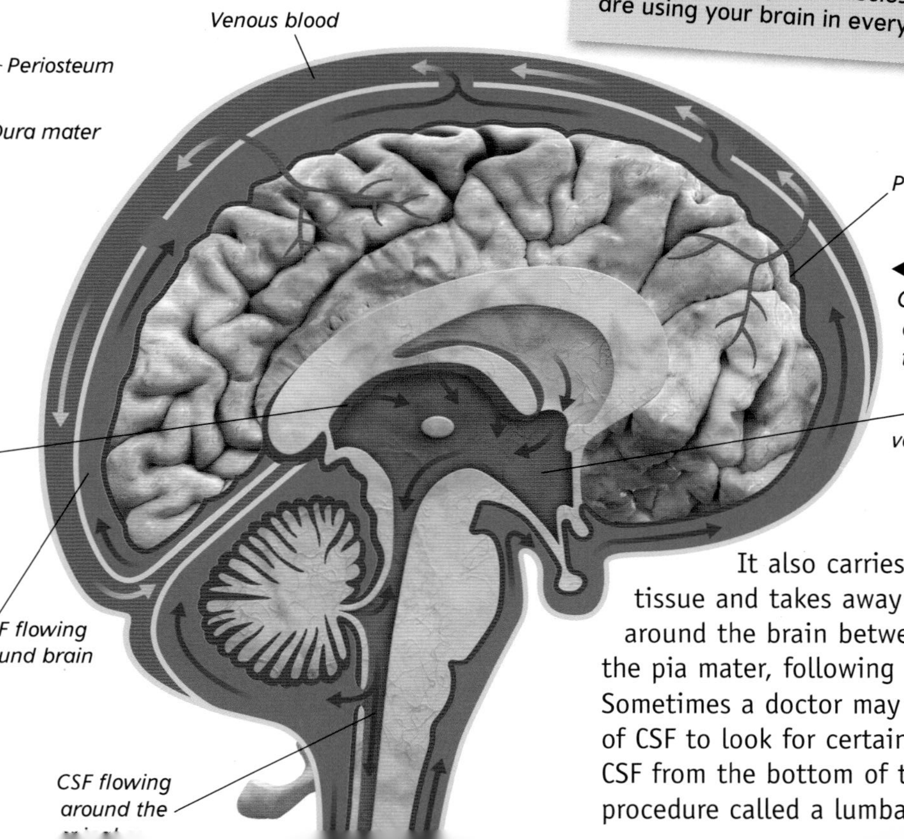
Venous blood
Choroid plexus where CSF is made
CSF flowing around brain
CSF flowing around the
Pia mater
Third ventricle

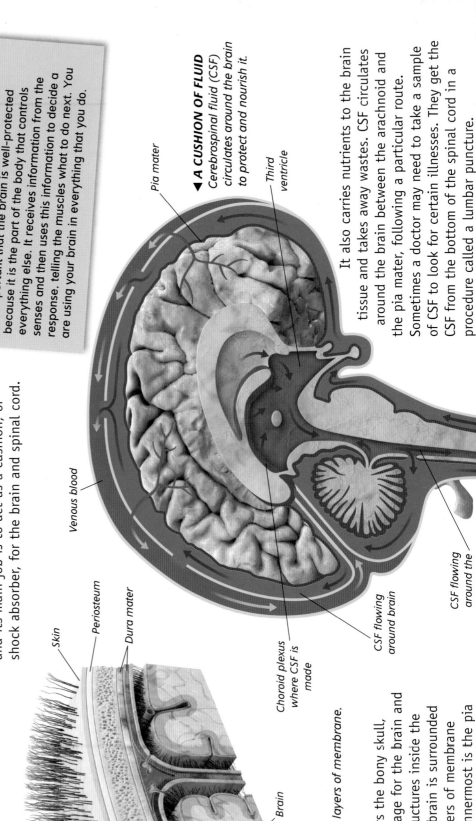

◀ A CUSHION OF FLUID
Cerebrospinal fluid (CSF) circulates around the brain to protect and nourish it.

It also carries nutrients to the brain tissue and takes away wastes. CSF circulates around the brain between the arachnoid and the pia mater, following a particular route. Sometimes a doctor may need to take a sample of CSF to look for certain illnesses. They get the CSF from the bottom of the spinal cord in a procedure called a lumbar puncture.

CONTROL CENTRE

It is important that the brain is well-protected because it is the part of the body that controls everything else. It receives information from the senses and then uses this information to decide a response, telling the muscles what to do next. You are using your brain in everything that you do.

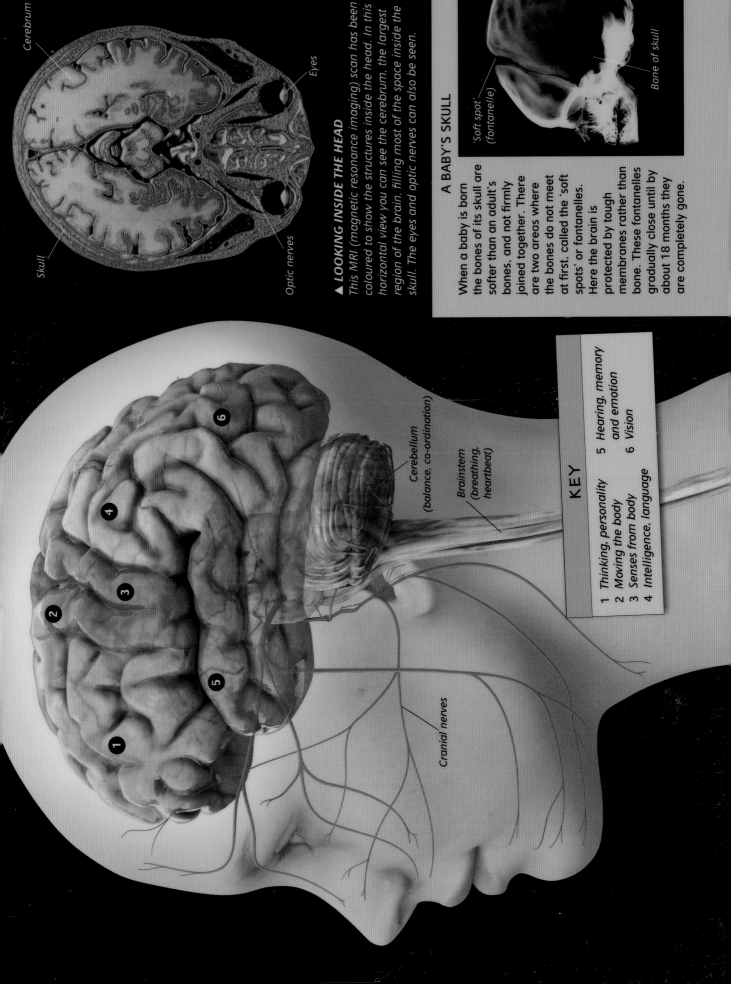

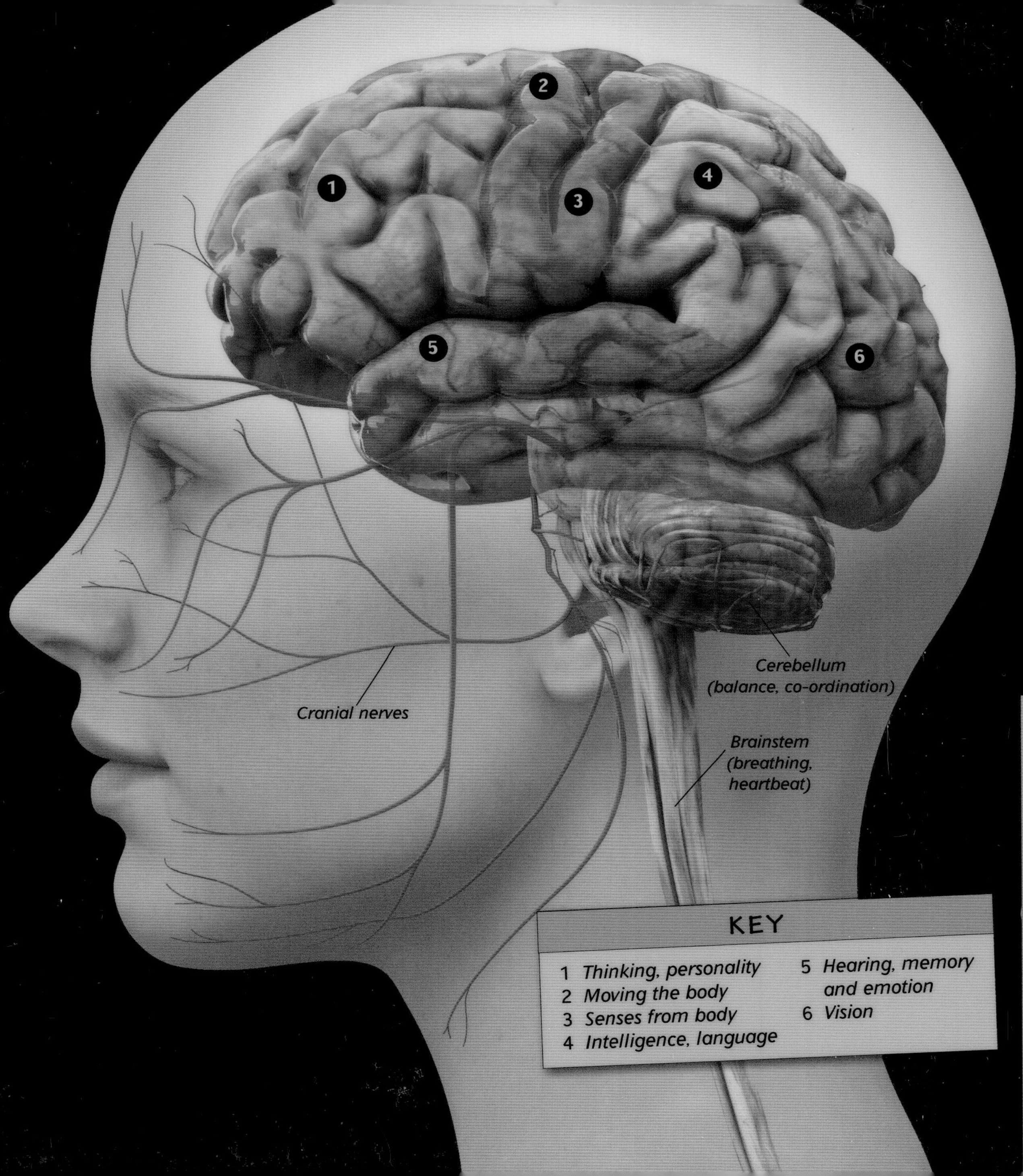
1
2
3
4
5
6
Cranial nerves
Cerebellum
(balance, co-ordination)
Brainstem
(breathing,
heartbeat)
KEY
1 Thinking, personality
2 Moving the body
3 Senses from body
4 Intelligence, language
5 Hearing, memory and emotion
6 Vision

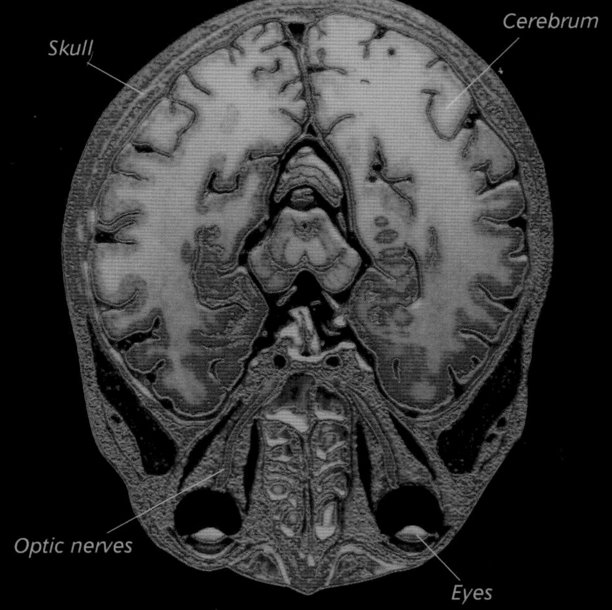
Skull
Cerebrum
Optic nerves
Eyes

▲ *LOOKING INSIDE THE HEAD*
This MRI (magnetic resonance imaging) scan has been coloured to show the structures inside the head. In this horizontal view you can see the cerebrum, the largest region of the brain, filling most of the space inside the skull. The eyes and optic nerves can also be seen.

A BABY'S SKULL

When a baby is born the bones of its skull are softer than an adult's bones, and not firmly joined together. There are two areas where the bones do not meet at first, called the 'soft spots' or fontanelles. Here the brain is protected by tough membranes rather than bone. These fontanelles gradually close until by about 18 months they are completely gone.

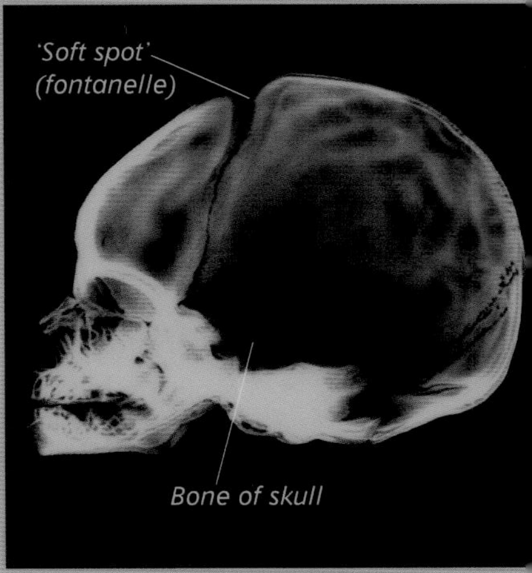
'Soft spot'
(fontanelle)
Bone of skull

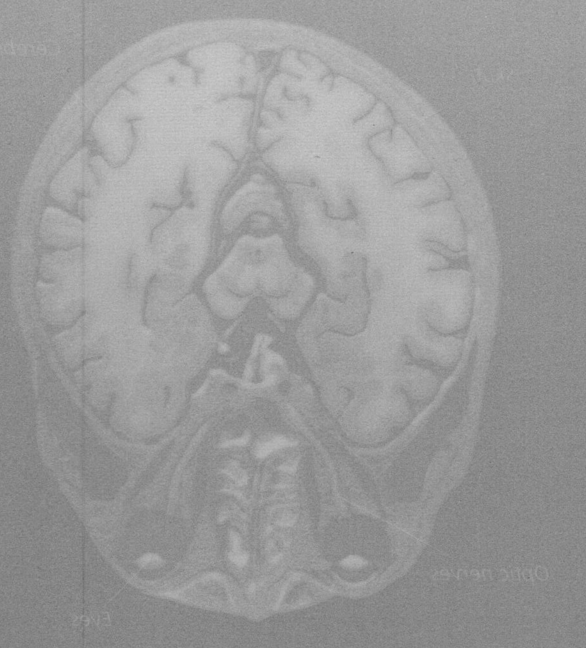
Cerebrum
Skull
Optic nerves
Eyes

▲ LOOKING INSIDE THE HEAD
This MRI (magnetic resonance imaging) scan has been coloured to show the structures inside the head. In this horizontal view you can see the cerebrum, the largest region of the brain, filling most of the space inside the skull. The eyes and optic nerves can also be seen.

A BABY'S SKULL

When a baby is born the bones of its skull are softer than an adult's bones, and not firmly joined together. There are two areas where the bones do not meet at first, called the 'soft spots' or fontanelles. Here the brain is protected by tough membranes rather than bone. These fontanelles gradually close until by about 18 months they are completely gone.

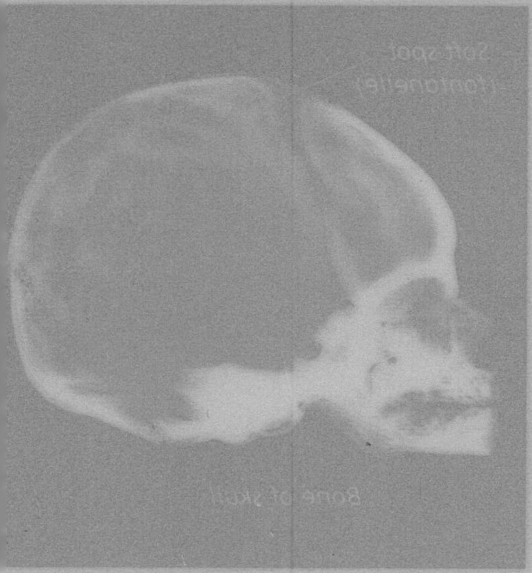
Soft spot (fontanelle)
Bone of skull

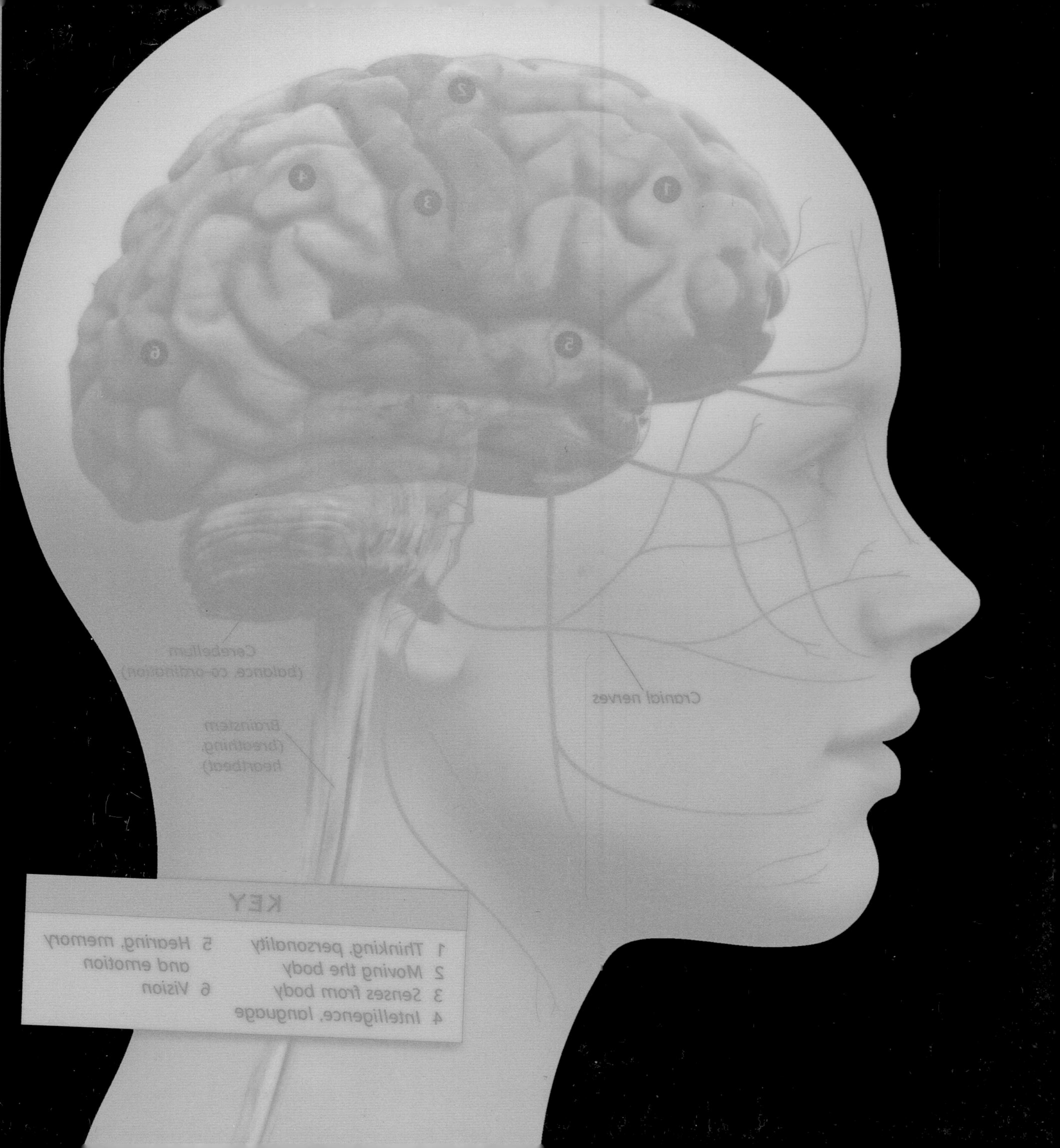
1
2
3
4
5
6
Cerebellum (balance, co-ordination)
Brainstem (breathing, heartbeat)
Cranial nerves

KEY
1 Thinking, personality
2 Moving the body
3 Senses from body
4 Intelligence, language
5 Hearing, memory and emotion
6 Vision

▶ INSIDE YOUR BRAIN
Protected by your skull, your brain is made up of many different but interconnected parts with different jobs to do.

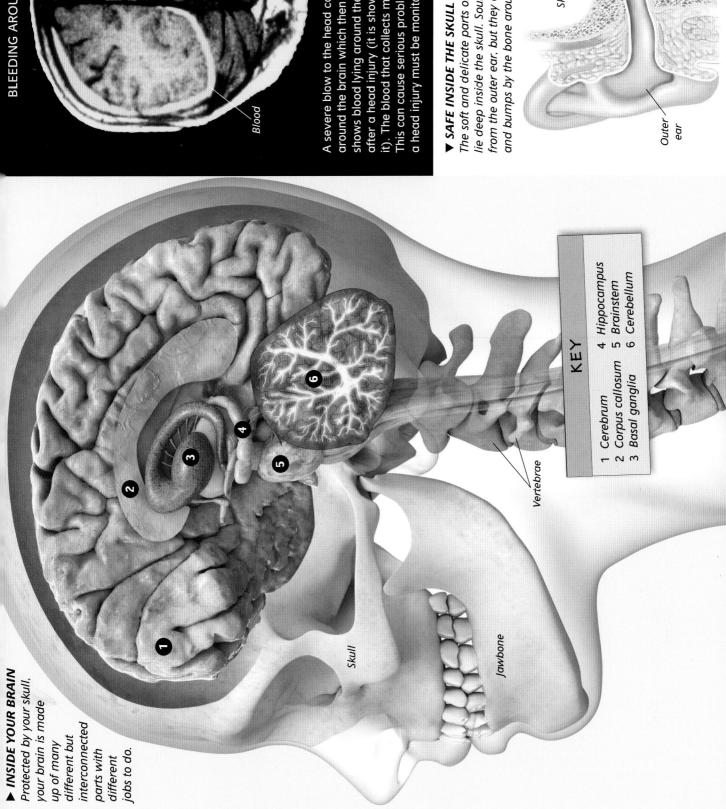

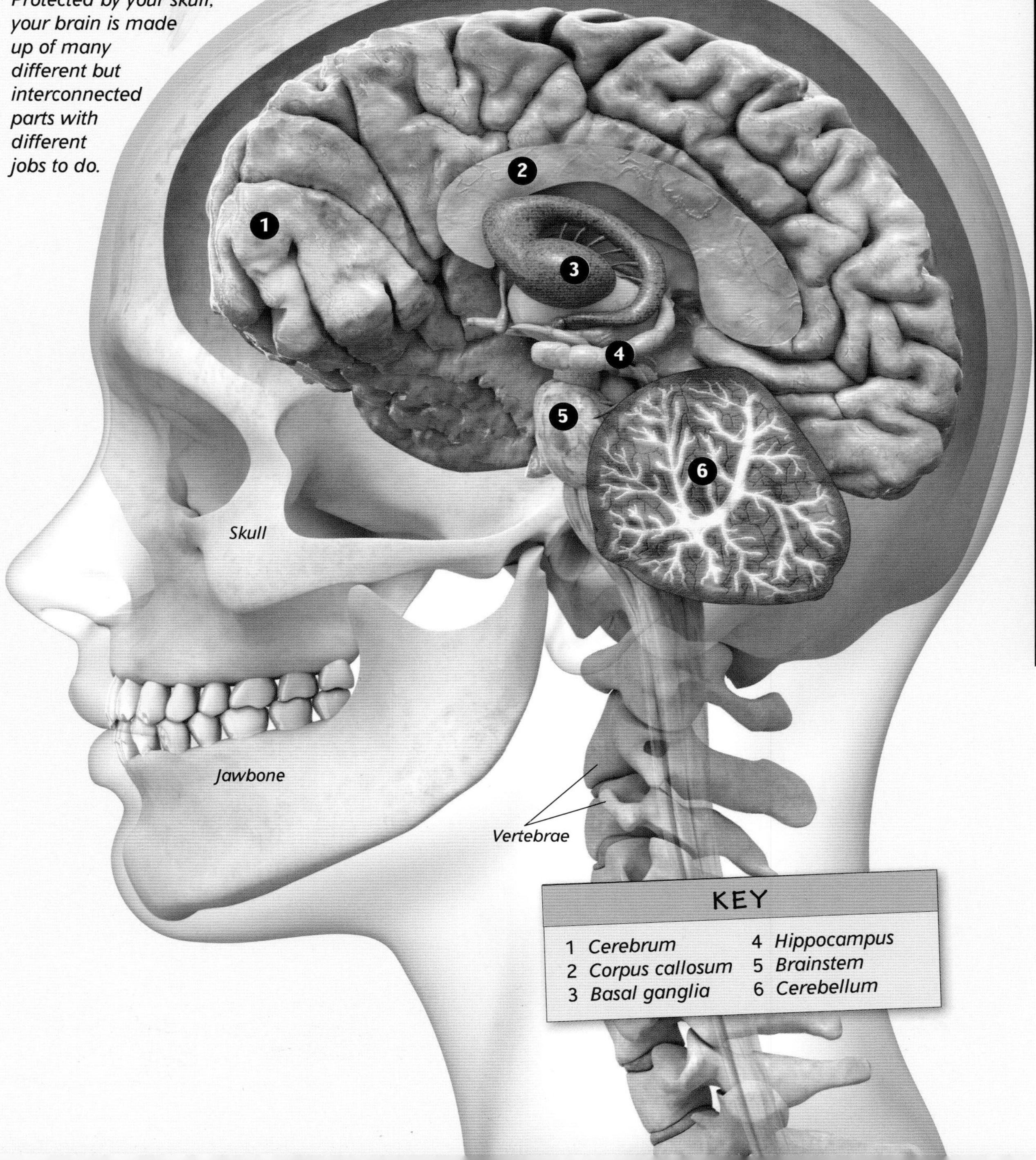

1
2
3
4
5
6
Skull
Jawbone
Vertebrae
KEY
1 Cerebrum
2 Corpus callosum
3 Basal ganglia
4 Hippocampus
5 Brainstem
6 Cerebellum

BLEEDING AROUND THE BRAIN

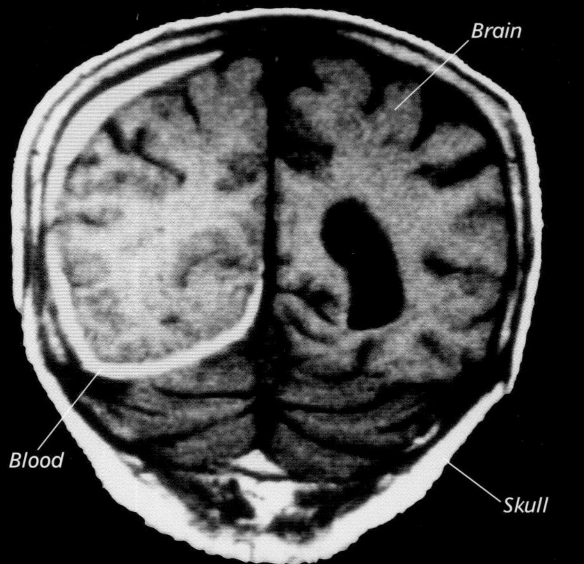

Brain
Blood
Skull

A severe blow to the head can tear tiny blood vessels around the brain which then bleed. This MRI scan shows blood lying around the right side of the brain after a head injury (it is shown in pink so you can see it). The blood that collects may then squeeze the brain. This can cause serious problems, so a person who has a head injury must be monitored closely.

▼ SAFE INSIDE THE SKULL
The soft and delicate parts of the middle and inner ear lie deep inside the skull. Sound is carried down to them from the outer ear, but they are protected from knocks and bumps by the bone around them.

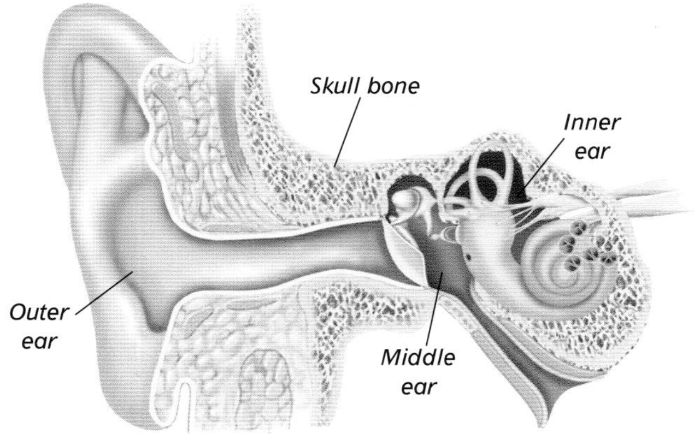

Skull bone
Inner ear
Outer ear
Middle ear

Reflexes

● **Reflexes are muscle movements** that are automatic – they happen without you thinking about them.

● **Inborn reflexes** are those you were born with, such as shivering when you are cold. The knee-jerk is an inborn reflex that makes your leg jerk upwards when the tendon below your knee is tapped.

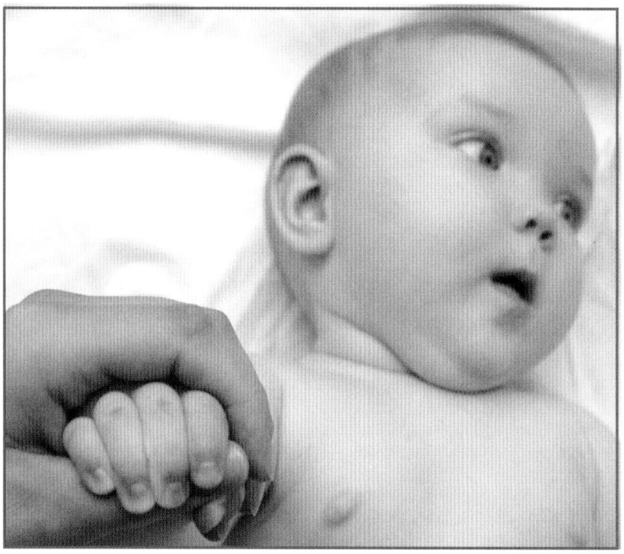

● **Primitive reflexes** are reflexes that babies have for a few months after they are born.

DID YOU KNOW?

Athletes often have lightning reflexes – their bodies react faster than their brains can process.

● **The grasping reflex** is a primitive reflex. It causes a baby's hand to automatically grip anything it touches.

● **Conditioned reflexes** are learnt through habit, as certain nerve pathways are used again and again.

● **Conditioned reflexes** help you do anything, from holding a cup to playing football without thinking.

● **Reflex reactions** occur when your safety demands a fast, automatic response.

● **Reflex reactions** bypass the brain. The alarm signal from the body part that has detected the pain sets off motor signals in the spinal cord to make you move.

● **A reflex arc** is the nerve circuit from sense to muscle via the spinal cord.

◀ *Even babies have reflexes – automatically grasping anything put into the palms of their hands.*

Sensory nerves

● **Sensory nerves** are those that carry information to the brain from sense receptors all over the body.

● **Each sense receptor** in the body is linked to the brain by a sensory nerve.

● **Most sensory nerves** feed their signals to the somatosensory cortex.

● **Massive bundles** of sensory nerve cells form the nerves that link major senses, such as vision, hearing, balance, taste and smell, to the brain.

● **Sensory information** from other regions of the body is carried by the paired spinal nerves – mixed nerves, that carry information to and from the brain. Each spinal nerve is associated with an area of the body.

● **In the skin**, many sense receptors are simply 'free', exposed sensory nerve-endings.

● **The brain interprets the signals** from sensory nerves in the skin so that you can tell the difference between touch, pain, hot and cold.

● **Different parts of the body** are more sensitive to the differences than others. This is because of the different amount of somatosensory cortex in the brain devoted to each region of the body.

● **Electrical signals** from the sensory receptors of the body travel to the brain along specific nerve pathways called ascending tracts.

● **Once the sensory signal** reaches the brain, processing of the information allows you to work out what the sensation (sensory signal) actually means. This is called sensory perception. For example, whether pressure on the skin is uncomfortable and where on the body it is felt.

◀ *Some of our most pleasant feelings, such as being hugged or stroked, are sent to the brain by sensory nerves.*

Motor nerves

- **Motor nerves** tell your muscles to move.
- **Every major muscle** in the body has many motor nerve-endings that instruct it to contract (tighten).
- **Motor nerves cross over** from one side of the body to the other at the top of your spinal cord. This means that signals from the right side of the brain go to the left side of the body, and vice versa.
- **Each motor nerve** is paired to a proprioceptor on the muscle and its tendons. This sends signals to the brain to say whether the muscle is tensed or relaxed.
- **If the strain** on a tendon increases, the proprioceptor sends a signal to the brain. The brain then adjusts the motor signals to that muscle to make it contract more or less.

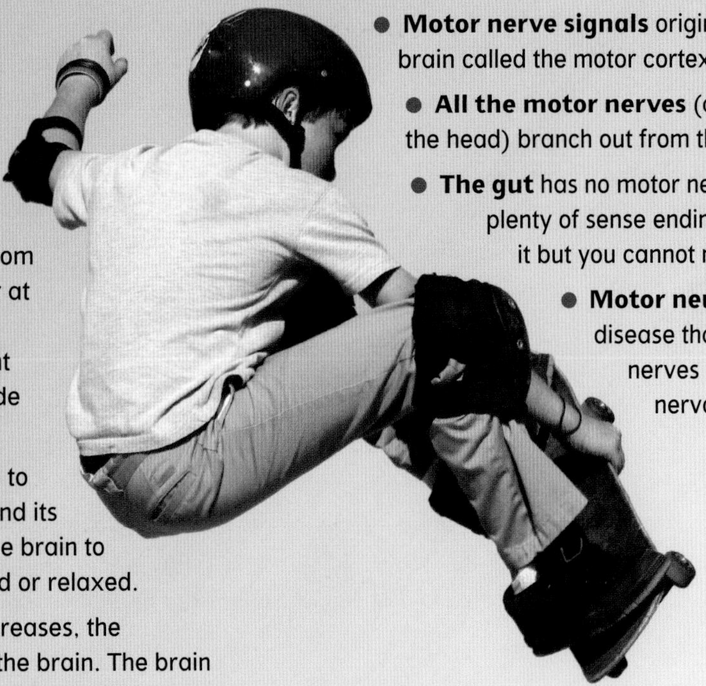

- **Motor nerve signals** originate in a part of the brain called the motor cortex.
- **All the motor nerves** (apart from those in the head) branch out from the spinal cord.
- **The gut** has no motor nerve-endings but plenty of sense endings, so you can feel it but you cannot move it consciously.
- **Motor neuron disease** is a disease that attacks motor nerves within the central nervous system.

▲ *Motor nerves fire to make muscles move.*

Cranial nerves

- **The cranial nerves** are part of the peripheral nervous system. There are 12 numbered pairs.
- **Cranial Nerve I** is called the olfactory nerve. It is an entirely sensory nerve carrying signals to the brain about smell.
- **Cranial Nerve II**, the optic nerve, is a sensory nerve that carries information about vision to the brain.
- **Cranial Nerves III, IV, and VI** are the oculomotor, trochlear and abducent nerves, which control eye movement.
- **Cranial Nerve V**, the trigeminal nerve, carries sensory information from the skin of the face and inside the nose to the brain, and controls the jaw muscles.
- **Cranial Nerve VII**, the facial nerve, controls the movement of the facial muscles to give expressions, and carries the sense of taste from the front of the tongue to the brain.
- **Cranial Nerve VIII** is called the vestibulocochlear nerve. It carries mostly sensory information about balance and hearing from the ear to the brain.
- **Cranial nerve IX, X and XI** are the vagus nerve, the glossopharyngeal nerve and the accessory nerve. Together, they control swallowing. The glossopharyngeal nerve also carries taste information from the back of the tongue. The vagus nerve controls many other functions including heart rate.
- **Cranial Nerve XII**, the hypoglossal nerve, controls the muscles of the tongue used when speaking and swallowing.

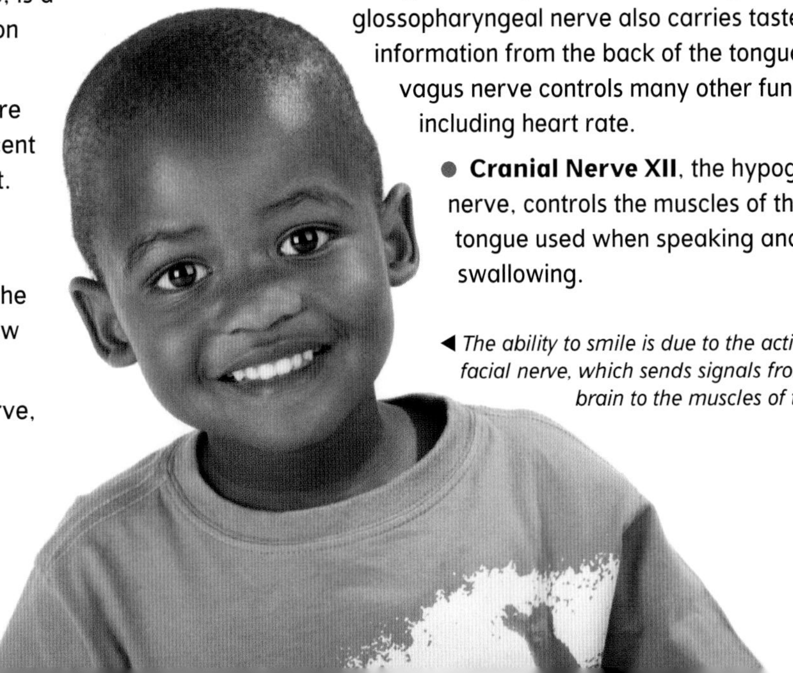

◀ *The ability to smile is due to the action of the facial nerve, which sends signals from the brain to the muscles of the face.*

Thinking

- **Some scientists** claim that humans are the only living things that are capable of conscious thought.
- **Most thoughts** appear to take place in the cerebrum (situated at the top of the brain), and different kinds of thought are linked to different areas. These are called association areas.
- **Each half of the cerebrum** is divided into four rounded segments called lobes: two at the front (frontal and temporal lobes) and two at the back (occipital and parietal lobes).
- **The frontal lobe** is linked to your personality and is the area in which your ideas form.
- **The temporal lobe** is the area in which you hear and understand what people say to you.
- **The occipital lobe** is the area in which you work out what your eyes are seeing.
- **The parietal lobe** is where you register touch, heat and cold, and pain.
- **The left side of the brain** (left hemisphere) controls the right side of the body. The right side (right hemisphere) controls the left side.
- **One half of the brain** is always dominant (in charge). Usually, the left is dominant, which is why 90 percent of people are right-handed.

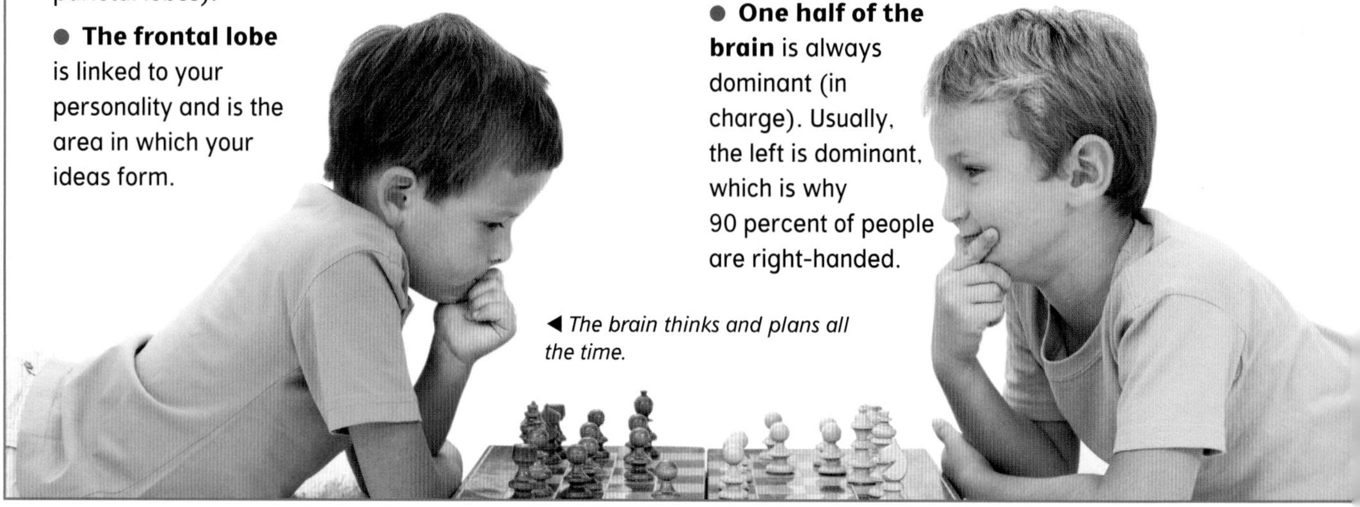

◀ *The brain thinks and plans all the time.*

Smell

- **Smells are scent molecules** that are carried in the air and breathed in through your nose.
- **The human nose** may be able to tell the difference between many millions of different chemicals.
- **Inside the nose**, scent molecules are picked up by a patch of cells called the olfactory epithelium.

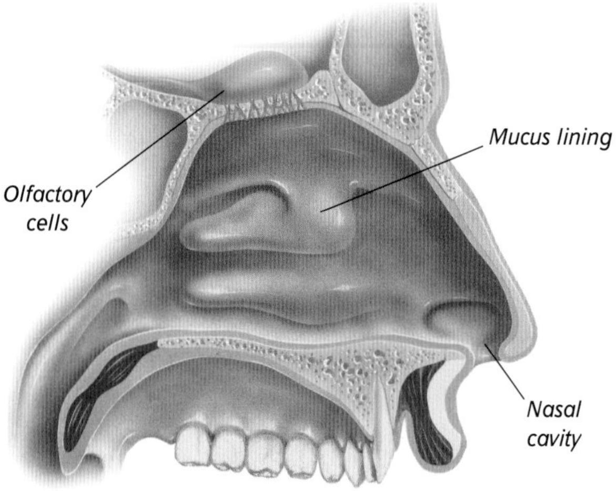
Olfactory cells
Mucus lining
Nasal cavity

▲ *The parts that detect smells are in the roof of the large chamber inside the nose.*

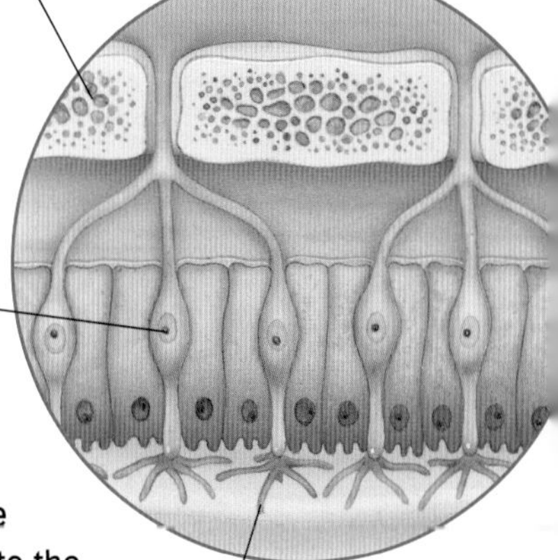
Bone
Olfactory cell
Micro-hair

▶ *Olfactory cells have micro-hairs facing into the nasal chamber to detect smell particles.*

- **Extensions of the receptor cells** pass through a piece of bone in the base of the skull to the olfactory bulb.
- **The olfactory bulb** then sends the electrical signals to the part of the brain that recognizes smell.
- **The part of the brain** that deals with smell is closely linked to the parts that deal with memories and emotions. This may be why smells can evoke memories.
- **By the age of 20**, you will have lost 20 percent of your sense of smell. By 60, you will have lost 60 percent of it.
- **The female hormone oestrogen** increases the sense of smell, so women are more sensitive to smells than men.

Hearing

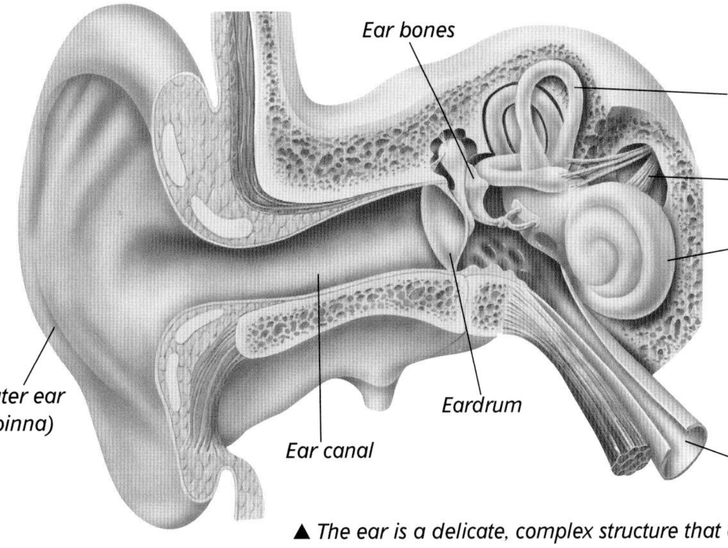
Ear bones
Semicircular canal (for balance)
Auditory nerve
Cochlea
Outer ear (pinna)
Eardrum
Ear canal
Eustachian tube to throat

▲ *The ear is a delicate, complex structure that can pick up the tiny variations in air pressure created by a sound.*

● **The ear** is a complex organ containing the mechanisms for hearing and balance.

● **Pinnae** are the ear flaps on the sides of your head that collect and funnel sound.

● **When the eardrum vibrates** it shakes three bones called ossicles – the smallest bones in the body.

● **The three ossicle bones** are the malleus (hammer), the incus (anvil) and the stapes (stirrup). They sit in a small air-filled chamber called the middle ear.

● **When the ossicles vibrate**, they transmit the vibration to the fluid of the cochlea (the organ of hearing).

● **The cochlea** is a fluid-filled organ that contains thousands of hair cells. These cells detect frequencies of vibration and send this information to the brain.

● **The semicircular canals** are three fluid-filled canals containing nerve endings that detect head movement. Messages from these nerve endings help the brain to control balance.

● **The Eustachian tube** connects the middle ear chamber to the back of the nose. It keeps the air pressure inside the ear equal to the pressure outside your head.

Vision

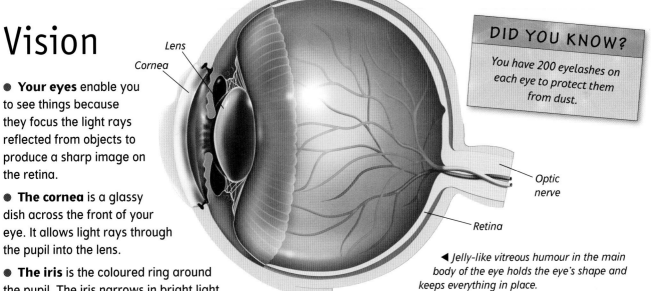

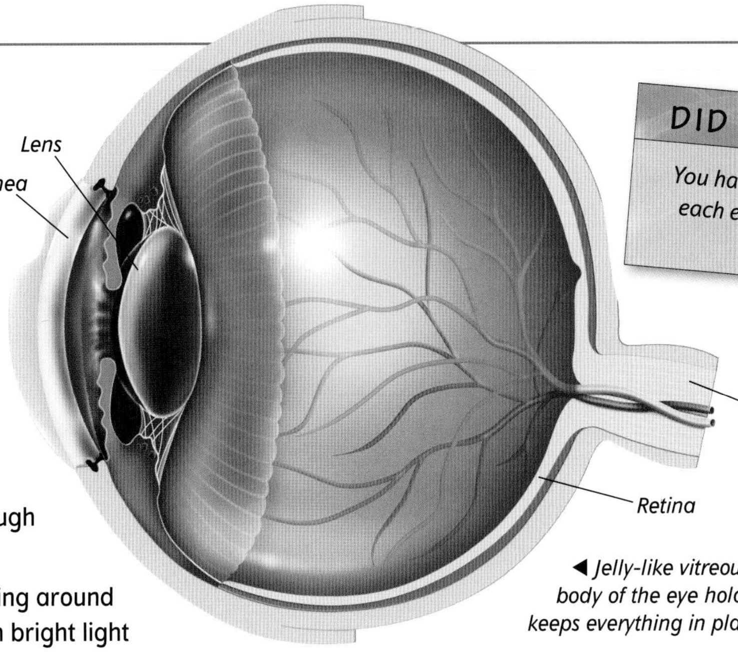
Lens
Cornea
Optic nerve
Retina

◀ *Jelly-like vitreous humour in the main body of the eye holds the eye's shape and keeps everything in place.*

DID YOU KNOW?

You have 200 eyelashes on each eye to protect them from dust.

● **Your eyes** enable you to see things because they focus the light rays reflected from objects to produce a sharp image on the retina.

● **The cornea** is a glassy dish across the front of your eye. It allows light rays through the pupil into the lens.

● **The iris** is the coloured ring around the pupil. The iris narrows in bright light and widens when light is dim.

● **The lens** is just behind the pupil. It bends and focuses the image onto the back of the eye.

● **The image on the retina** is upside down because the light rays are bent. The brain turns the image the right way up when interpreting the information.

● **The back of the eye** is lined with millions of cells. This lining is called the retina, and it registers the picture and sends signals to the brain via the optic nerve.

● **There are two kinds** of light-sensitive cell in the retina – rods and cones. Rods can work even in dim light, but cannot detect colours. Cones respond to colour.

● **Some kinds of cone** are sensitive to red light, some to green and some to blue.

● **Your eyes** each give you a slightly different view of the world. Your brain combines the two views to give an impression of depth.

Taste

- **Taste allows you to tell** whether food is safe to eat or should be avoided.
- **Taste receptors** detect food chemicals dissolved in saliva (spit) in the mouth. They are found mainly on the tongue's surface inside structures called taste buds.
- **Taste buds** are tiny cups that contain taste receptor cells. Long projections on these cells stick out of the taste bud so that they are always in saliva.
- **There are around 10,000 taste buds** on the tongue. There are also a few inside the cheeks and in the throat.
- **When a food chemical** is detected, the taste receptor sends a signal via the facial nerve to the brain.
- **Taste and flavour** are different – there are at least five basic tastes, and many flavours.
- **The detection of flavour** is an interaction between the senses of taste and smell. Food tastes bland when you have a cold because you lose this interaction when your nose is blocked.
- **The basic tastes** are umami (savoury), sweet, salty, sour and bitter.

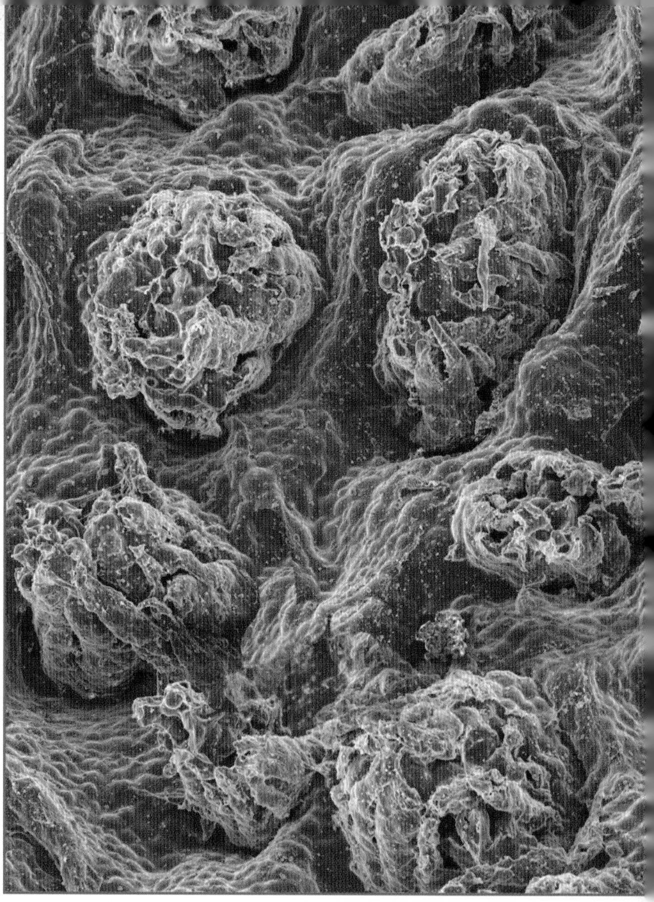

▲ *This powerful microscope picture of the surface of the tongue shows in pink the papillae which contain the taste buds.*

Touch

- **Nerve endings in the skin** can detect touch, pressure, pain, heat and cold.
- **There are sense receptors** everywhere in your skin, but places like your face have more than your back.
- **There are 200,000** heat and cold receptors in your skin, plus 500,000 touch and pressure receptors, and nearly 3 million pain receptors.
- **Free nerve-endings** respond to all kinds of skin sensation and are almost everywhere in your skin.
- **There are specialized receptors** in certain places, each named after their discoverer.
- **Pacini's and Meissner's corpuscles** react instantly to sudden pressure.
- **Krause's end-bulbs**, Merkel's discs and Ruffini's corpuscles respond to steady pressure.
- **Krause's end-bulbs** are also sensitive to cold.

DID YOU KNOW?

The speed of nerve signals from the skin to the brain varies according to the amount of pressure the sensors in your skin feel.

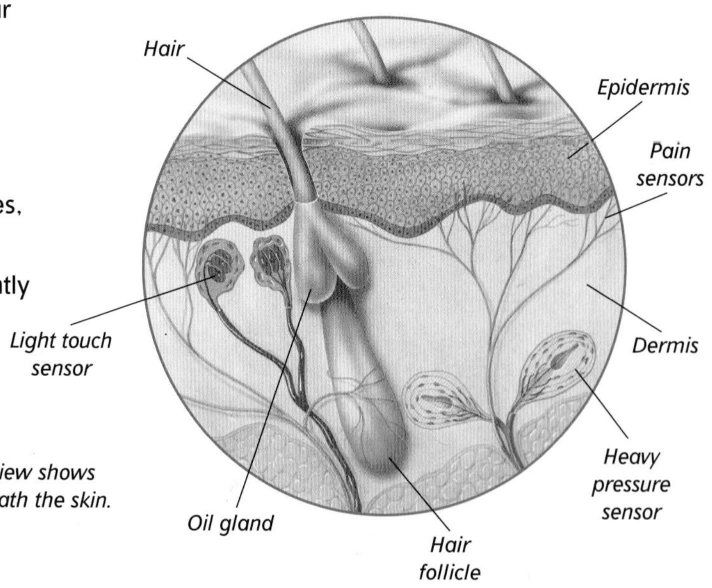
Hair
Epidermis
Pain sensors
Dermis
Heavy pressure sensor
Hair follicle
Oil gland
Light touch sensor

▶ *This magnified view shows touch sensors beneath the skin.*

Balance

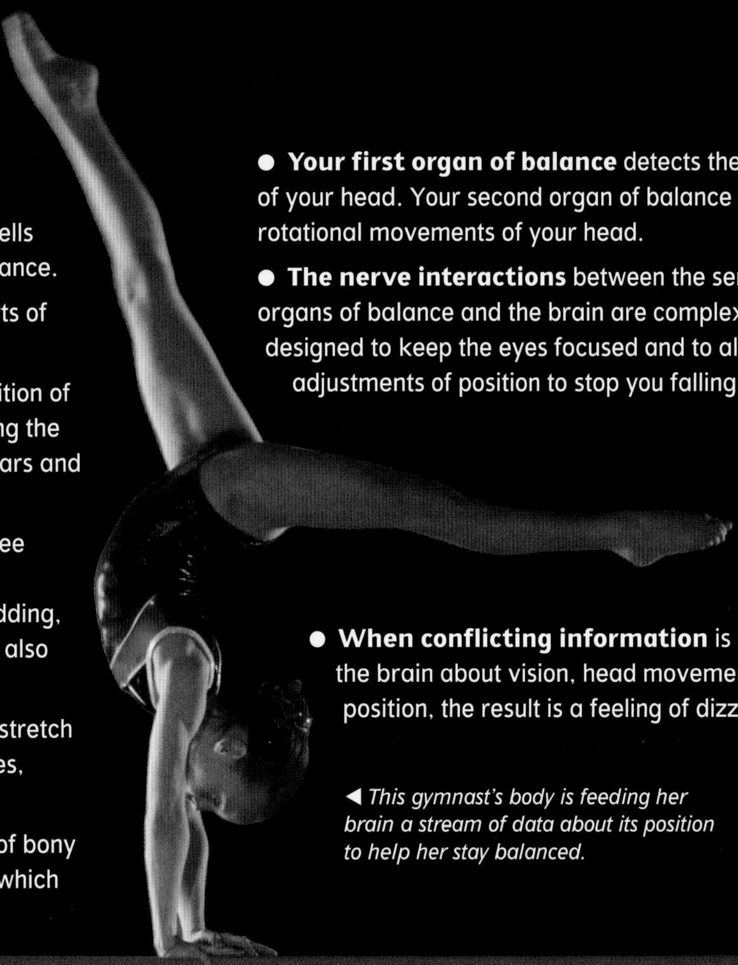

- **To stay upright**, the body sends a continual stream of data about its position to the brain – and the brain tells the body how to move to keep its balance.
- **Balance** is controlled in many parts of the brain, including the cerebellum.
- **The brain** finds out about the position of the body from many sources, including the eyes, the semicircular canals in the ears and proprioceptors.
- **The semicircular canals** are three fluid-filled loops in the inner ear that detect head movement, including nodding, shaking and turning your head. They also detect how fast the head is moving.
- **Proprioceptors** are position and stretch sensors that are found in skin, muscles, tendons and in every joint.
- **Your inner ear** contains a maze of bony chambers called the bony labyrinth, which contains your organs of balance.
- **Your first organ of balance** detects the position of your head. Your second organ of balance detects rotational movements of your head.
- **The nerve interactions** between the sensory organs of balance and the brain are complex. They are designed to keep the eyes focused and to allow quick adjustments of position to stop you falling.
- **When conflicting information** is received by the brain about vision, head movement and body position, the result is a feeling of dizziness.

◀ *This gymnast's body is feeding her brain a stream of data about its position to help her stay balanced.*

Co-ordination

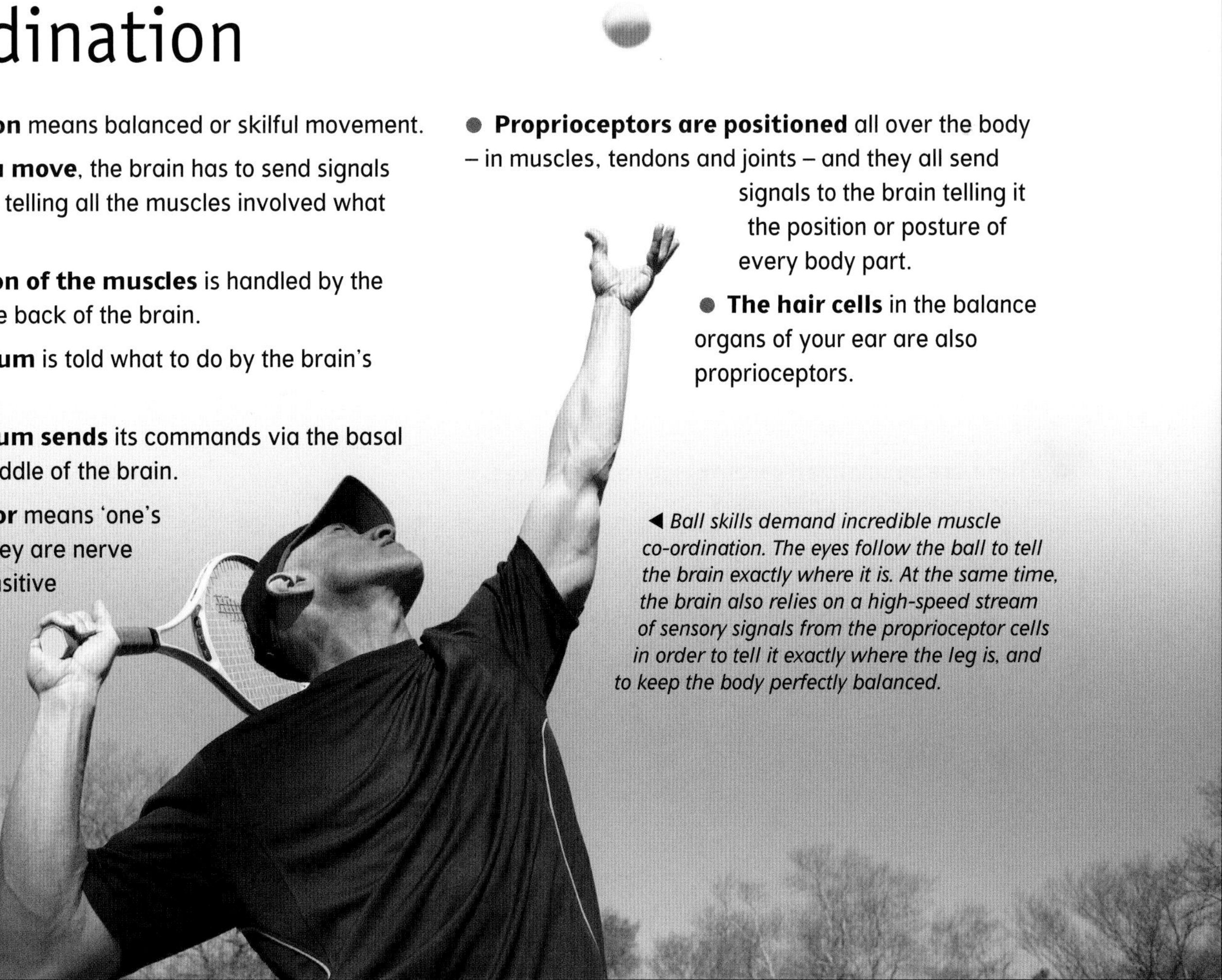

- **Co-ordination** means balanced or skilful movement.
- **To make you move**, the brain has to send signals out along nerves telling all the muscles involved what to do.
- **Co-ordination of the muscles** is handled by the cerebellum at the back of the brain.
- **The cerebellum** is told what to do by the brain's motor cortex.
- **The cerebellum sends** its commands via the basal ganglia in the middle of the brain.
- **Proprioceptor** means 'one's own sensors'. They are nerve cells that are sensitive to movement, pressure or stretching.
- **Proprioceptors are positioned** all over the body – in muscles, tendons and joints – and they all send signals to the brain telling it the position or posture of every body part.
- **The hair cells** in the balance organs of your ear are also proprioceptors.

◀ *Ball skills demand incredible muscle co-ordination. The eyes follow the ball to tell the brain exactly where it is. At the same time, the brain also relies on a high-speed stream of sensory signals from the proprioceptor cells in order to tell it exactly where the leg is, and to keep the body perfectly balanced.*

Mood

- **Mood is your state of mind** – whether you are happy or sad, angry or afraid, overjoyed or depressed.
- **Moods and emotions** seem to be strongly linked to the structures in the centre of the brain, where unconscious activities are controlled.
- **Moods** have three elements – how you feel, what happens to your body, and what they make you do.
- **Scientists are only** just beginning to discover how moods and emotions are linked to particular parts of the brain.
- **Certain memories or experiences** are so strongly linked in your mind that they can trigger a certain mood.
- **It is possible that the bacteria** normally living in your intestines affect your mood. Substances made by these bacteria can affect nerves and the immune system, which in turn affect the brain.

▶ *Changes in the body can alter the way you feel – the act of smiling can make you feel more positive.*

DID YOU KNOW?

In one experiment, people injected with adrenaline found terrible jokes much funnier!

Memory

- **When you remember something**, it is thought that the brain stores it by creating new nerve connections.
- **There are three types of memory** – sensory, short-term and long-term.
- **Sensory memory** is the impression that new information makes on the mind. It lasts for only a fraction of a second.
- **Short-term memory** is information that the brain stores for a few seconds, like a phone number remembered long enough to dial.
- **Long-term memory** is memory that can last for months or maybe even your whole life.
- **The brain** has two kinds of long-term memory, called declarative and non-declarative memories.
- **Non-declarative** memories are skills you teach yourself by practising, such as playing badminton or the flute.
- **Declarative memories** are either episodic or semantic.
- **Episodic memories** are memories of striking events in your life, such as breaking your leg or your first day at a new school. You not only recall facts, but sensations.
- **Semantic memories** are facts such as dates. The brain seems to store these in the left temporal lobe.

◀ *Learning to play the guitar involves non-declarative memory, in which nerve pathways become reinforced by repeated use. This is why practising is so important.*

Sleeping

● **When you are asleep**, your body functions go on as normal. But your body may save energy and do routine repairs.

● **Lack of sleep** can be dangerous. A newborn baby needs 18–20 hours sleep a day. An adult needs 7–8 hours.

▲ *We all shut our eyes to sleep. When the body is asleep, the brain's activity pattern changes and the heartbeat slows.*

● **Sleep is controlled** in the brainstem.

● **The activity of the brain** when awake and asleep can be investigated by placing electrodes on the skull that pick up the electrical activity inside the head. This investigation is called an electroencephalogram (EEG). Using this technique, wave patterns of electrical activity have been identified and named.

● **When you sleep**, the pattern to the electricity created by the firing of the brain's nerve cells becomes more regular.

● **For the first 90 minutes**, your sleep gets deeper and the brain waves become stronger.

● **After 90 minutes of sleep**, your eyes begin to flicker from side to side under their lids. This is called Rapid Eye Movement (REM) sleep. You are hard to wake up.

● **REM sleep** is thought to occur when you are dreaming.

● **While you sleep**, ordinary deeper sleep alternates with spells of REM lasting up to half an hour.

Temperature

● **The inside of your body** stays at a constant temperature of 37°C (98°F), rising a few degrees only when you are ill.

● **The body creates heat** by burning food in its cells, especially the 'energy sugar' glucose.

● **Even when you are resting**, your body generates so much heat that you are comfortable only when the air is slightly cooler than you are.

● **Your body loses heat** as you breathe in cool air and breathe out warm air.

● **The body's temperature control** is the tiny hypothalamus in the brain.

● **Sensors in the skin**, in the body's core, and in the blood around the hypothalamus transmit signals to the hypothalamus about body temperature.

● **If it is too hot**, the hypothalamus sends signals to the skin telling it to sweat more. Signals also tell blood vessels in the skin to widen – this increases the blood flow, so the heat loss from your blood becomes greater.

▶ *Sweat is made in the sweat glands. It cools the body by letting warm water out, and the moisture cools the skin as it evaporates.*

● **If it is too cold**, the hypothalamus sends signals to the skin to cut back skin blood flow, as well as signals to tell the muscles to generate heat by shivering.

● **If it is too cold**, the hypothalamus may also stimulate the thyroid gland to send out hormones to make your cells burn energy faster and so make more heat.

Circulation

- **Circulation** is the system of tubes called blood vessels that carries blood from the heart to all body tissues and back again.
- **Blood circulation** was discovered in 1628 by the English physician William Harvey (1578–1657), who built on the ideas of Matteo Colombo.
- **Each of the body's** 600 billion cells gets fresh blood once every few minutes or less.

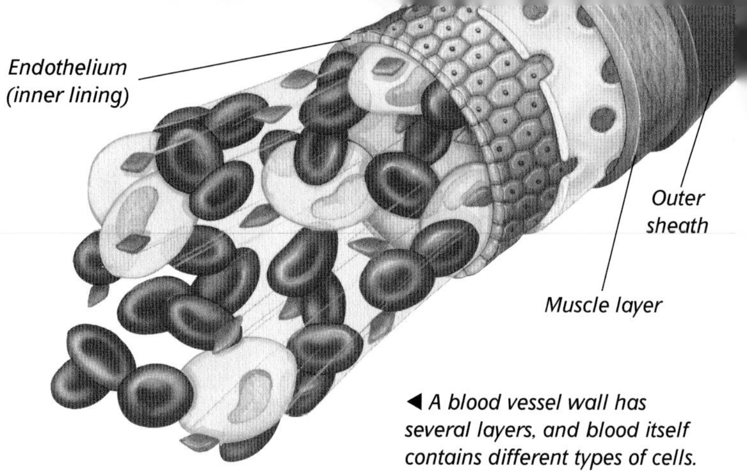
Endothelium (inner lining)
Outer sheath
Muscle layer

◀ *A blood vessel wall has several layers, and blood itself contains different types of cells.*

- **On the way out** from the heart, blood is pumped through vessels called arteries and arterioles.
- **On the way back** to the heart, blood flows through venules and veins.
- **Blood flows** from the arterioles to the venules through the tiniest tubes called capillaries.
- **The blood circulation** has two parts – the pulmonary and the systemic.
- **The pulmonary circulation** is the short section that carries blood that is low in oxygen from the right side of the heart to the lungs for 'refuelling'. It then returns oxygen-rich blood to the left side of the heart.
- **The systemic circulation** carries oxygen-rich blood from the left side of the heart all around the body, and returns blood that is low in oxygen to the right side of the heart.
- **In the blood**, oxygen is carried by the haemoglobin in red blood cells.
- **For each outward-going artery** there is usually an equivalent returning vein.

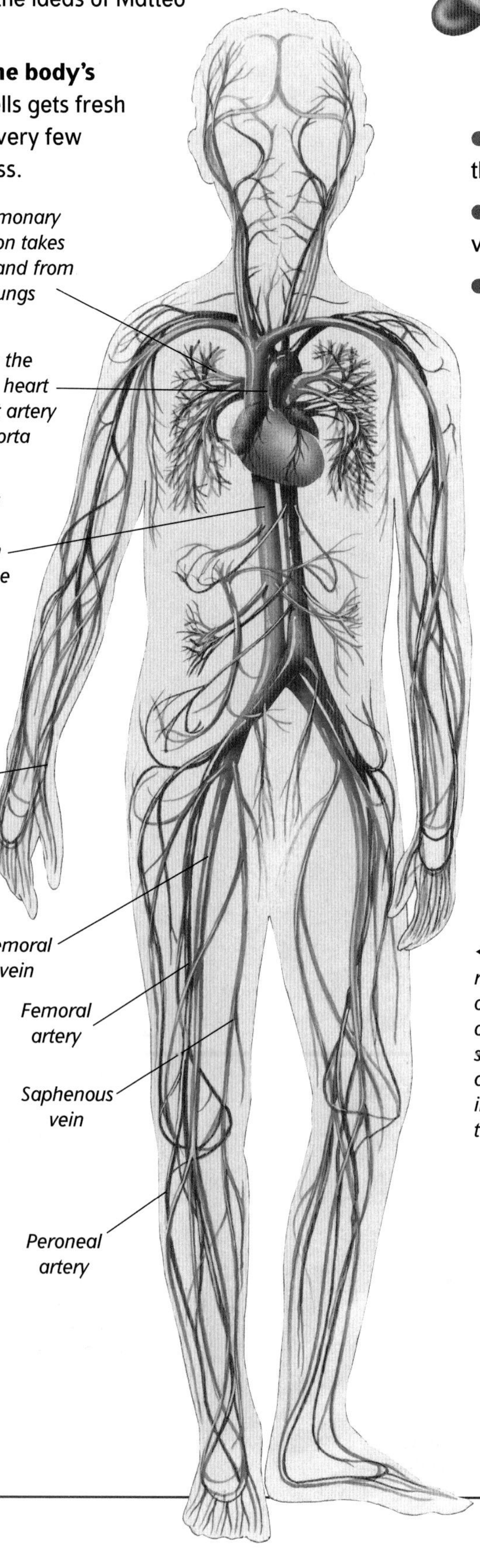
The pulmonary circulation takes blood to and from the lungs
Blood leaves the left side of the heart through a giant artery called the aorta
Blood returns to the heart through main veins called the vena cavae
Radial artery
Femoral vein
Femoral artery
Saphenous vein
Peroneal artery

◀ *Blood circulates continuously round and round the body through an intricate series of tubes called blood vessels. Bright red, oxygen-rich blood is pumped from the left side of the heart through vessels called arteries and arterioles. Blood that is low in oxygen returns to the right of the heart through veins and venules.*

DID YOU KNOW?

It takes less than 90 seconds on average for the blood to circulate through all of the body's 100,000 km of blood vessels!

The heart

● **The heart** is the size of a clenched fist. It is inside the middle of the chest, and slightly to the left. It is a powerful pump made almost entirely of muscle.

● **To pump blood** out through your arteries, the heart contracts (tightens) and relaxes automatically about 70 times a minute.

● **The two sides** of the heart are separated by a muscle wall called the septum.

● **The right side** is smaller and weaker, and it pumps blood only to the lungs. The stronger left side pumps blood around the body.

● **Each side of the heart** has two chambers. There is an atrium at the top where blood accumulates (builds up) from the veins, and a ventricle below that contracts to pump blood out into the arteries.

DID YOU KNOW?

During an average lifetime, the heart pumps 200 million l of blood – enough to fill New York's Central Park to a depth of 15 m.

● **Each of the heart's four chambers** ejects about 70 ml of blood with each beat.

● **There are two valves** in each side of the heart to make sure that blood flows only one way – a large one between the atrium and the ventricle, and a small one at the exit from the ventricle into the artery.

● **The coronary arteries** supply the heart. If they become clogged, the heart muscle may be short of blood and stop working. This is what happens in a heart attack.

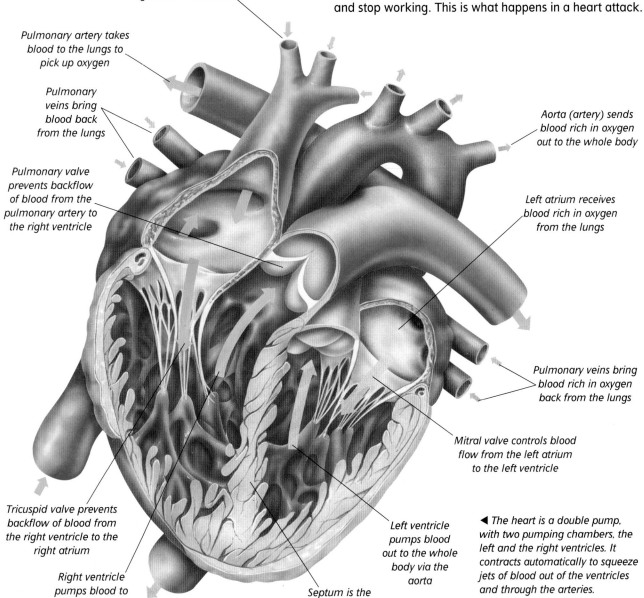

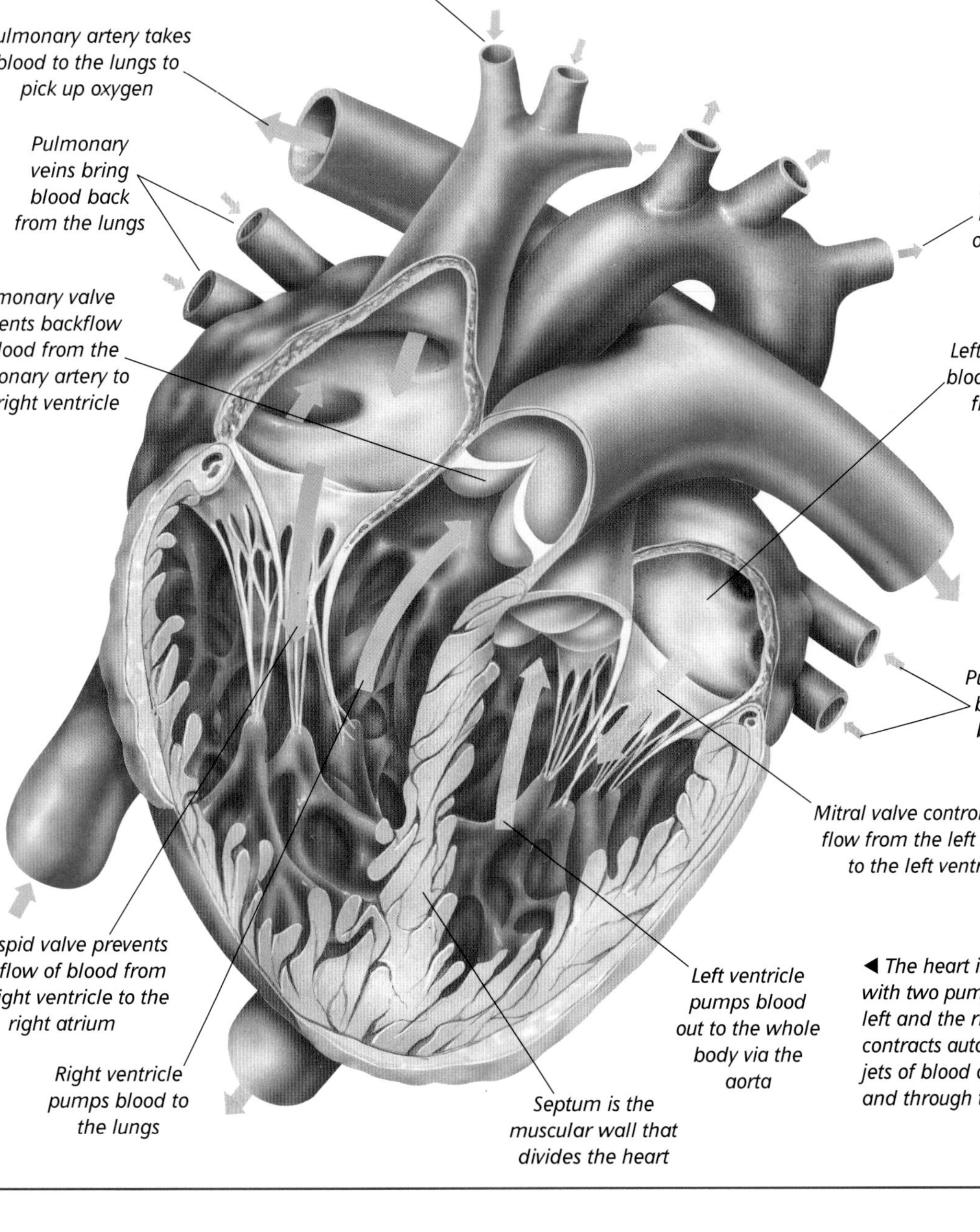
Superior vena cava (vein) brings blood low in oxygen back from the body to the right side of the heart
Pulmonary artery takes blood to the lungs to pick up oxygen
Pulmonary veins bring blood back from the lungs
Pulmonary valve prevents backflow of blood from the pulmonary artery to the right ventricle
Aorta (artery) sends blood rich in oxygen out to the whole body
Left atrium receives blood rich in oxygen from the lungs
Pulmonary veins bring blood rich in oxygen back from the lungs
Mitral valve controls blood flow from the left atrium to the left ventricle
Tricuspid valve prevents backflow of blood from the right ventricle to the right atrium
Right ventricle pumps blood to the lungs
Septum is the muscular wall that divides the heart
Left ventricle pumps blood out to the whole body via the aorta

◄ The heart is a double pump, with two pumping chambers, the left and the right ventricles. It contracts automatically to squeeze jets of blood out of the ventricles and through the arteries.

Heartbeat

- **The heartbeat** is the regular squeezing of the heart muscle to pump blood around the body.
- **The heartbeat has two phases** – systole (contraction) and diastole (resting).
- **Systole begins** when muscle contraction sweeps across the heart squeezing blood from the atria (blood receiving chambers) into the ventricles (pumping chambers).
- **When the contraction** reaches the ventricles, they squeeze blood into the arteries.
- **In diastole**, the heart muscle relaxes and the atria fill with blood again.
- **The rate of beating** is controlled by a special group of nerve cells called a pacemaker. Nerve signals from the brain control the pacemaker, making it go faster or slower as required.

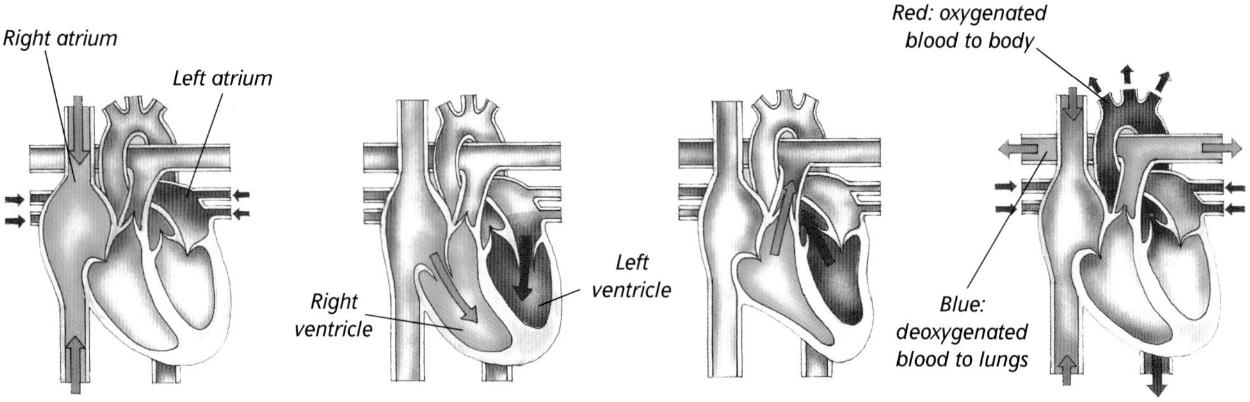
Right atrium
Left atrium
Right ventricle
Left ventricle
Red: oxygenated blood to body
Blue: deoxygenated blood to lungs

▲ *Blood floods into the relaxed atria.*

▲ *The wave of contraction squeezes blood into ventricles.*

▲ *Blood is squeezed out of the ventricles into the arteries.*

▲ *Blood starts to fill up the now relaxed atria again.*

Pulse

- **Your pulse** is the powerful high-pressure surge or wave that runs through your blood and vessels as the heart contracts strongly with each beat.
- **You can feel your pulse** by pressing two fingertips on the inside of your wrist, where the radial artery nears the surface.
- **Other pulse points** include the carotid artery in the neck and the brachial artery inside the elbow.

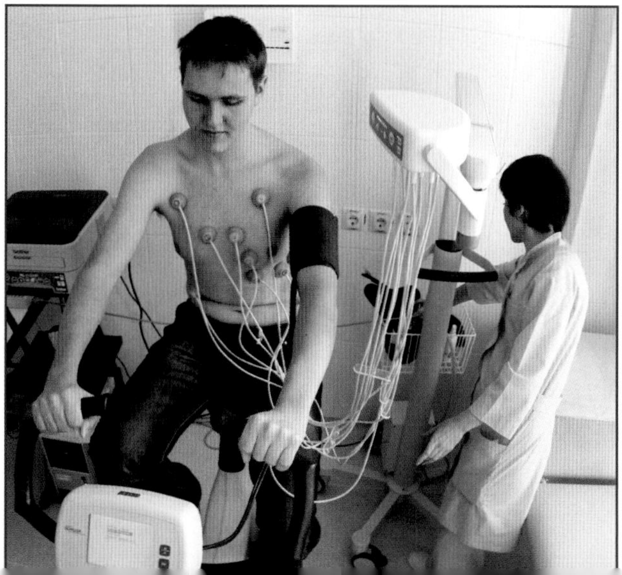

- **Checking the speed of the pulse** is a good way of finding out how healthy someone is.
- **Normal pulse rates** vary between 50 and 100 beats a minute. The average for a man is about 71, for a woman it is 80, and for children it is about 85.
- **Tachycardia** is the medical word for an abnormally fast heartbeat rate.
- **Someone who has tachycardia** when sitting down may have drunk too much coffee or tea, or taken drugs, or be suffering from anxiety or a fever, or have heart disease.
- **Bradycardia** is an abnormally slow heart rate.
- **Arrhythmia** is an abnormality in a person's heart rhythm.
- **Anyone with a heart problem** may be connected to a machine called an electrocardiogram (ECG) to monitor their heartbeat.

◀ *By monitoring how much heart rate goes up and down during exercise, an ECG can show how healthy someone's heart is.*

Valves

- **Valves are crucial** in the circulation of your blood and lymph fluid, ensuring that liquids flow only one way.
- **The heart has four valves** to make sure blood flows only one way through it.
- **On each side of the heart** there is a large valve between the atrium and the ventricle, and a smaller one where the arteries leave the ventricle.
- **The mitral valve** is the large valve on the left. The tricuspid valve is the large valve on the right.
- **The aortic valve** is the smaller valve on the left. The pulmonary is the smaller valve on the right.
- **Heart valves** can sometimes get stiff and narrowed, or may start to leak. This makes the heart work harder and can cause heart failure.
- **A faulty heart valve** may be replaced with a valve from a human or pig heart, or a mechanical valve.
- **Valves in the arteries and veins** are simply flaps that open only when the blood is flowing one way.
- **The lymphatic system** also has its own small valves to ensure lymph fluid is squeezed only one way.

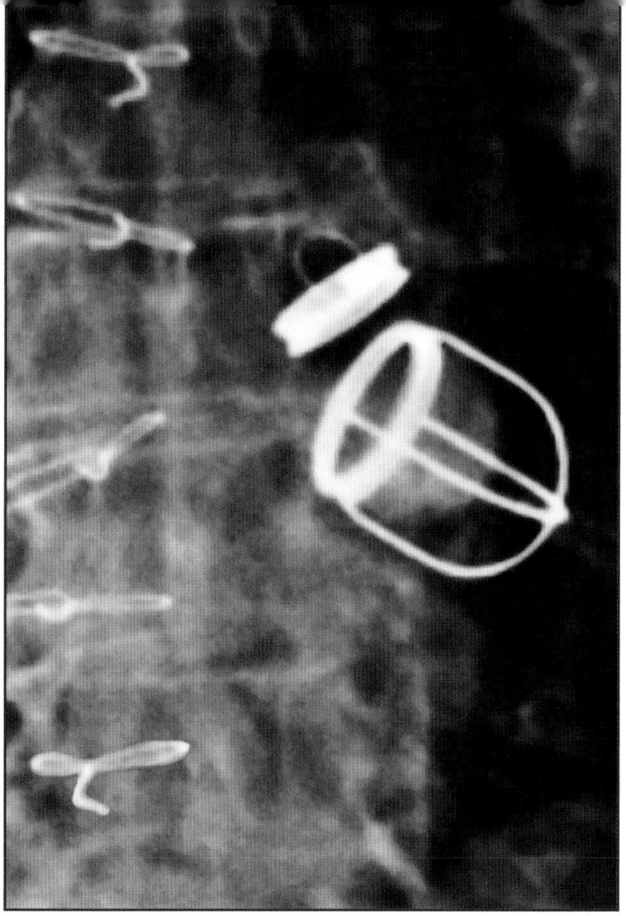

▲ *An X-ray of a patient who has had both the mitral and aortic valves of their heart replaced with artificial heart valves.*

Arteries and veins

DID YOU KNOW?

At any moment, 75 percent of the body's blood is in the veins.

- **An artery** is a tube-like blood vessel that carries blood away from the heart. Systemic arteries transport blood rich in oxygen around the body.
- **An arteriole** is a smaller branch off an artery. Arterioles branch into microscopic capillaries.
- **Arteries run alongside** most of the veins that return blood to the heart.
- **Arteries have thicker, stronger walls** than veins, and can expand or relax to control the blood flow.
- **Veins are blood vessels** that carry blood back to the heart. The body cells have taken the oxygen they need from the blood, so it is low in oxygen.
- **When blood** is low in oxygen, it is red-brown in colour. Oxygenated blood, carried by the arteries, is bright red.
- **The only veins** that carry oxygenated blood are the four pulmonary veins – they carry blood from the lungs to the heart.
- **The two largest veins** in the body are the vena cavae that flow into the heart from above and below.
- **Most large veins** have flaps inside them that act as valves to make sure that the blood only flows one way.
- **Unlike arteries**, veins collapse when empty because their walls are thin.
- **Blood is helped** through the veins by surrounding muscles squeezing the vein walls.

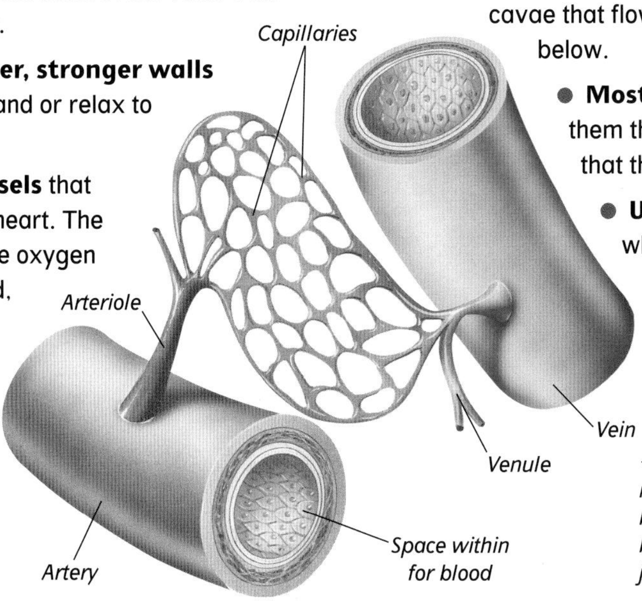
Capillaries
Arteriole
Artery
Space within for blood
Venule
Vein

◀ *This illustration shows how the main kinds of blood vessel in the body are connected. The artery (red) branches into tiny capillaries, which join up to supply the vein (blue).*

Capillaries

- **Capillaries** are the smallest of all the blood vessels, only visible under a microscope. They link the arterioles to the venules.
- **Capillaries** were discovered by Marcello Malphigi in 1661. There are 10 billion capillaries in the body, and the largest is just 0.2 mm wide.
- **Each capillary** is about 0.5–1 mm in length.
- **Capillary walls** are only one cell thick, which makes it easy for chemicals to pass through them.
- **Blood passes oxygen**, food and waste to and from each one of your body cells through the capillary walls.

DID YOU KNOW?

The average capillary is 0.001 mm in diameter – just wide enough for red blood cells to pass through one at a time.

- **Tissues which are very active**, such as muscles, liver and kidneys, have a particularly high number of capillaries.
- **Capillaries** allow more blood to reach the surface when you are warm, and less blood to reach the surface to save heat when you are cold.

◀ *You generate heat when exercising, which the body tries to lose by opening up capillaries in the skin, turning it red.*

Blood

- **Blood is the liquid** that circulates around the body. It carries oxygen and food to body cells, and takes carbon dioxide and waste away. It fights infection, keeps you warm and distributes chemicals.
- **Blood is made up** of red cells, white cells and platelets, all carried in a liquid called plasma. Plasma is 90 percent water, but also contains hundreds of other substances, including nutrients and hormones.

1
2
3

- **Oxygen turns blood bright red** when you bleed. In your veins it can be almost brown.
- **Platelets are tiny pieces of cell** that make blood clots form to stop bleeding.
- **Blood clots** also involve a lacy, fibrous network made from a protein called fibrin.
- **Most people's blood** belongs to one of four groups or types – A, O, B and AB. O is the most common.
- **Blood is also** either Rhesus positive (Rh+) or Rhesus negative (Rh–).
- **If your blood is Rh+ and your group is A**, your blood group is said to be A positive. If your blood is Rh– and your group is O, you are O negative, and so on.
- **When you are given blood** from another person's body it is called a transfusion. Your body will only accept blood from certain groups that match yours.
- **Blood transfusions** are given when someone has lost too much blood because of an injury or operation. It is also given to replace diseased blood.

◀ *When you are injured, red blood cells (1) and platelets (2) leak out into the surrounding tissues and a sticky substance called fibrin (3) is produced to help heal the wound.*

Blood cells

- **The blood has two main kinds of cell** – red cells and white cells – plus pieces of cell called platelets.
- **Red cells** are button-shaped and mainly contain red protein called haemoglobin.

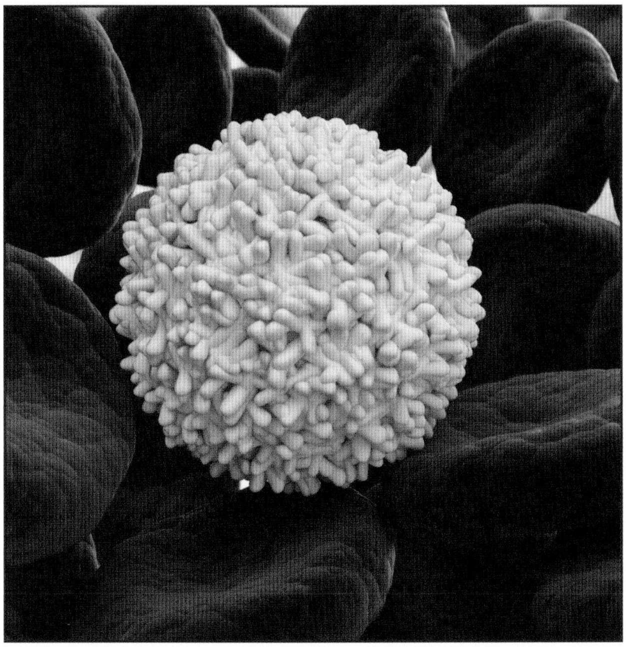

DID YOU KNOW?

Red blood cells have a lifespan of only four months, so the body is constantly making more to replace them.

- **Haemoglobin** allows red blood cells to transport oxygen around your body.
- **Red cells** also contain enzymes that the body uses to make certain chemical processes happen.
- **White blood cells** are big cells called leucocytes and most types are involved in fighting infections.
- **Most white cells** contain tiny little grains and are called granulocytes.
- **Most granulocytes** are giant white cells called neutrophils. They are the blood's cleaners, and their task is to eat up invaders.
- **Eosinophils and basophils** are granulocytes that are involved in fighting disease and allergies. Some release antibodies that help fight infection.

◀ *Button-shaped red blood cells carry oxygen through the blood. Spiky ball-shaped white blood cells help your body fight infection.*

Marrow

- **Some bones** contain a core of jelly-like substance called marrow.
- **Bone marrow** can be red or yellow, depending on whether it has more blood tissue or fat tissue.
- **Red bone marrow** is the body's factory where all blood cells, apart from some white cells, are made.
- **All bone marrow** is red when you are a baby, but as you grow older, more and more turns yellow.
- **In adults**, red marrow is only found in the spine, breastbone, ribs, shoulder blades, pelvis and the skull.
- **Yellow bone marrow** is a store for fat, but it may turn to red marrow when you are ill.
- **The many different** kinds of blood cell all start life in red marrow as one type of cell called a stem cell. Different blood cells develop as stem cells divide and re-divide.
- **Some stem cells** divide to form red blood cells and platelets.

▶ *Inside most bones is a core called marrow. The red marrow (shown here in green) of some bones is the body's blood cell factory, making 5 million new cells a day.*

- **Some stem cells** divide to form lymphoblasts. These divide in turn to form various different kinds of white cells – monocytes, granulocytes and lymphocytes.
- **The white cells** made in bone marrow play a key part in the body's immune system. This is why bone marrow transplants can help people with illnesses that affect their immune system.

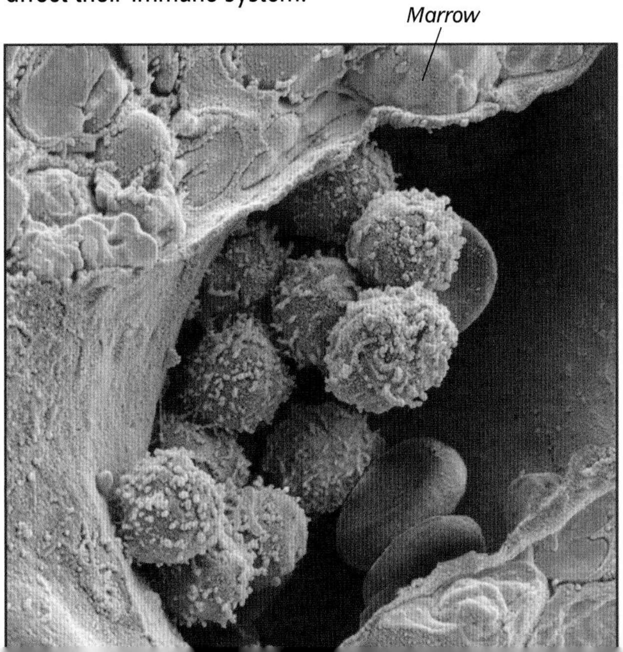
Marrow

Inside the chest

The body needs a constant supply of oxygen in order to stay alive. The heart and lungs work together within the chest to get oxygen from the air and to send it out around the body in the bloodstream.

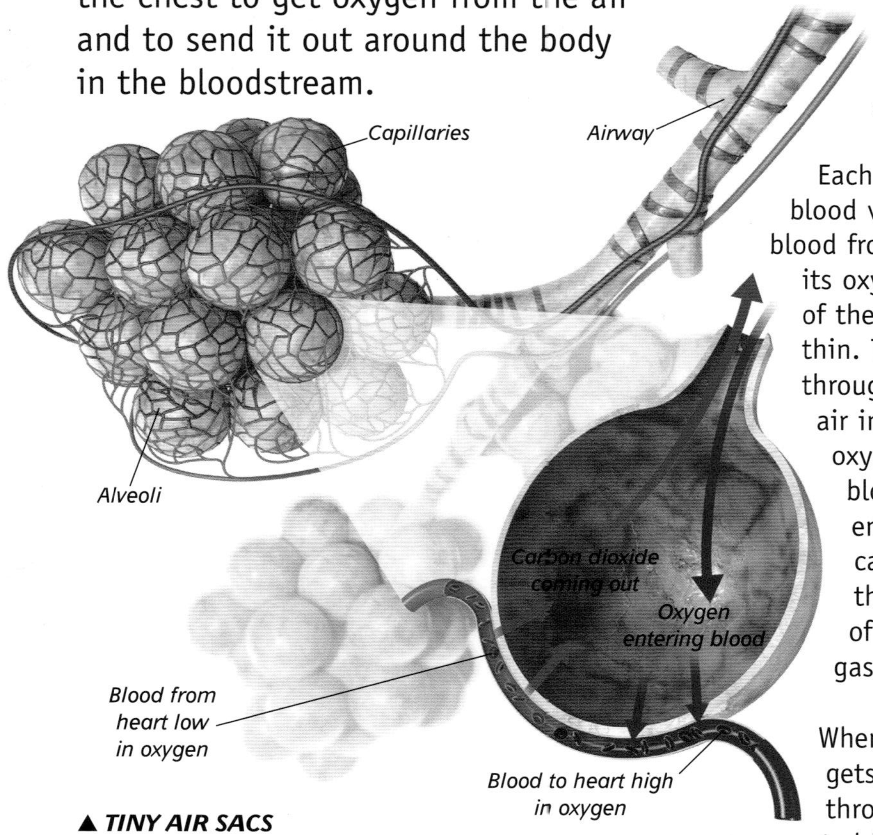
Capillaries
Airway
Alveoli
Carbon dioxide coming out
Oxygen entering blood
Blood from heart low in oxygen
Blood to heart high in oxygen

▲ *TINY AIR SACS*
The millions of tiny air sacs (alveoli) in the lungs are where oxygen enters the bloodstream and waste carbon dioxide comes out.

When a person breathes in, air is sucked in through the nose and mouth, and carried down to the lungs through the trachea (windpipe).

At the bottom, the trachea divides into two large air tubes, the bronchi, which each carry the air into a lung. Within the lungs the air passages divide again and again until they end in tiny clusters of air sacs called alveoli. These look like bunches of grapes, and there are millions of them in each lung.

Each alveolus is surrounded by very small blood vessels called capillaries. These bring blood from the heart, which has had a lot of its oxygen used up by the body. The walls of the alveolus and capillaries are very thin. This means that oxygen can pass through. When a person breathes in, the air inside the alveolus has a lot of oxygen in it so this passes into the blood. At the same time that oxygen enters the blood, the waste gas carbon dioxide comes out and into the air in the alveolus. This swapping of oxygen and carbon dioxide is called gas exchange.

When a person breathes out the body gets rid of the waste carbon dioxide through the nose and mouth. The newly oxygenated blood in the capillaries around the alveoli travels back to the heart, which then pumps it to all parts of the body. This process occurs continuously throughout a person's whole life. The heart and lungs work together to bring the body the oxygen it needs to survive.

► *CARRYING OXYGEN*
Oxygen is carried in the blood by red blood cells, attached to a special protein called haemoglobin. Haemoglobin picks up oxygen in the lungs and carries it to the body's tissues where it is needed.

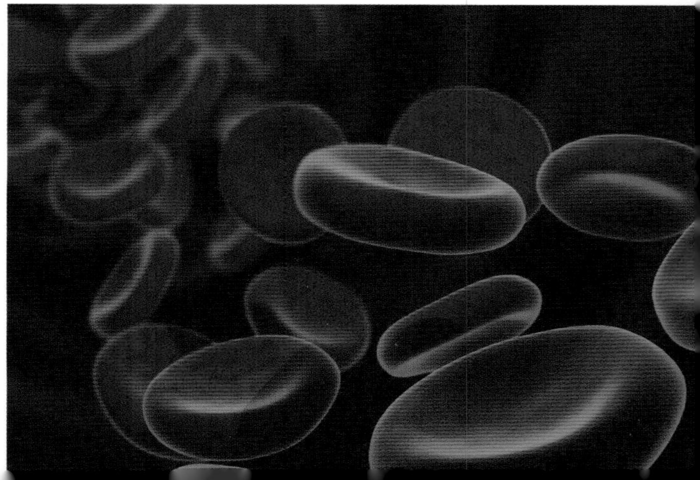

NEEDING MORE OXYGEN

The body needs a certain amount of oxygen all the time, but during exercise the muscles are more active and need more oxygen. So the heart beats faster, and breathing becomes faster and deeper. After exercise, the heart and breathing go back to normal, but this may take a little while.

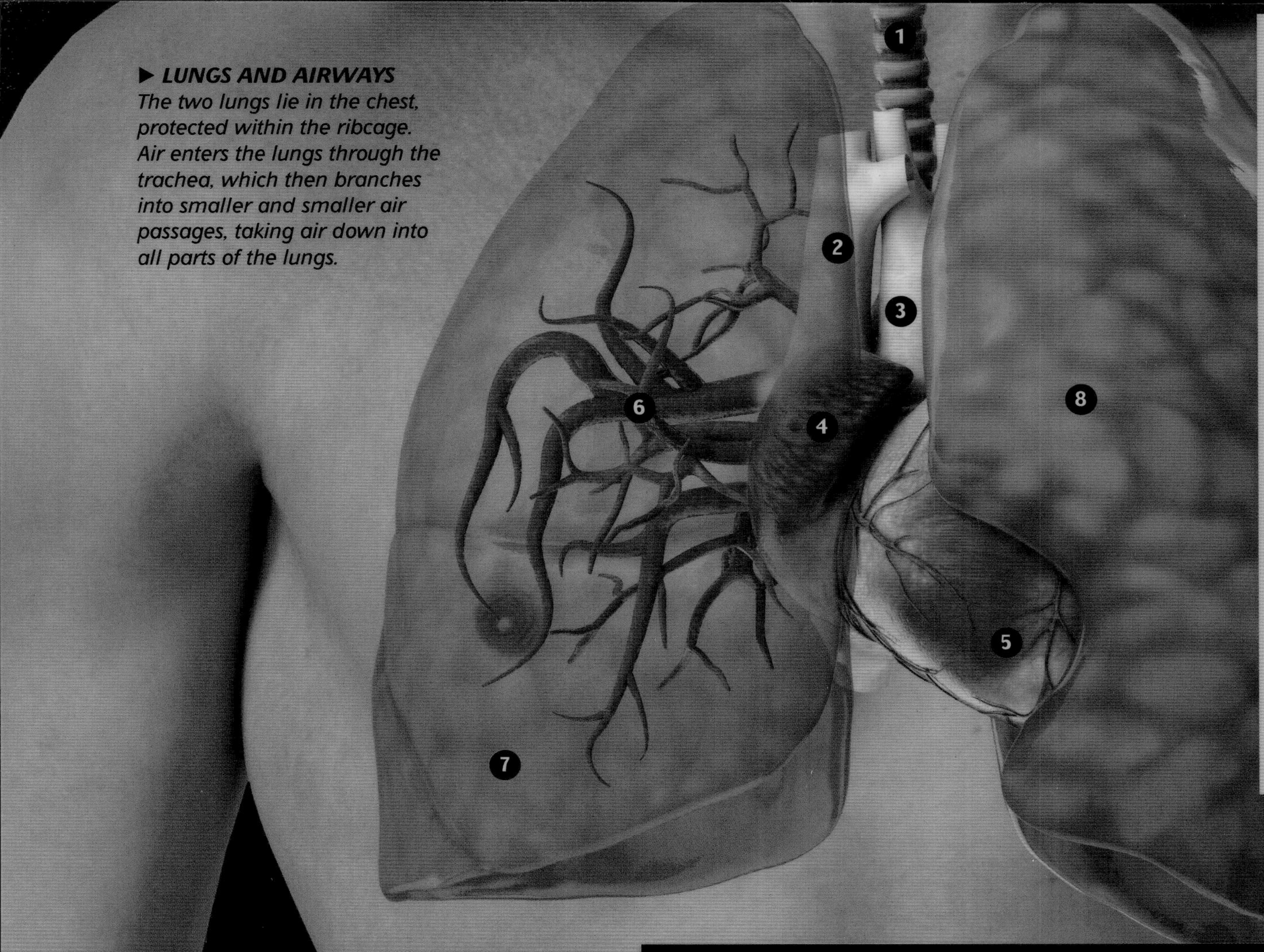
1
2
3
4
5
6
7
8

► ***LUNGS AND AIRWAYS***
The two lungs lie in the chest, protected within the ribcage. Air enters the lungs through the trachea, which then branches into smaller and smaller air passages, taking air down into all parts of the lungs.

KEY

1 *Trachea (windpipe)*
2 *Superior vena cava*
3 *Aorta*
4 *Right atrium of heart*
5 *Ventricles of heart*
6 *Blood vessels in lung*
7 *Right lung*
8 *Left lung*

ASTHMA

Asthma is a condition that affects the airways, which are more sensitive than normal. If someone has asthma and they come into contact with something that irritates the lungs, the airways become narrower. This is because the muscles in their walls contract, the lining of the airway becomes inflamed and swells, and the person produces more sticky mucus (phlegm). When the airway is narrower it is harder to breathe and they get asthma symptoms, such as wheezing, chest tightness or a cough. People can take medicines to help stop this happening.

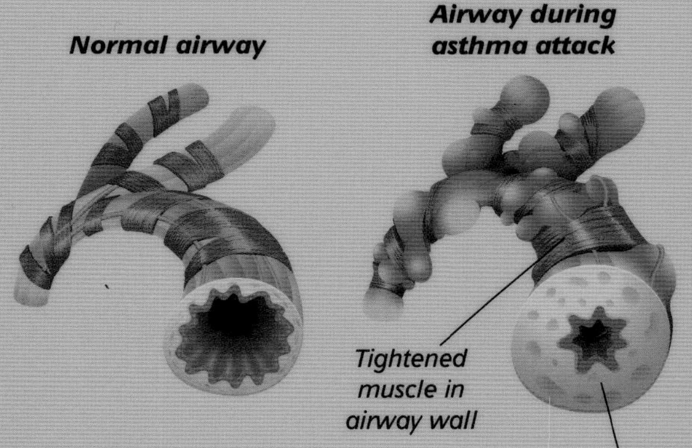
Normal airway
Airway during asthma attack
Tightened muscle in airway wall
Wall inflamed and thickened

SMOKING DAMAGES LUNGS

Smoking tobacco damages the lungs and stops blood from carrying as much oxygen as it should. This CT (computerized tomography) scan of the lungs shows emphysema – a serious medical condition where smoking damages the walls of the alveoli in the lungs. It leaves areas where there is one large air sac instead of many tiny ones. This makes it harder for a person to get the oxygen they need and they become short of breath.

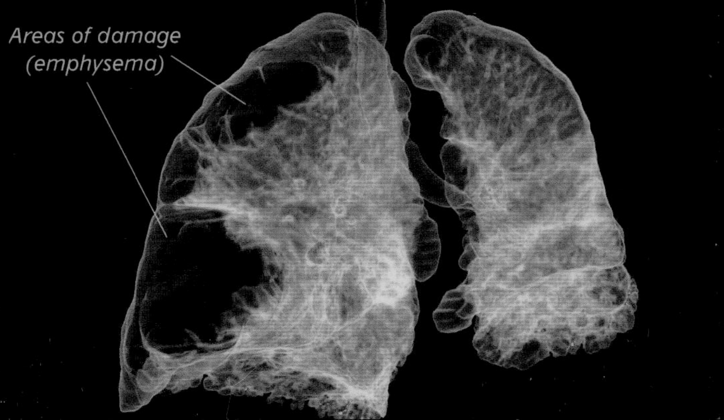
Areas of damage (emphysema)

ASTHMA

Asthma is a condition that affects the airways, which are more sensitive than normal. If someone has asthma and they come into contact with something that irritates the lungs, the airways become narrower. This is because the muscles in their walls contract, the lining of the airway becomes inflamed and swells, and the person produces more sticky mucus (phlegm). When the airway is narrower it is harder to breathe and they get asthma symptoms, such as wheezing, chest tightness or a cough. People can take medicines to help stop this happening.

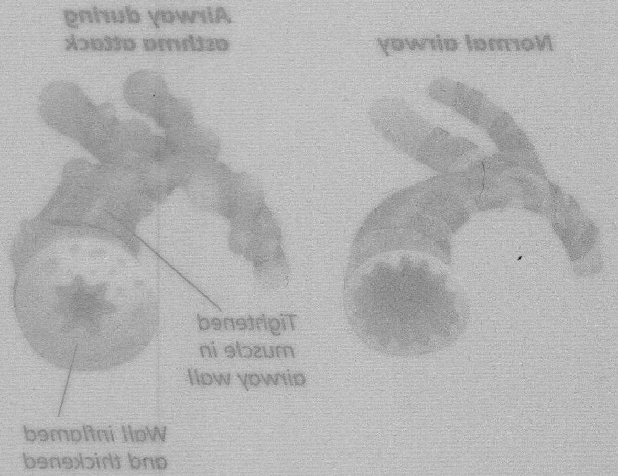

Normal airway
Airway during asthma attack
Tightened muscle in airway wall
Wall inflamed and thickened

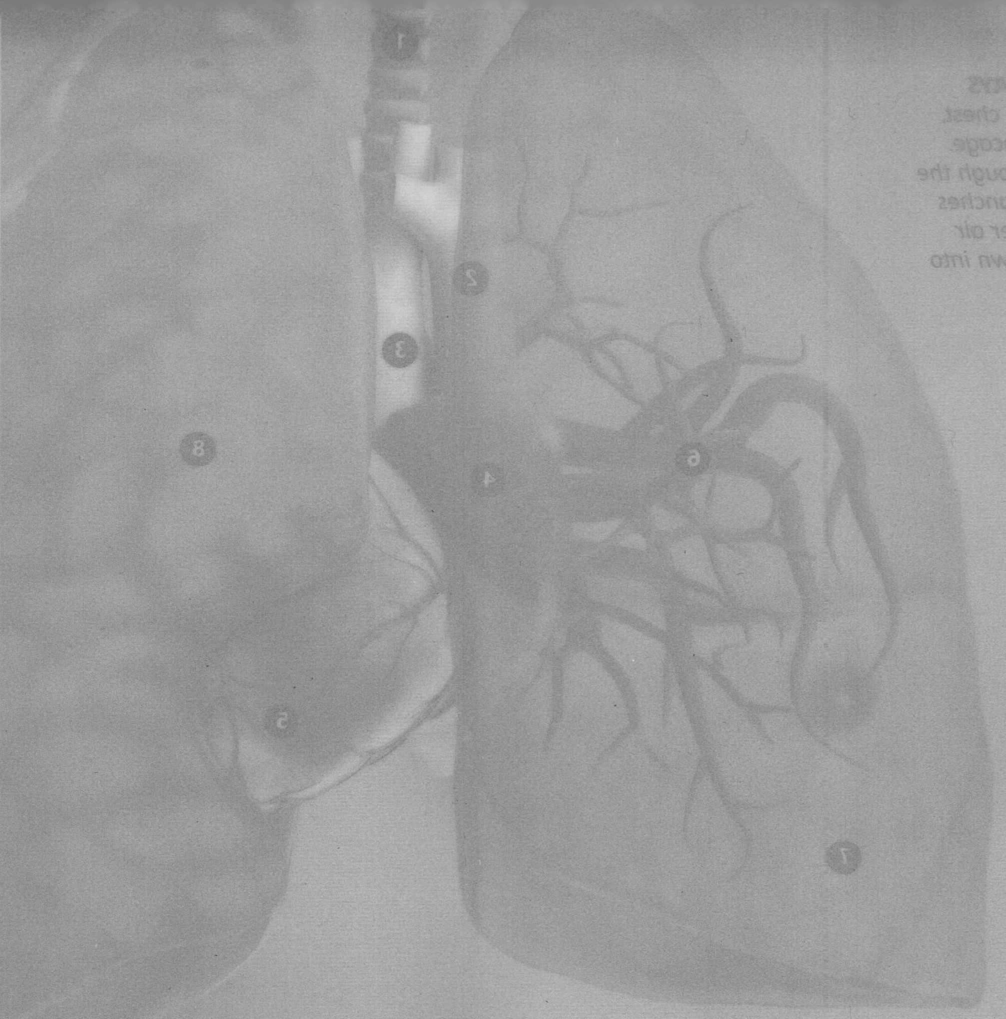

1
2
3
4
5
6
7
8

► LUNGS AND AIRWAYS
The two lungs lie in the chest, protected within the ribcage. Air enters the lungs through the trachea, which then branches into smaller and smaller air passages, taking air down into all parts of the lungs.

KEY

1 Trachea (windpipe)
2 Superior vena cava
3 Aorta
4 Right atrium of heart
5 Ventricles of heart
6 Blood vessels in lung
7 Right lung
8 Left lung

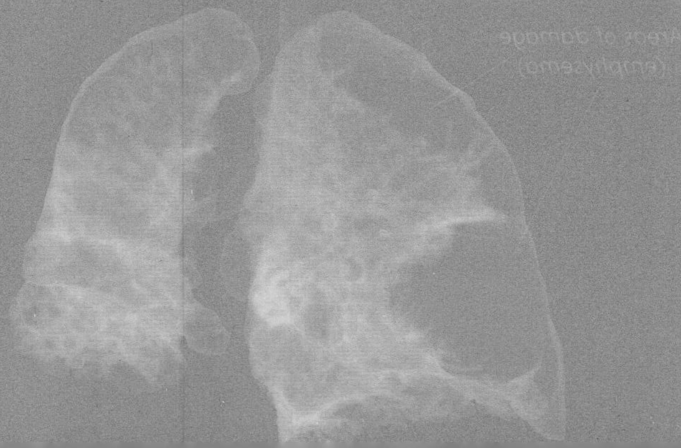

Areas of damage (emphysema)

SMOKING DAMAGES LUNGS

Smoking tobacco damages the lungs and stops blood from carrying as much oxygen as it should. This CT (computerized tomography) scan of the lungs shows emphysema – a serious medical condition where smoking damages the walls of the alveoli in the lungs. It leaves areas where there is one large air sac instead of many tiny ones. This makes it harder for a person to get the oxygen they need and they become short of breath.

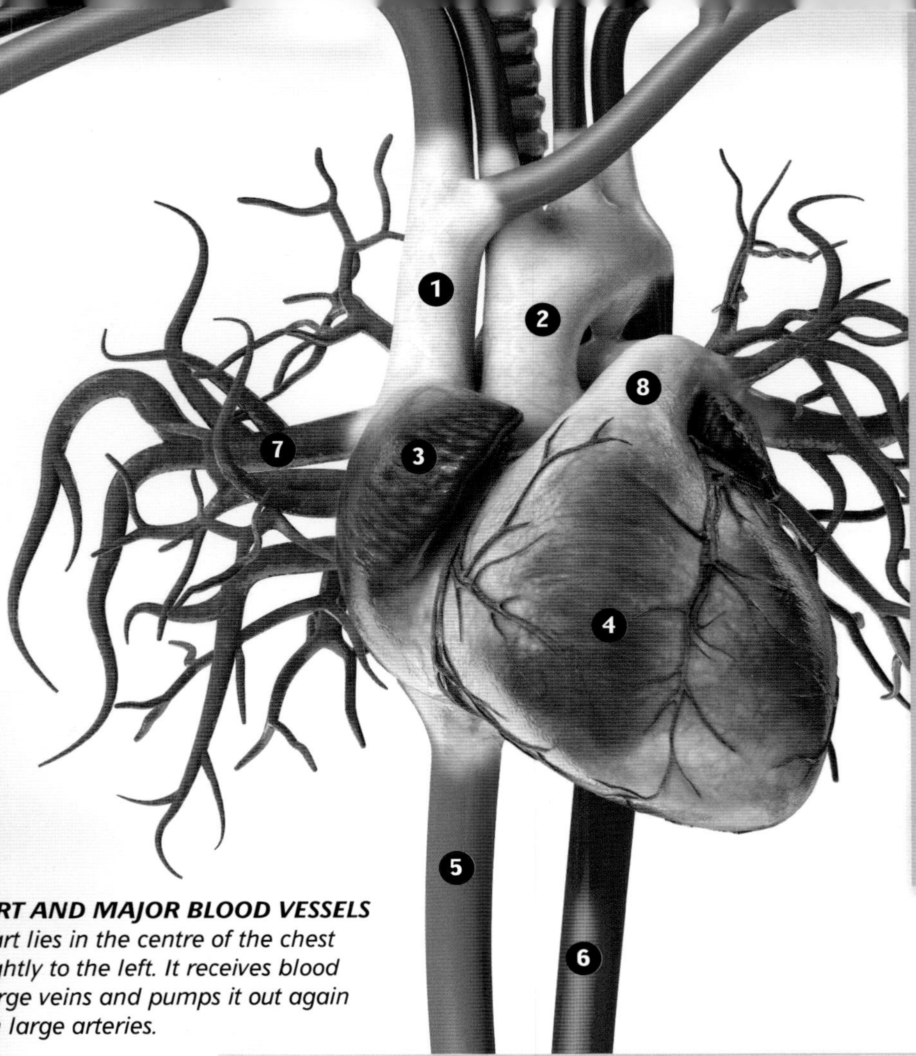
1
2
3
4
5
6
7
8

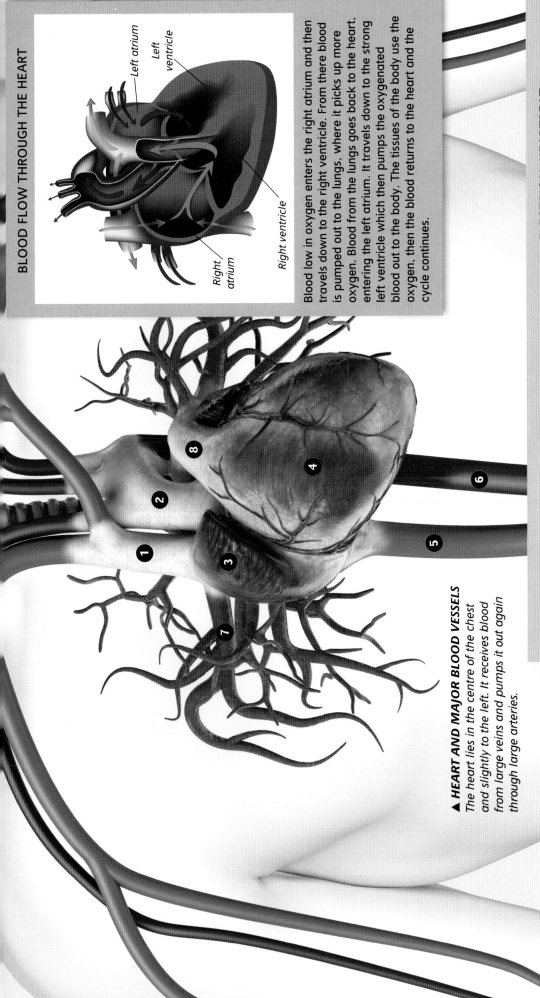

▲ ***HEART AND MAJOR BLOOD VESSELS***
The heart lies in the centre of the chest and slightly to the left. It receives blood from large veins and pumps it out again through large arteries.

KEY

1 *Superior vena cava*
2 *Aorta*
3 *Right atrium of heart*
4 *Ventricles of heart*
5 *Inferior vena cava*
6 *Descending aorta*
7 *Blood vessels in lung*
8 *Pulmonary trunk*

BLOOD FLOW THROUGH THE HEART

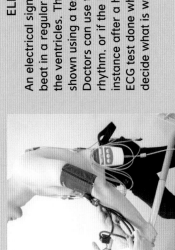

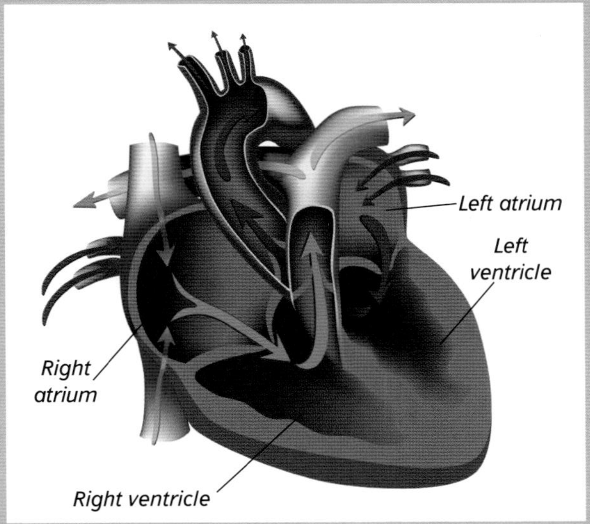
Left atrium
Left ventricle
Right atrium
Right ventricle

Blood low in oxygen enters the right atrium and then travels down to the right ventricle. From there blood is pumped out to the lungs, where it picks up more oxygen. Blood from the lungs goes back to the heart, entering the left atrium. It travels down to the strong left ventricle which then pumps the oxygenated blood out to the body. The tissues of the body use the oxygen, then the blood returns to the heart and the cycle continues.

ELECTRICAL HEARTBEAT

An electrical signal travels down the heart to make it beat in a regular pattern. First the atria contract, then the ventricles. The electrical activity in the heart can be shown using a test called an ECG (electrocardiogram). Doctors can use this test to see if there is an abnormal rhythm, or if the heart has become damaged, for instance after a heart attack. Sometimes, having the ECG test done while a person exercises helps doctors to decide what is wrong.

The respiratory system

DID YOU KNOW?

Your throat is linked to your ears by tubes, which open when you swallow to balance air pressure.

▶ *The respiratory system includes the upper and lower airways, which branch into the lungs.*

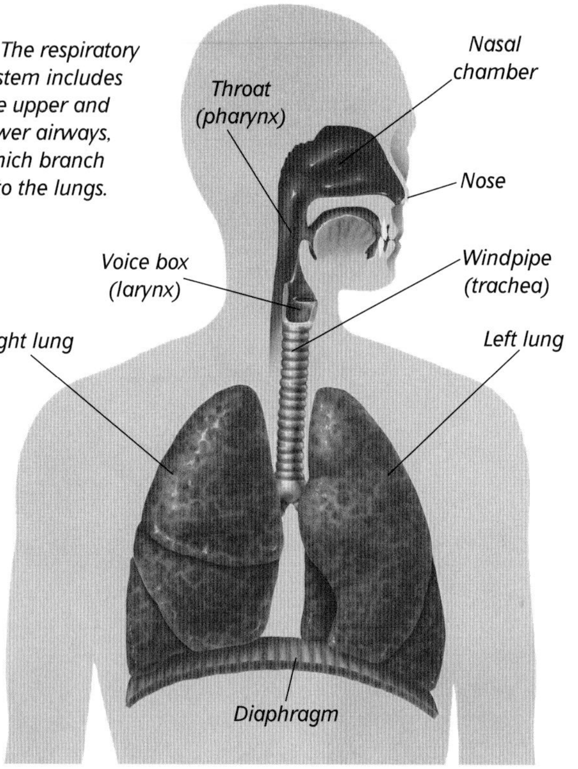
Nasal chamber
Throat (pharynx)
Nose
Voice box (larynx)
Windpipe (trachea)
Right lung
Left lung
Diaphragm

- **The respiratory system** includes the lungs and the airways. The airways allow the passage of air in and out between the nose and the lungs when breathing.
- **The airways are described** as upper and lower. The division between upper and lower is at the level of the voice box (larynx).
- **The upper airways** include the nose, throat (pharynx) and voice box (larynx).
- **The lower airways** include the windpipe (trachea), its branches and the airways of the lungs.
- **The mouth** is part of the airway only when vocalizing (speaking, shouting and singing) or when the nose is blocked.
- **The pharynx** allows the passage of food as well as air. It is the tube at the back of the nose and mouth and below the back of the tongue.
- **The tonsils and adenoids** are swellings of lymph tissue that protect the airways from infection, especially in young children. They get smaller as you grow older.
- **The tonsils** are at the back of the mouth. You can see them on either side of the throat when you open your mouth wide.
- **The adenoids** are at the back of the nose.
- **The sinuses** are chambers containing air within the bones of the skull that form the face and forehead. If mucus blocks them when you get a cold, you may get pain in your face and teeth.

▼ *When you run fast, your muscles need extra oxygen, so your lungs must work hard to take in more air.*

Breathing

● **You breathe** because every cell in your body needs a continuous supply of oxygen to burn glucose, the high-energy substance from digested food.

● **Scientists call breathing 'respiration'**. Breathing in is called 'inhalation' and breathing out, 'exhalation'.

● **Oxygen is taken into the lungs**, and then carried in the blood to cells. Waste carbon dioxide from the cells is returned in the blood to the lungs, to be breathed out.

● **The diaphragm** is the sheet of muscle below your chest. It works with your chest muscles to make you breathe.

● **Speaking and singing** depend on the larynx (voice box) in the neck. This has bands of tissue called the vocal cords, which vibrate as air is breathed out over them.

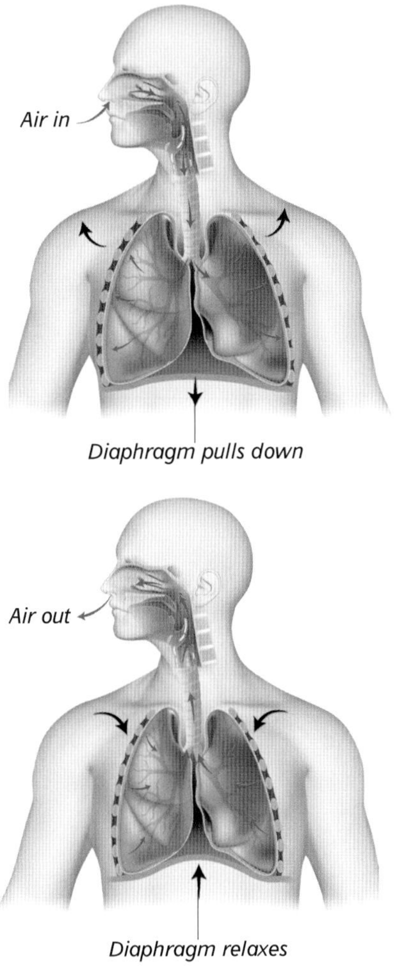
Air in
Diaphragm pulls down
Air out
Diaphragm relaxes

● **When you are silent**, the vocal cords are apart, and air passes between them freely. When you speak or sing, the cords tighten across the airway and vibrate to make sounds.

● **The tighter** the vocal cords are stretched, the more high-pitched the sounds you make will be.

● **The basic sound** produced by the vocal cords is 'aah'. By changing the shape of your mouth, lips and tongue, you can change this simple sound into letters and words.

● **Men's vocal cords** are longer than women's, so they vibrate more slowly and produce a deeper sound.

◀ *Breathing uses two main sets of muscles, the diaphragm and those between the ribs.*

The lungs

● **The lungs** are a pair of spongy organs inside your chest.

● **Each lung** is divided into lobes. The right lung has three, but the left lung has only two, to allow room for the heart.

● **Each lung** is surrounded by a double-layered membrane called the pleura. Fluid between them lubricates the movement of the lungs during breathing.

● **When you breathe in**, air rushes in through your nose or mouth, down your trachea (windpipe) and into the airways in your lungs.

● **The two biggest airways** are called bronchi. They branch into smaller airways called bronchioles.

● **The surface** of the airways is protected by a film of mucus. The lining cells have tiny hairs that waft the mucus towards the nose and mouth to clean the airways.

● **The bronchioles** end at groups of tiny 'bubbles' called alveoli.

● **Alveoli** are covered by tiny blood vessels, and alveoli walls are one cell thick – thin enough to let oxygen and carbon dioxide seep through.

▼ *A powerful microscope picture of the lining of the lungs showing the tiny hairs (cilia).*

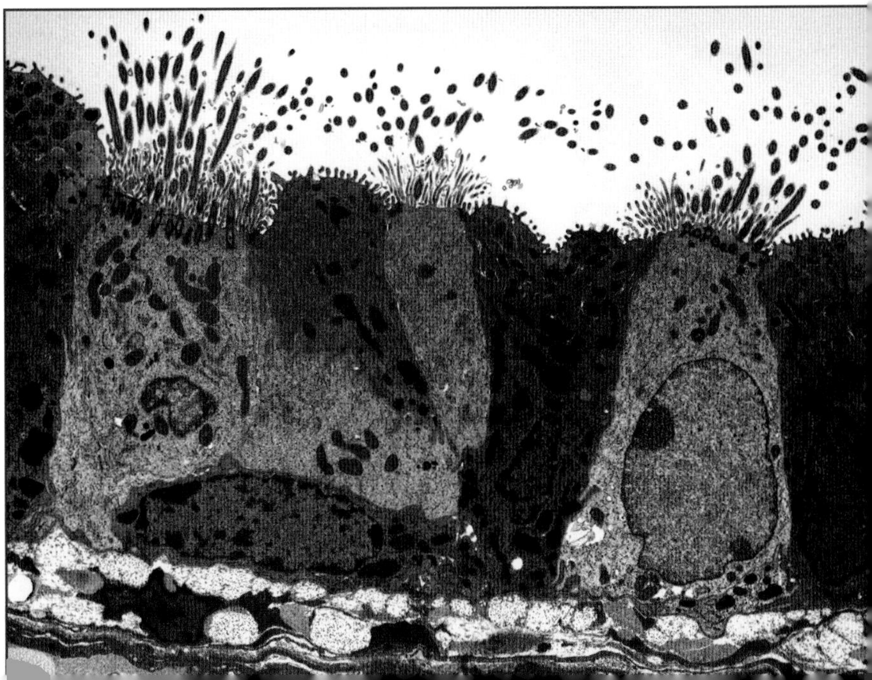

The skeleton

- **The skeleton** is a rigid framework of bones, which provides an anchor for the muscles, supports the skin and other organs, and protects vital organs.
- **An adult's skeleton has 206 bones** joined together by ligaments.
- **A baby's skeleton has 300** or more bones, but some of these fuse (join) together as the baby grows older.
- **The parts of an adult skeleton** that have fused into one bone include the skull and the pelvis.
- **The skeleton** has two main parts – the axial skeleton and the appendicular skeleton.
- **The axial skeleton** is the 80 bones of the upper body. It includes the skull, the vertebrae of the backbone, the ribs and the breastbone. The arm and shoulder bones are suspended from it.
- **The appendicular skeleton** is the other 126 bones – the arm and shoulder bones, and the leg and hip bones. It includes the femur (thigh bone), the body's longest bone.
- **The word skeleton** comes from the ancient Greek word for 'dry'.
- **Most women and girls** have smaller and lighter skeletons than men and boys.

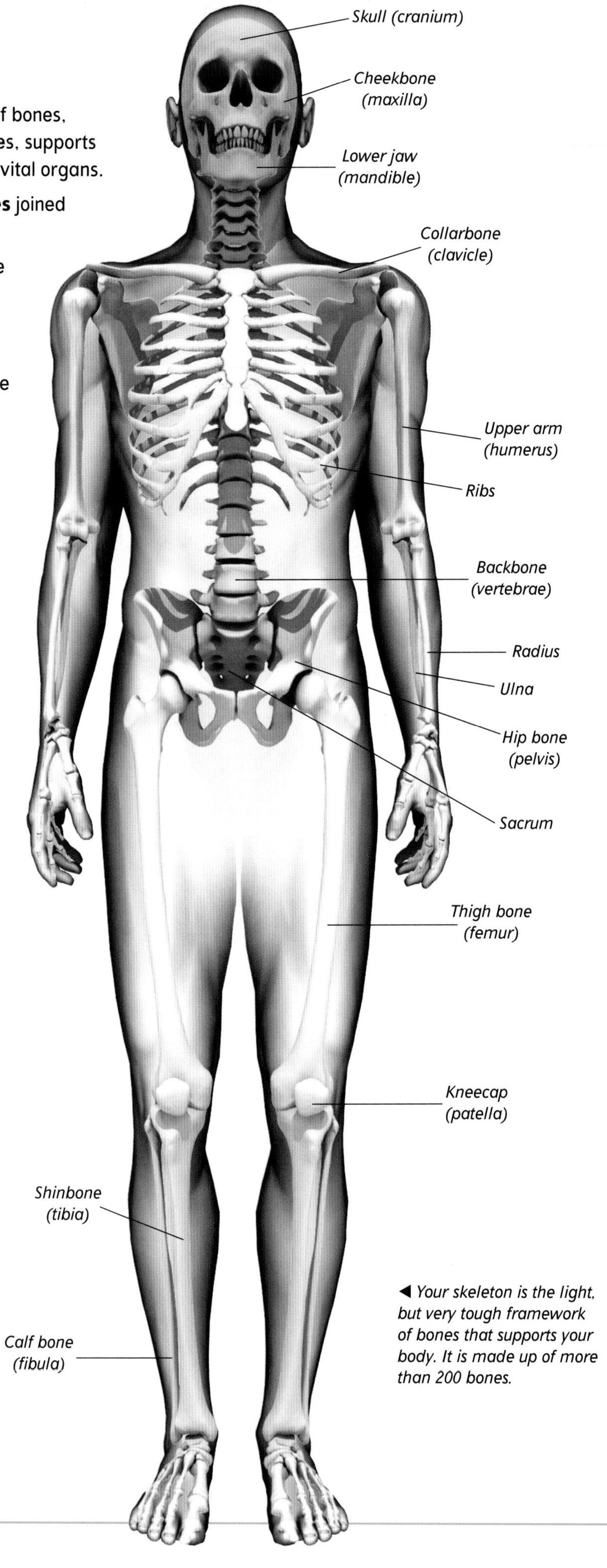
Skull (cranium)
Cheekbone (maxilla)
Lower jaw (mandible)
Collarbone (clavicle)
Upper arm (humerus)
Ribs
Backbone (vertebrae)
Radius
Ulna
Hip bone (pelvis)
Sacrum
Thigh bone (femur)
Kneecap (patella)
Shinbone (tibia)
Calf bone (fibula)

◀ *Your skeleton is the light, but very tough framework of bones that supports your body. It is made up of more than 200 bones.*

DID YOU KNOW?

There are 27 bones in each of your hands and 26 bones in each of your feet.

Bones

- **Bones** can cope with twice the squeezing pressure that granite can, or four times the stretching tension that concrete can, before breaking. Weight for weight, bone is at least five times as strong as steel.
- **Bones are so light** that they only make up 14 percent of your body's total weight.
- **Bones get their rigidity** from hard deposits of minerals such as calcium and phosphate.
- **Bones get their flexibility** from tough, elastic, rope-like fibres of collagen.
- **The hard outside of bones** (compact bone) is reinforced by strong rods called osteons. The inside (spongy bone) is a light honeycomb made of thin supporting bars (trabeculae), which are angled to take stress. Some bones have a core of jelly-like bone marrow.
- **Bones are living tissue** packed with cells called osteocytes. Each osteocyte is housed in its own hole, or lacuna.
- **In some parts of each bone**, there are special cells called osteoblasts that make new bone. In other parts, cells called osteoclasts break up old bone.
- **Bones grow** by getting longer near the end – at a region called the epiphyseal plate.

▼ *Bones are strong but light, with a complicated structure.*

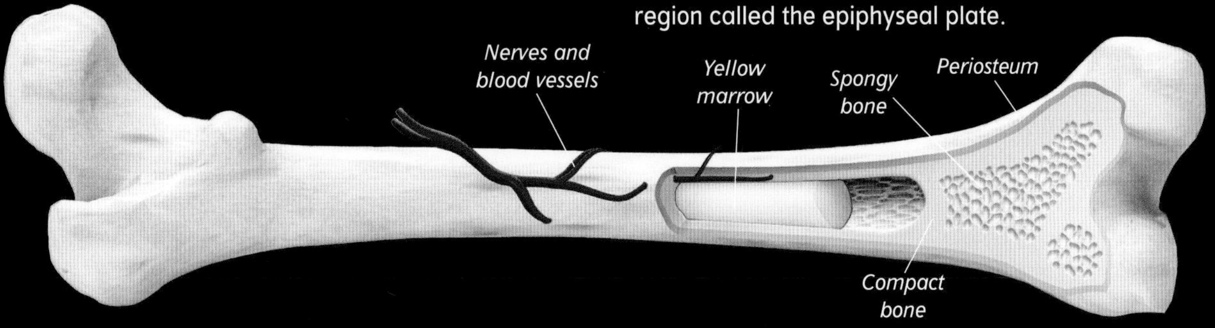
Nerves and blood vessels
Yellow marrow
Spongy bone
Periosteum
Compact bone

The skull

- **The skull** (cranium) is the hard bone case that protects your brain.
- **The skull looks** as though it is a single bone. In fact, it is made up of 22 separate bones, cemented together along rigid joints called sutures.
- **The dome** on top is called the cranial vault. It is made from eight curved pieces of bone fused (joined) together.
- **A baby has soft spots** called fontanelles in its skull because the bones join slowly over about 18 months.
- **As well as the sinuses** of the nose, the skull has four large cavities – the cranial cavity for the brain, the nasal cavity (the nose) and two orbits for the eyes.

DID YOU KNOW?

Archaeologists can use computer analysis of ancient skulls to reconstruct the faces of people who died long ago.

- **There are holes in the skull** to allow blood vessels and nerves through, including the optic nerves to the eyes and the olfactory tracts to the nose.
- **The biggest hole** is in the base of the skull. It is called the foramen magnum, and the brain stem goes through it to meet the spinal cord.
- **In the 19th century**, people called phrenologists thought they could work out people's characters from little bumps on their skulls.

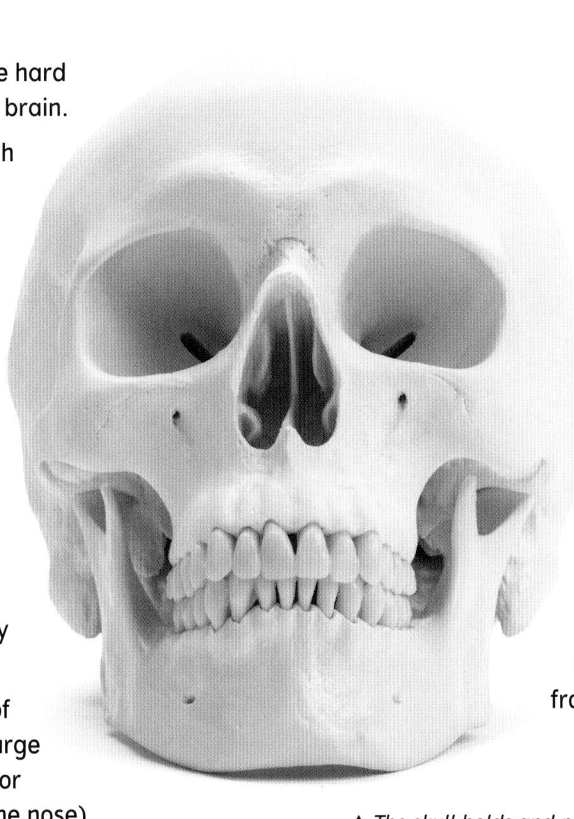

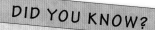

▲ *The skull holds and protects the brain. It is made of a number of bones that fuse together.*

Backbone

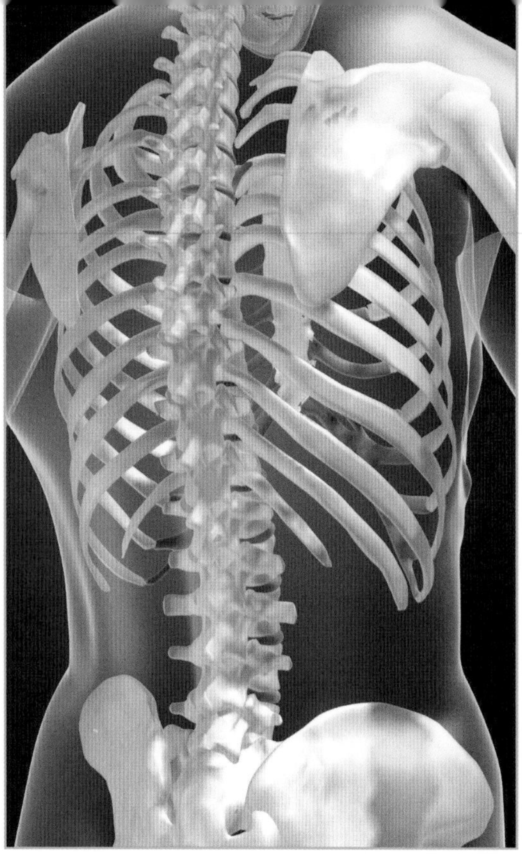

DID YOU KNOW?

The story character the Hunchback of Notre Dame suffered from kyphosis – excessive curving of the spine.

◀ *The backbone is not straight – its 33 vertebrae curve into an S-shape.*

● **The backbone** (spine) extends from the base of the skull down to the hips.

● **It is a column** of drum-shaped bones called vertebrae (singular, vertebra). There are 33 altogether. Some of these fuse (join) as the body grows.

● **Each vertebra** is linked to the next by facet joints, which are like tiny ball-and-socket joints.

● **The vertebrae are separated** by discs of rubbery material.

● **The bones of the spine** are divided into five groups from top to bottom. These are the cervical (7 bones), the thoracic (12 bones), the lumbar (5 bones), the sacrum (5 fused bones), and the coccyx (4 fused bones).

● **The cervical spine** is the vertebrae of the neck. The thoracic spine is the back of the chest, and each bone has a pair of ribs attached to it. The lumbar spine is the small of the back.

● **A normal spine** curves in an S-shape – the cervical spine curves forwards, the thoracic section backwards, the lumbar forwards, and the sacrum backwards.

● **On the back** of each vertebra is a bridge called the spinal process. The bridges on each bone link to form a tube that holds the spinal cord, the body's central bundle of nerves.

Ribs

● **The ribs** are the thin, flattish bones that curve around your chest.

● **The rib bones**, the backbone and the breastbone combine to make up the rib cage.

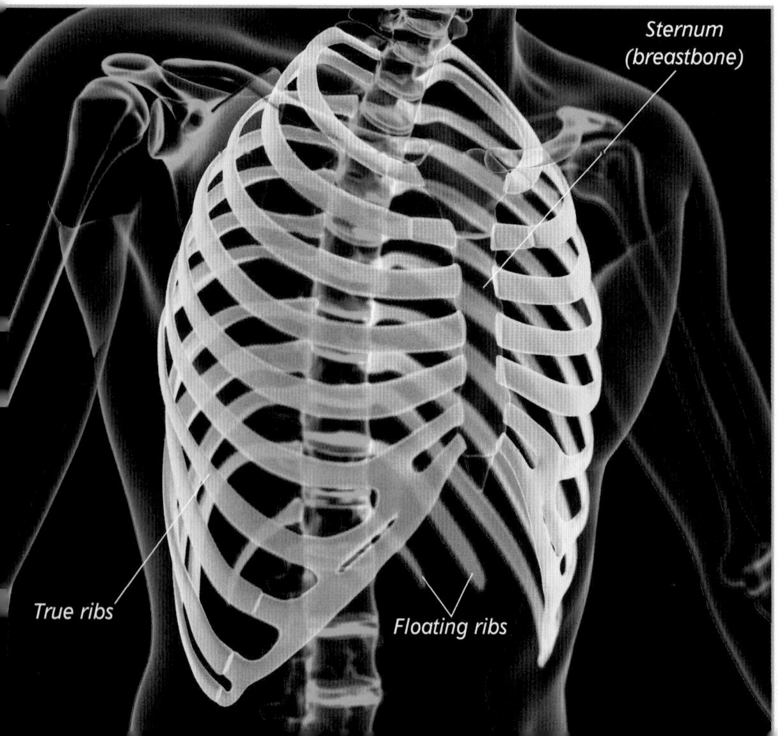
Sternum (breastbone)
True ribs
Floating ribs

● **The rib cage** protects vital organs such as the heart, lungs, liver, kidneys and stomach.

● **You have 12 pairs** of ribs altogether.

● **Seven pairs** of your ribs are true ribs. Each of these ribs is attached to the breastbone via a strip of costal cartilage, and curves around to join one of the vertebrae that make up the backbone.

● **There are three pairs** of false ribs. These are attached to vertebrae but are not linked to the breastbone. Instead, each rib is attached to the rib above it by cartilage.

● **There are two pairs** of floating ribs. These are attached only to the vertebrae of the backbone.

● **The gaps between the ribs** are called intercostal spaces. They hold sheets of muscle that expand and relax the chest during breathing.

● **The bones of the ribs** contain red marrow and are one of the body's major blood-cell factories.

◀ *The ribs provide a framework for the chest and form a protective cage around the heart, lungs and other organs.*

The pelvis

- **The pelvis** has two main functions. It allows movement of the body, such as walking and running, and it supports and protects the internal organs of the abdomen and pelvic cavity.
- **The pelvis** is a strong and sturdy ring of bone which is formed by the two hip bones, the sacrum and the coccyx. These are held firmly together by strong ligaments.
- **Each hip bone** is itself made up of three bones – the ilium, the ischium and the pubis. These fuse together to form one solid structure that contains the socket half of the ball-and-socket hip joint.
- **The sacrum** is a wedge-shaped bone made up of five vertebrae that have become fused together. The back of the sacrum is roughened, where muscles attach to it.
- **The coccyx**, or tailbone, forms the lowest part of the spine. It is a small, triangular-shaped bone made up by the fusing of four tiny vertebrae.
- **A woman's pelvis** is much wider than a man's. This is because the opening has to be wide enough for a baby to pass through when it is born.
- **Experts can** usually tell the sex of a skeleton by looking at the pelvis.

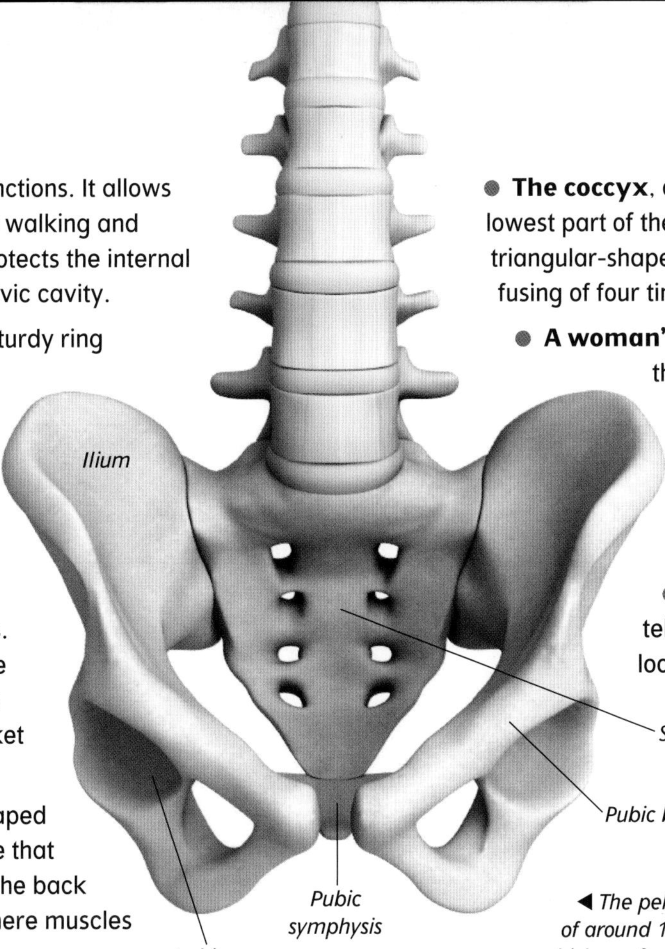
Ilium
Sacrum
Pubic bone
Pubic symphysis
Ischium

◀ *The pelvis is a strong ring made up of around 15 smaller bones, many of which are fused together.*

Hands and feet

- **Half of the bones** in the body are in the hands and the feet. Each hand has 27 bones, and each foot has 26.
- **The bones** in the hands and feet are arranged in a rather similar way. The first part is the wrist and ankle, then there is a longer middle part (the metacarpals and metatarsals), and finally the furthest part, the fingers and toes (phalanges).
- **The functions of the hands and feet** are very different, which is why the shape of the hand is different to the shape of the foot.
- **The wrist** is made up of eight carpal bones, which are all slightly different shapes. The individual bones are named for the shape they resemble – for example, the scaphoid bone is named from the Greek word for 'boat-shaped'.
- **There are five long metacarpals** in each hand, supporting the palm. Fourteen bones called phalanges make up the fingers and thumb.
- **Seven tarsal bones** make up the ankle and heel. Together with five long metatarsal bones and strong ligaments, they form the arches of the foot, which help carry the weight of the body. The toes contain 14 small phalanges.
- **There are many tiny joints** within the hands and feet, letting the bones move against each other. Muscles attach to the bones to allow the foot, and especially the hand, to move in many different ways.

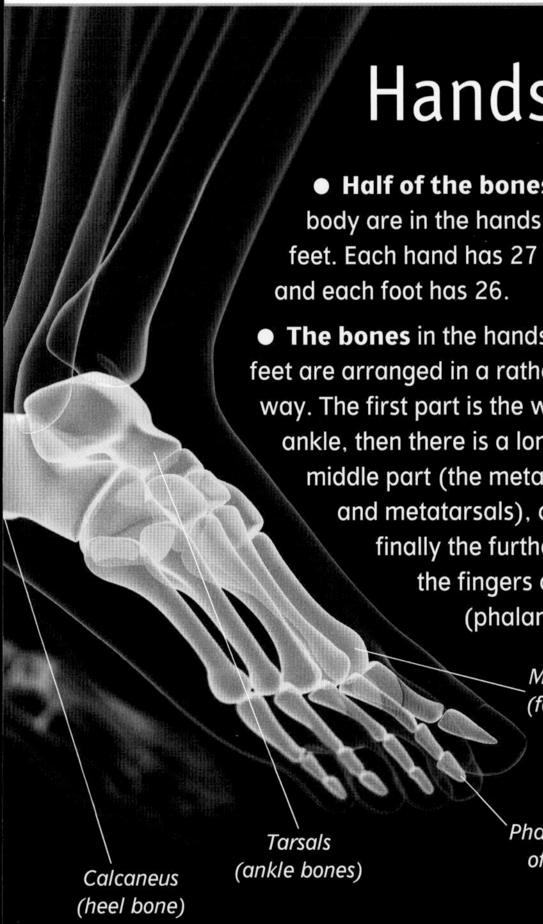
Metatarsals (foot bones)
Phalanges of toes
Tarsals (ankle bones)
Calcaneus (heel bone)

▲ *The 26 bones of the feet provide support for the weight of the body.*

Muscles and bones

The muscular system and skeleton work together to allow the body to move or maintain its position. Muscles also help the bones support and protect internal organs and softer parts of the body.

Each muscle and bone within the body has a particular job to do, and is just the right size and shape to do that job. The largest bone in the body is the femur (thigh bone), which gives a person height and lets them walk and run. The smallest bone is the stapes (stirrup bone) inside the ear, which transmits sound.

The largest muscle is the gluteus maximus, in the bottom, which lets a person move their hip and thigh. The smallest is the stapedius, which attaches to the stapes and helps protect the ear from loud sounds.

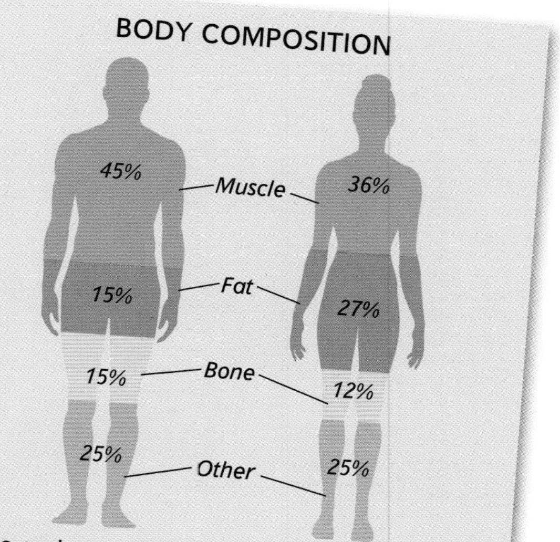
BODY COMPOSITION
45%
Muscle
36%
15%
Fat
27%
15%
Bone
12%
25%
Other
25%

Bone and muscle make up about 60 percent of an average man's weight, and nearly 50 percent of an average woman's weight.

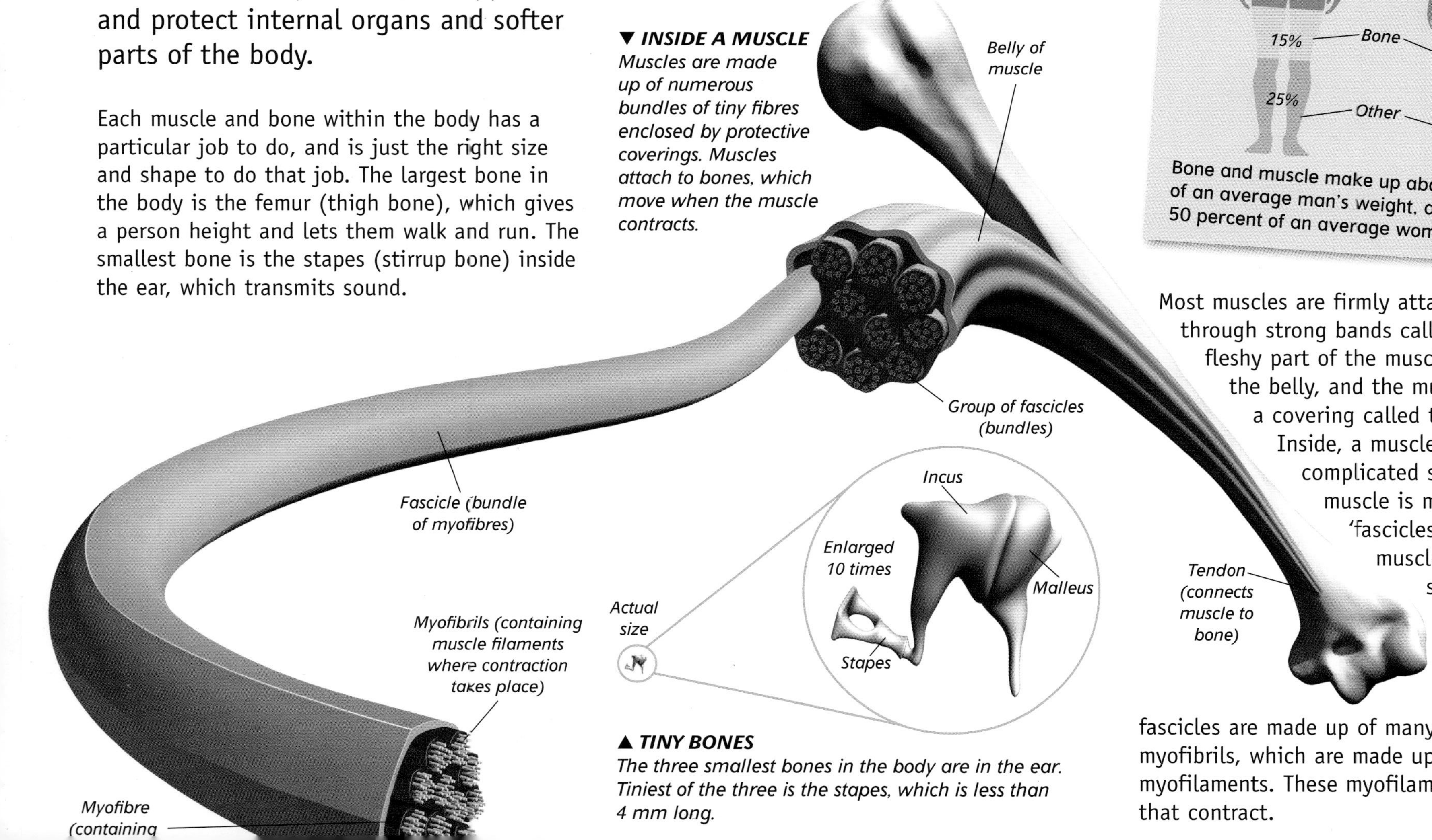
Belly of muscle
Group of fascicles (bundles)
Fascicle (bundle of myofibres)
Myofibrils (containing muscle filaments where contraction takes place)
Myofibre (containing
Tendon (connects muscle to bone)
Actual size
Enlarged 10 times
Incus
Malleus
Stapes

▼ *INSIDE A MUSCLE*
Muscles are made up of numerous bundles of tiny fibres enclosed by protective coverings. Muscles attach to bones, which move when the muscle contracts.

▲ *TINY BONES*
The three smallest bones in the body are in the ear. Tiniest of the three is the stapes, which is less than 4 mm long.

Most muscles are firmly attached to two bones through strong bands called tendons. The fleshy part of the muscle in the middle is the belly, and the muscle is enclosed in a covering called the epimysium. Inside, a muscle has quite a complicated structure. Each muscle is made up of many 'fascicles', bundles of small muscle fibres (myofibres) surrounded by a covering called the perimysium. The small muscle fibres inside the fascicles are made up of many long, thin myofibrils, which are made up of many tiny myofilaments. These myofilaments are the parts that contract.

LIVING BONES

When we see bones they appear to be dead and dry. But inside a living body bones are actually active, living tissues that can grow and repair themselves. They are strong, yet light and flexible. Bones contain cells, blood vessels and nerves. These all lie within a framework of hard, non-living material containing minerals such as calcium and phosphorus.

The cells inside bones have different jobs to do. Some break down bone tissue (osteoclasts) and some build it up again (osteoblasts). Working together, these cells can change the shape of a bone or repair it if it breaks.

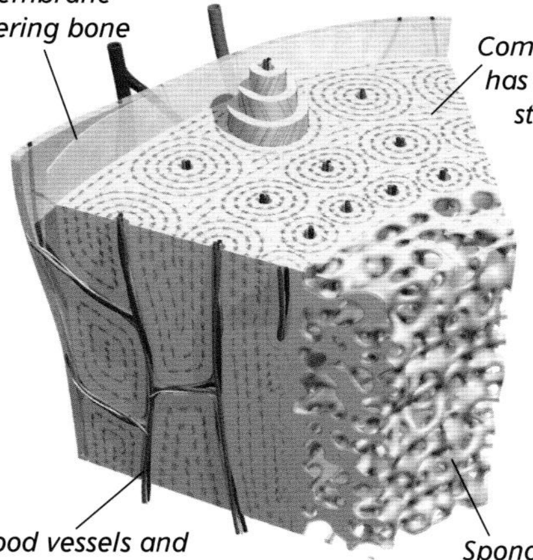
Periosteum – membrane covering bone
An osteon – a sub unit of compact bone
Compact bone has a regular structure
Blood vessels and nerves inside bone
Spongy bone

▼ STRONG BONES
Bones support the body and, together with the muscles, allow a person to move. Bones move against each other at joints, and are held together by strong ligaments.

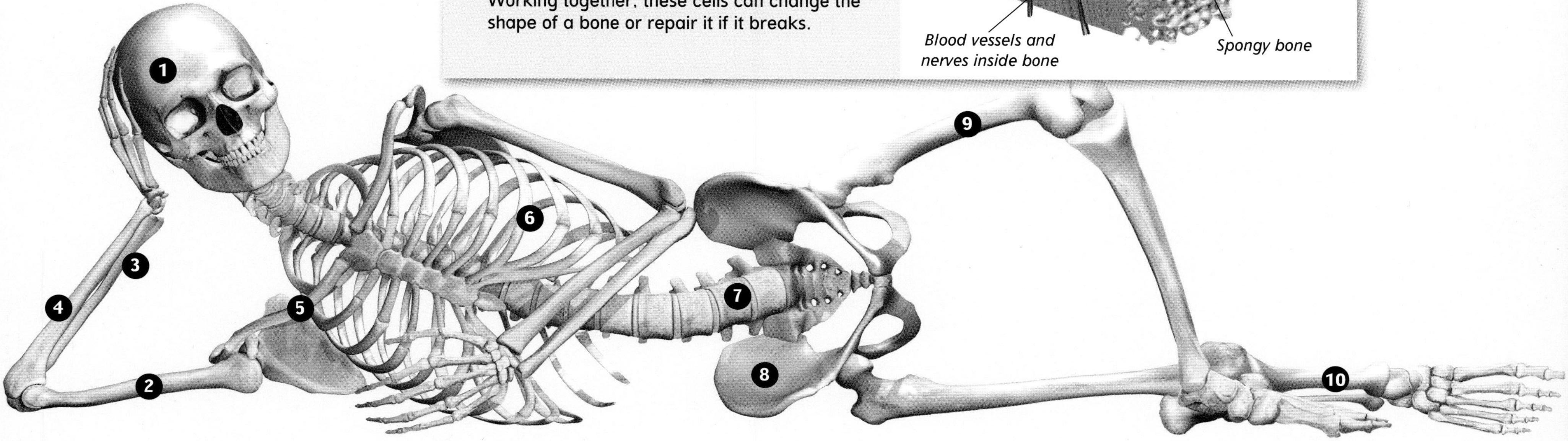
1
2
3
4
5
6
7
8
9
10

WORN OUT JOINTS

As people get older their joints can become worn out, stiff and painful. This is called osteoarthritis and is very common. People with osteoarthritis can do exercises and take medicines to ease the discomfort. But sometimes the joint becomes so worn out that it is best to be replaced with a new man-made joint. These are usually made of metal and special plastics, and are fitted in a surgical operation. The joints that are most commonly replaced with man-made joints are the hip and the knee.

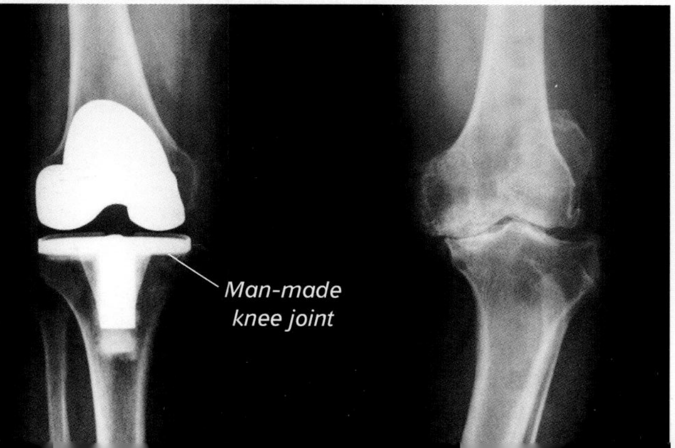
Man-made knee joint

KEY	
1 *Skull*	6 *Ribs*
2 *Humerus*	7 *Spine*
3 *Radius*	8 *Hip bone*
4 *Ulna*	9 *Thigh bone*
5 *Collarbone*	10 *Shinbone*

Teeth

- **Milk teeth** are the 20 teeth that start to appear when a baby is about six months old. Around the age of six, you start to grow your adult teeth – 16 in the top row and 16 in the bottom.
- **Molars** are the strong teeth with flattish tops (crowns) at the back of your mouth. Most people have three pairs on each side. The third molars at the back of the jaws are called wisdom teeth because they normally come through the gums (erupt) in early adulthood.
- **Incisors** are the four pairs of teeth at the front of your mouth. They have sharp edges for cutting food.
- **Canines** are the two pairs of pointed teeth behind the incisors. Their shape is good for piercing food.
- **The premolars** are the four pairs of teeth between the molars and the canines.

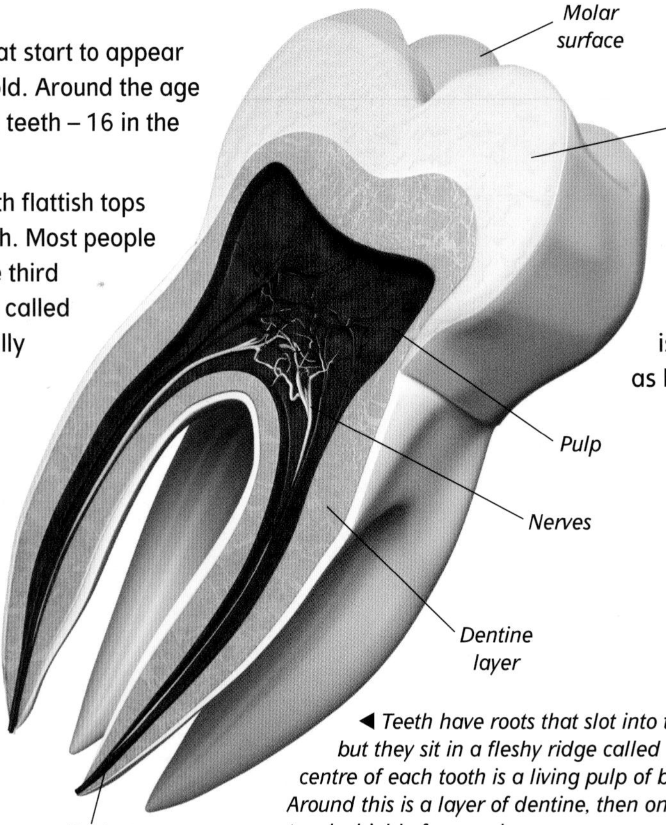
Molar surface
Coating of enamel
Pulp
Nerves
Dentine layer
Root canal

- **The enamel** on teeth is the body's hardest substance. Dentine inside teeth is softer but still hard as bone.

◀ Teeth have roots that slot into the jawbones, but they sit in a fleshy ridge called the gums. In the centre of each tooth is a living pulp of blood and nerves. Around this is a layer of dentine, then on top of that a tough shield of enamel.

Cartilage

- **Cartilage is a rubbery substance** used in various places around the body. You can feel cartilage in your ear flap if you move it back and forward.
- **Cartilage is made from cells** called chondrocytes embedded in a jelly-like ground substance with fibres of collagen, all wrapped in an envelope of tough fibres.
- **The three types of cartilage** are hyaline, fibrous and elastic.
- **Hyaline cartilage** is the most widespread in your body. It is semi-transparent, pearly white and quite stiff.
- **Hyaline cartilage** is used in many of the joints between bones to cushion them against impacts.
- **Fibrous cartilage** is really tough. It is found between the bones of the spine and in the knee.
- **Cartilage in the knee** makes two dish shapes called menisci between the thigh and shin bones. Footballers often damage these cartilages.

DID YOU KNOW?

Osteoarthritis is when joint cartilage breaks down, making movements painful.

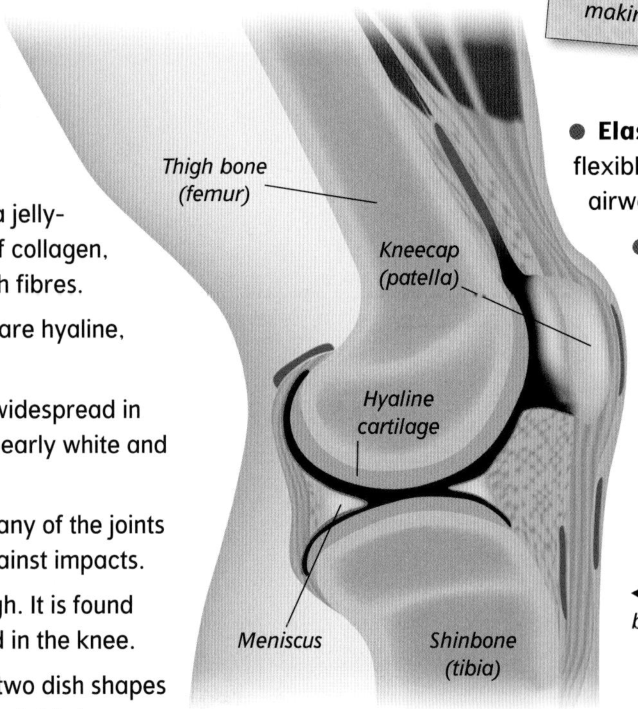
Thigh bone (femur)
Kneecap (patella)
Hyaline cartilage
Meniscus
Shinbone (tibia)

- **Elastic cartilage** is very flexible and used in your airways, nose and ears.
- **Cartilage grows** more quickly than bone, and the skeletons of babies in the womb are mostly cartilage, which gradually ossifies (hardens to bone).

◀ The knee is the body's biggest single joint.

Joints

- **Body joints** are places where bones meet.
- **Most body joints** let bones move, but different kinds of joint let them move in different ways.
- **Hinge joints**, such as the elbow, let the bones swing to and fro in two directions in a similar way to door hinges.
- **In ball-and-socket joints**, such as the hip, the rounded end of one bone sits in the cup-shaped socket of the other and can move in almost any direction.
- **Swivel joints** turn like a wheel on an axle. Your head can swivel to the left or to the right on your spine.
- **Saddle joints**, such as those in the thumb, have the bones interlocking like two saddles. These joints allow great mobility with considerable strength.

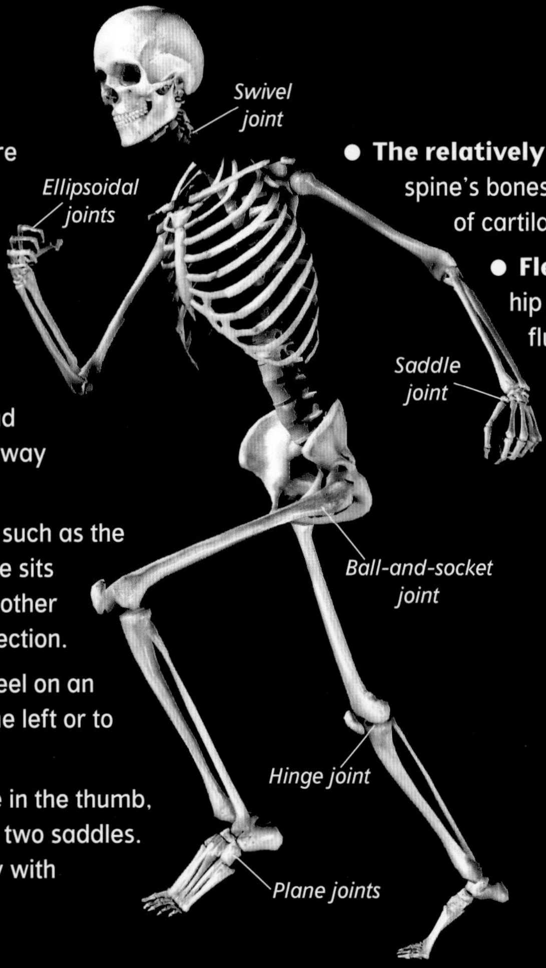
Swivel joint
Ellipsoidal joints
Saddle joint
Ball-and-socket joint
Hinge joint
Plane joints

- **The relatively inflexible joints** between the spine's bones (vertebrae) are cushioned by pads of cartilage.
- **Flexible synovial joints** such as the hip joint are lubricated with synovial fluid and cushioned by cartilage.
- **The knee joint can bend**, straighten and (when slightly bent) rotate.

◀ *Synovial joints allow the body to move in many ways so we can walk, run, play and work.*

Tendons and ligaments

- **Tendons are cords** that tie a muscle to a bone or a muscle to another muscle. Most are rope-like bundles of fibre. A few are flat sheets called aponeuroses.
- **Tendon fibres** are made from a rubbery substance called collagen.
- **Your fingers are mainly moved** by muscles in the forearm, connected to the fingers by long tendons.
- **The Achilles tendon** pulls up the heel at the back.
- **Tendons** can transmit a force of up to five times your body weight.
- **Ligaments** are cords attached to bones on either side of a joint to strengthen it. They are made up of bundles of collagen and a stretchy substance called elastin.
- **Ligaments** also support various organs, including the liver, bladder and uterus (womb).

DID YOU KNOW?

The Achilles tendon is named after the Greek hero Achilles whose only weakness was his heel.

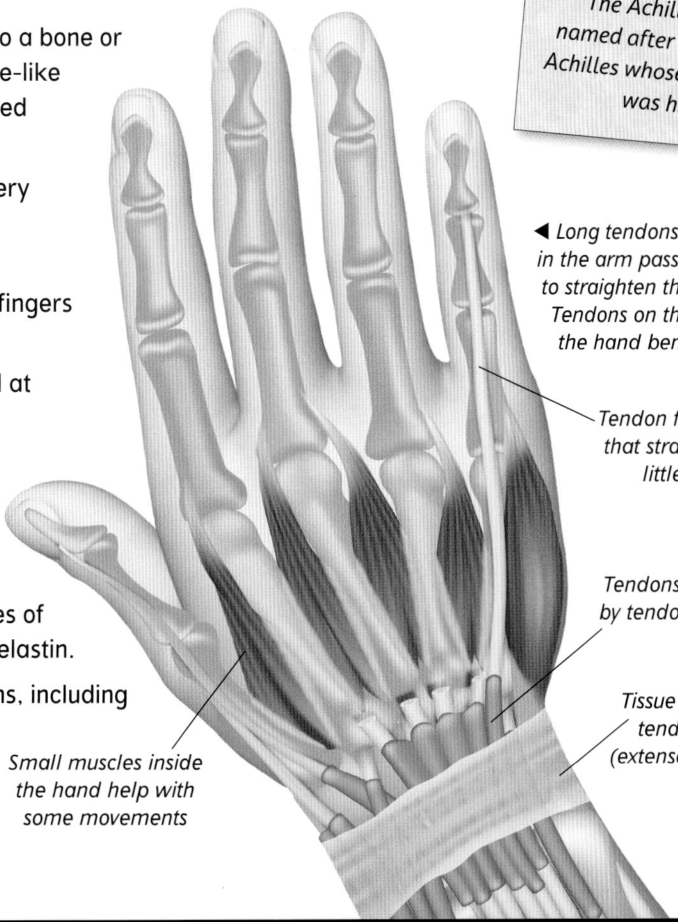
Tendon from muscle that straightens the little finger
Tendons protected by tendon sheathes
Tissue band holding tendons in place (extensor retinaculum)
Small muscles inside the hand help with some movements

◀ *Long tendons from muscles in the arm pass over the wrist to straighten the fingers. Tendons on the other side of the hand bend the fingers.*

Muscles

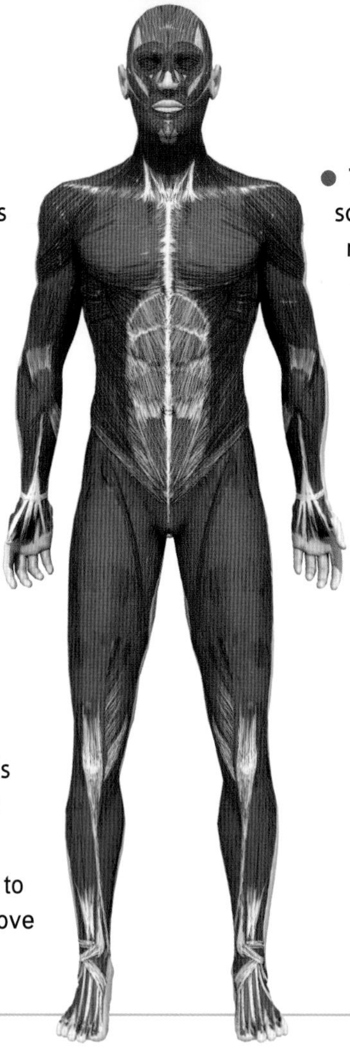

● **Muscles are special fibres** that contract (tighten) and relax to move parts of the body.

● **Voluntary muscles** are all the muscles you can control by thought, such as arm muscles. Involuntary muscles are those that work automatically, such as the muscles that move food through your intestine.

● **Most voluntary muscles** cover the skeleton and are called skeletal muscles. Most involuntary muscles form sacs or tubes such as the intestine.

● **Heart muscle** is a unique type of muscle. It has cells that work in a similar way to nerve cells, transmitting the signals for waves of muscle contraction to sweep through it.

● **Most skeletal muscles** are attached to two bones across a joint. Their job is to move those bones closer to each other.

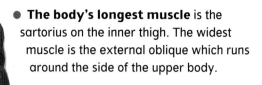

● **The body's longest muscle** is the sartorius on the inner thigh. The widest muscle is the external oblique which runs around the side of the upper body.

◀ *Most of the muscle in the body is skeletal muscle. There are around 640 skeletal muscles and they make up about half the weight of your body.*

DID YOU KNOW?

Your body's smallest muscle is the stapedius, inside the ear – it is about as big as this l.

Muscle movement

● **Most muscles** are long and thin and work by contracting (becoming shorter), sometimes by up to half their length.

● **Skeletal muscles** are made of cells that have many nuclei in a long fibre, called a myofibre. Muscles are made from hundreds or thousands of these fibres.

● **Muscle fibres** are made from strands called myofibrils, each marked with dark bands, giving the muscle its name of stripy or 'striated' muscle.

● **The stripes** in muscle are bands of two substances, actin and myosin, which interlock. When a signal comes from the brain, chemical 'hooks' on the myosin yank the actin filaments along, shortening the muscle.

● **Skeletal muscles** have two types of fibres – fast twitch and slow twitch.

● **Fast twitch fibres** contract faster and more forcibly, while slow twitch fibres contract slowly but can maintain contraction for longer.

▶ *The more we use our muscles, the stronger they become.*

108

Cells

- **Cells** are the basic building blocks of your body. Most are so tiny you would need 10,000 to cover a pinhead.
- **There are over 200 different kinds** of cell in your body, including nerve cells, skin cells, blood cells, bone cells, fat cells, muscle cells and many more.
- **A cell** is basically a little parcel of chemicals with a thin membrane (casing) of protein and fat. The membrane holds the cell together, but lets nutrients in and waste out.
- **Inside the cell** is a liquid called cytoplasm, and floating in this are various minute structures called organelles.
- **At the centre** of the cell is the nucleus – this is the cell's control centre and it contains DNA.
- **Each cell** is a dynamic chemical factory, and the cell's team of organelles is continually busy – ferrying chemicals to and fro, breaking up unwanted chemicals, and putting together new ones.
- **Some of the biggest cells** in the body are nerve cells. Although the main nucleus of a nerve cell is microscopic, the tails of some can extend for one metre or more through the body, and be seen even without a microscope.
- **Red blood cells** are among the smallest cells in the body. These are just 0.0075 mm across and have no nucleus.
- **Most body cells** are continually being replaced by new ones. The main exceptions are nerve cells – these are long-lived, but rarely replaced.

DID YOU KNOW?

The body contains more than 50 billion billion cells!

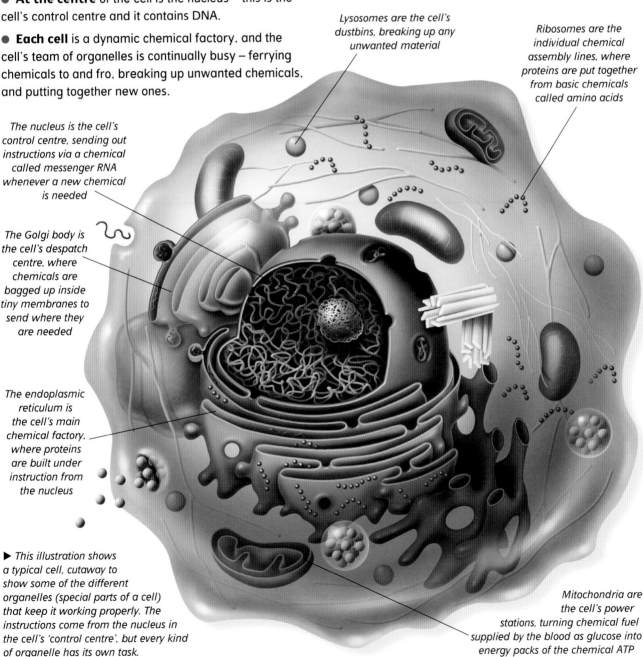

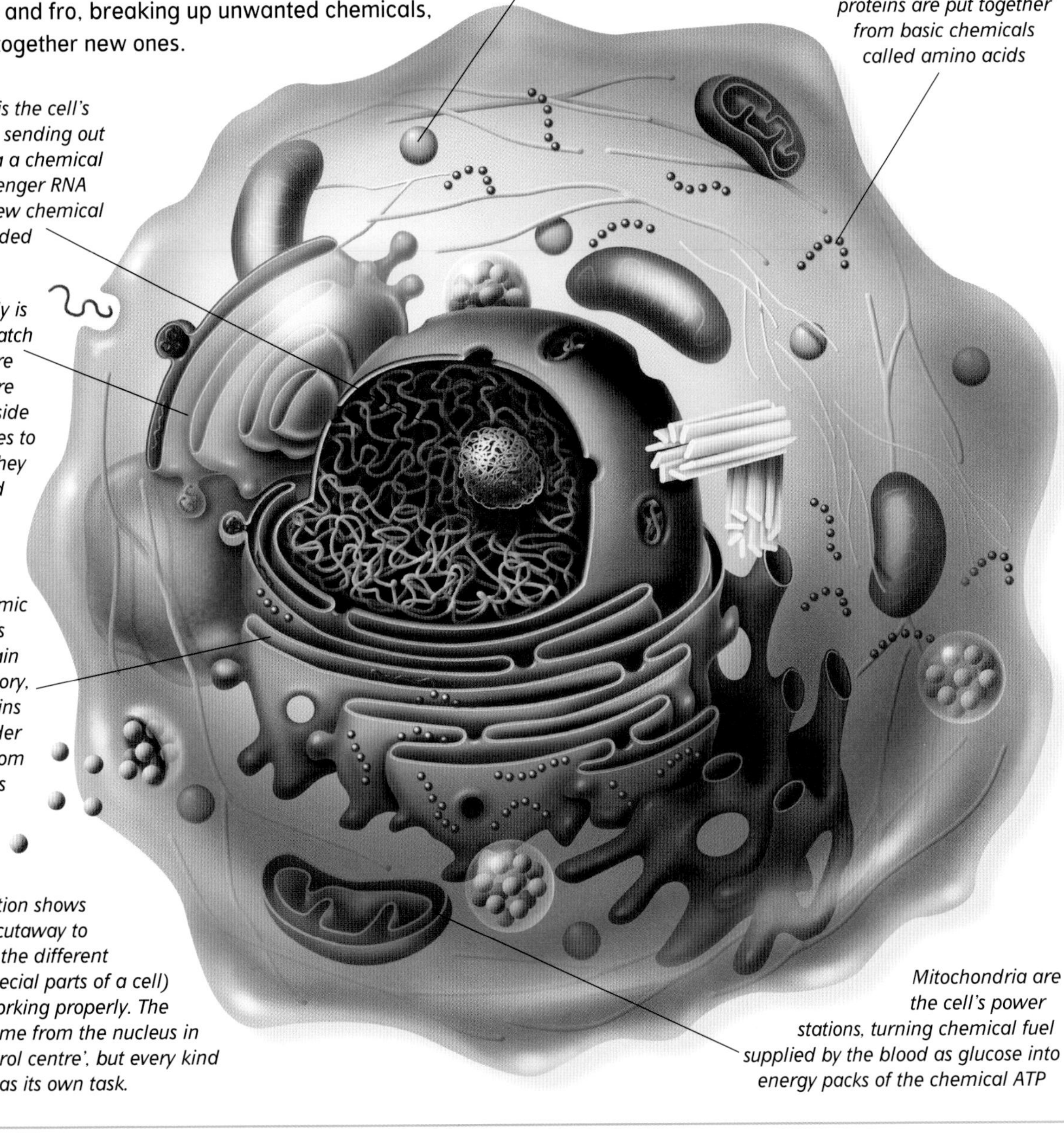
Lysosomes are the cell's dustbins, breaking up any unwanted material
Ribosomes are the individual chemical assembly lines, where proteins are put together from basic chemicals called amino acids
The nucleus is the cell's control centre, sending out instructions via a chemical called messenger RNA whenever a new chemical is needed
The Golgi body is the cell's despatch centre, where chemicals are bagged up inside tiny membranes to send where they are needed
The endoplasmic reticulum is the cell's main chemical factory, where proteins are built under instruction from the nucleus
Mitochondria are the cell's power stations, turning chemical fuel supplied by the blood as glucose into energy packs of the chemical ATP

▶ *This illustration shows a typical cell, cutaway to show some of the different organelles (special parts of a cell) that keep it working properly. The instructions come from the nucleus in the cell's 'control centre', but every kind of organelle has its own task.*

Tissue and organs

- **Each of the many different kinds of cell** in your body combines to make substances called tissues.
- **As well as cells**, some tissues include other materials.
- **Connective tissues** are made from particular cells (such as fibroblasts), plus two other materials – long fibres of protein (such as collagen) and a matrix. Matrix is the substance in which cells are embedded.
- **Connective tissue** holds all the other kinds of tissue together in various ways. Tendons, cartilage and the adipose tissue that makes fat are connective tissues.
- **Bone and blood** are both specialized forms of connective tissue.
- **Epithelial tissues** are thin layers of cells that cover and line various parts of the body. Skin is a type of epithelial tissue.

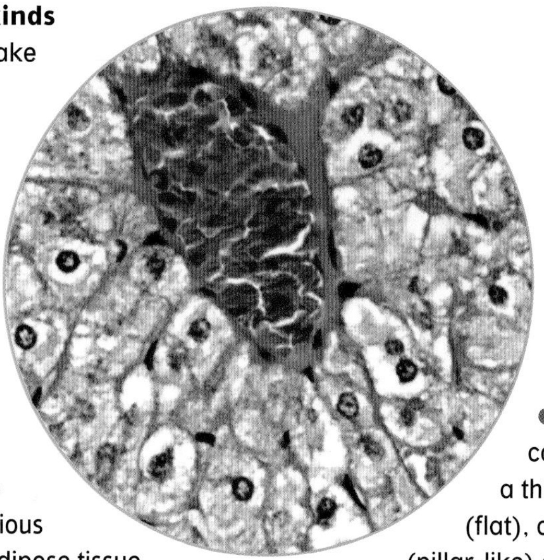

◀ *Liver tissue is made from densely packed liver cells, as shown in this highly magnified photograph.*

- **Epithelial tissue** may combine three kinds of cell to make a thin waterproof layer – squamous (flat), cuboid (box-like) and columnar (pillar-like) cells.
- **Nerve tissue** is made mostly from neurons (nerve cells), plus the Schwann cells (a type of cell that provides insulation) that coat them.
- **Organs** are made from combinations of tissues. The heart is made mostly of muscle tissue, but also includes epithelial and connective tissue.

DID YOU KNOW?

The body is made entirely from tissue and tissue fluid (liquid that fills the space between cells).

Skin

- **Acting as a protective coat**, skin shields your body from the weather and from infection, and helps to keep it at just the right temperature.
- **Skin is your largest sense receptor**, responding to touch, pressure, heat and cold.
- **Vitamin D is made** for your body by the skin from exposure to sunlight.
- **The epidermis** (the outer layer of skin) continually produces cells from underneath, which then pile up and gradually die. This covering of layers of dead cells contains a tough protein called keratin that protects the body.
- **Below the epidermis** is a thick layer of living cells called the dermis, which contains the sweat glands.

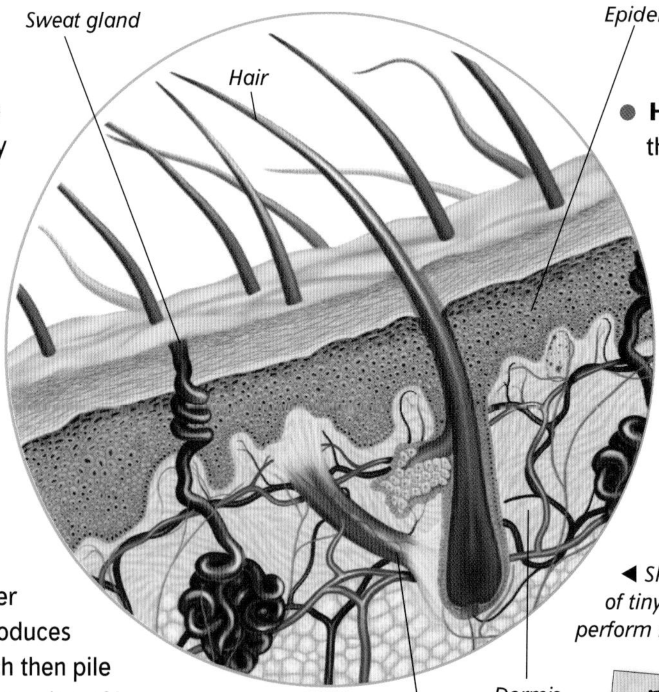

Sweat gland
Hair
Epidermis
Dermis
Erector pili muscle

◀ *Skin has several layers, and lots of tiny structures within it to help it perform its many functions.*

- **Hair roots** have tiny muscles that pull the hair upright when you are cold, giving you goose bumps.
- **Skin is 6 mm thick** on the soles of your feet, and just 0.5 mm thick on your eyelids.
- **The epidermis** contains cells that make the dark pigment melanin that determines skin colour.

DID YOU KNOW?

Even though its thickness averages just 2 mm, your skin gets one-eighth of all your blood supply.

Hair

- **Many mammals** have thick hair all over their skin, but human body hair is so short and fine that it gives the appearance of bare skin.
- **Lanugo** is the very fine hair babies are covered in when they are inside the womb, from the fourth month of pregnancy onwards.
- **Vellus hair** is fine, downy hair that grows all over your body until you reach puberty.
- **Terminal hair** is the coarser hair on your head, as well as the hair that grows on men's chins and around an adult's genitals.
- **The colour of your hair** depends on how much there are of pigments called melanin and carotene in the hairs.
- **Hair is red or auburn** if it contains carotene.
- **Black, brown and blonde hair** gets its colour from black melanin.
- **Each hair** is rooted in a pit called the hair follicle. The hair is held in place by its club-shaped tip, the bulb.
- **Hair grows** as cells fill with a material called keratin and die, and pile up inside the follicle.

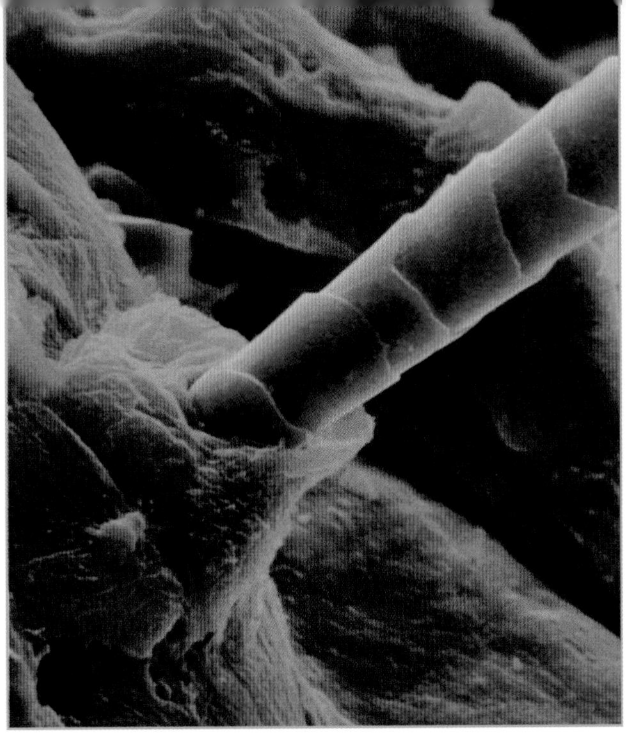

▲ *A microscopic view of a hair. It is only alive and growing at its root, in the base of the follicle. The shaft that sticks out of the skin is dead, and is made of flat cells stuck firmly together.*

- **The average person** has 120,000 head hairs and each grows about 3 mm per week.

Nails

- **A nail is a tough plate** that covers the surface of the end of each finger and toe.
- **Fingernails form a firm layer** at the back of the fingertip. This stops the flexible fingertip from bending too much, so we can feel, press and pick up small items more easily without damage.
- **Each nail** is a special growth of the epidermis (outer layer of the skin).
- **Nails are made** from the tough protein keratin.
- **A nail**, like a hair, grows at its root, which is under the skin at its base, and slides slowly along the finger. The root is the only living part of the nail.
- **The skin at the base of the nail** from which the nail grows is called the matrix.
- **The blood flow to the nail** is less visible at the nail base, leaving a paler, crescent-shaped area of nail visible. This is called the lunula.
- **Nails grow faster** in summer than in winter, and faster by day than by night.
- **Nails lengthen** by about half a millimetre, on average, each week.

DID YOU KNOW?

Toenails require 12 to 18 months to completely regrow.

▶ *A nail has its root under the skin and grows along the nail bed – the skin underneath it.*

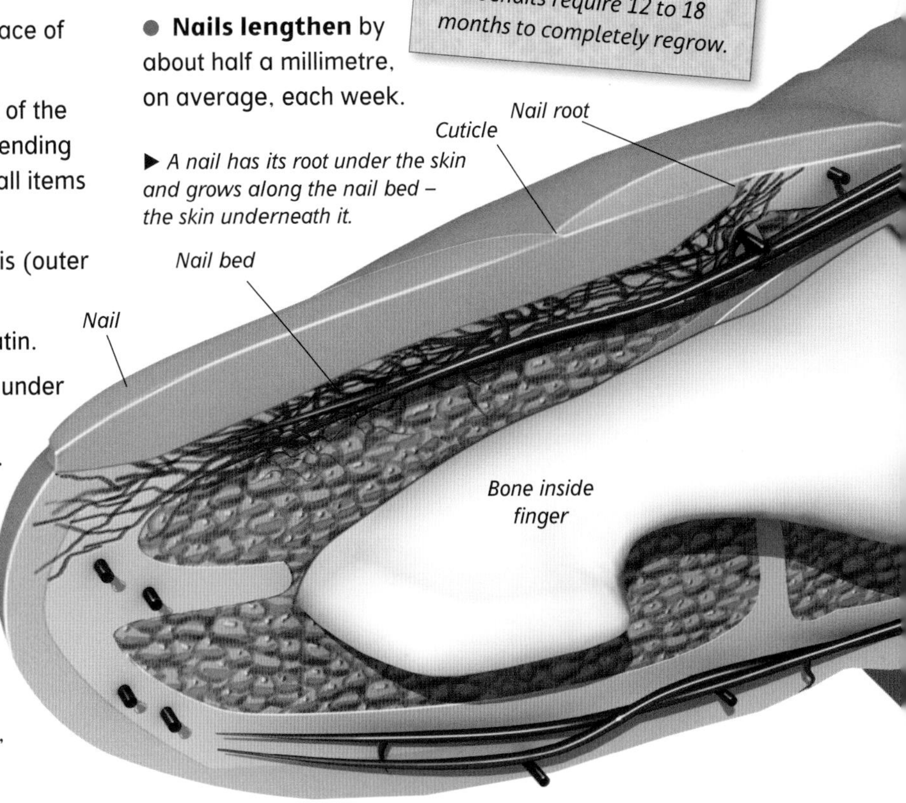
Nail root
Cuticle
Nail bed
Nail
Bone inside finger

Inside the abdomen

The abdomen contains many different organs all fitting closely together, filling the space between the diaphragm and the pelvis. It looks very confusing, but actually everything is quite organized, rather like a 3-dimensional jigsaw.

The soft abdominal organs are protected by the bones of the ribcage, spine and pelvis, and by the abdominal muscles all around. There are also pads of fat in certain places inside the abdomen to support and cushion the organs. Many organs in the abdomen have slippery coverings, with thin layers of liquid between them. This lets them slip and slide against each other when they need to, for example, when food needs to move down the intestines.

When doctors need to find out if there is a medical problem inside the abdomen there are a number of things they can do. They will ask their patient about any symptoms they have, such as pain or vomiting. They may feel the abdomen with their hands or even listen with a stethoscope. They may send samples of the patient's urine, faeces or blood to the laboratory.

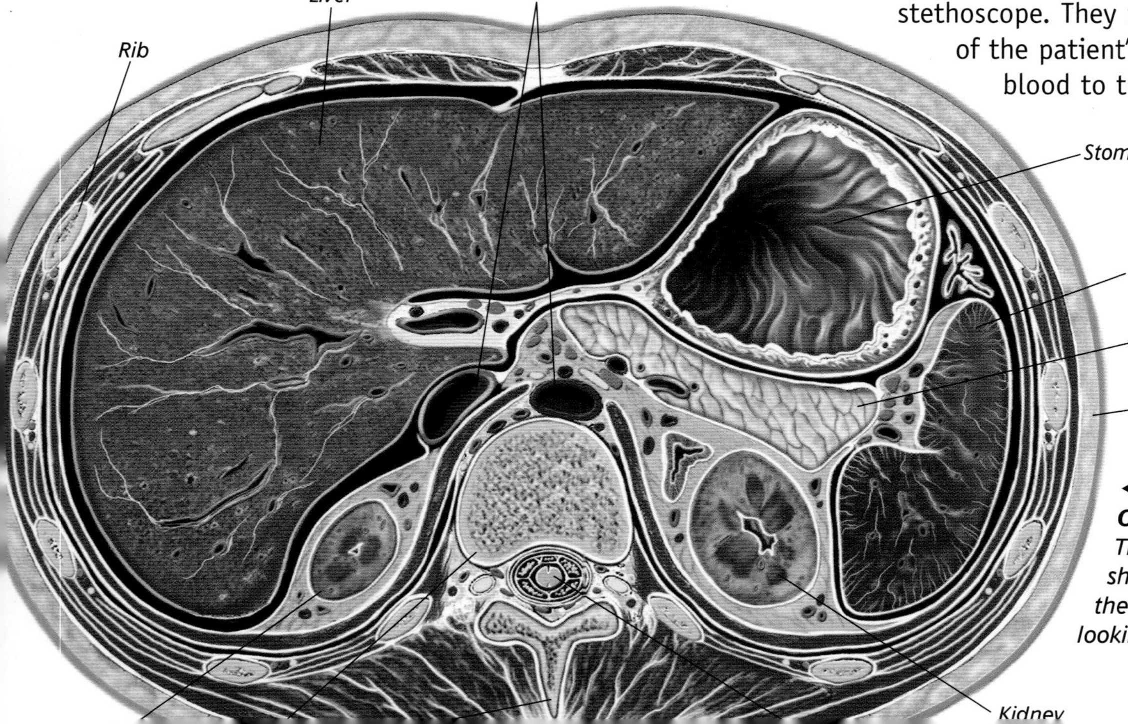
Liver
Main blood vessels
Rib
Stomach
Spleen
Pancreas
Layers of skin, fat and muscle
Kidney

◄ CROSS SECTION OF THE ABDOMEN
This cross section shows the organs inside the upper abdomen, looking from below.

STAYING HEALTHY

Most of the organs inside the abdomen deal with digestion of food, absorption of nutrients and removal of solid and liquid waste. People can help their organs do this properly by eating a healthy balanced diet and drinking plenty of water.

Sometimes doctors use a machine to scan inside the abdomen. These may use sound waves (ultrasound scan), X-rays (CT, computerized tomography scan) or magnetism (MRI, magnetic resonance imaging).

▼ LOOKING INSIDE
Special instruments called endoscopes can be used to look inside the abdomen.

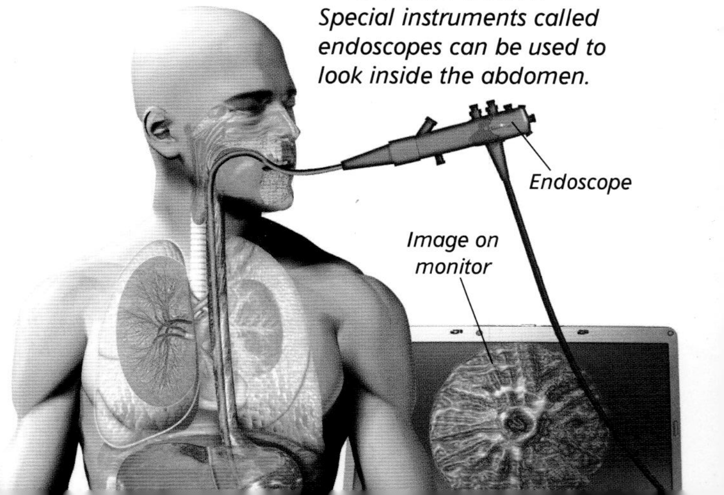
Endoscope
Image on monitor

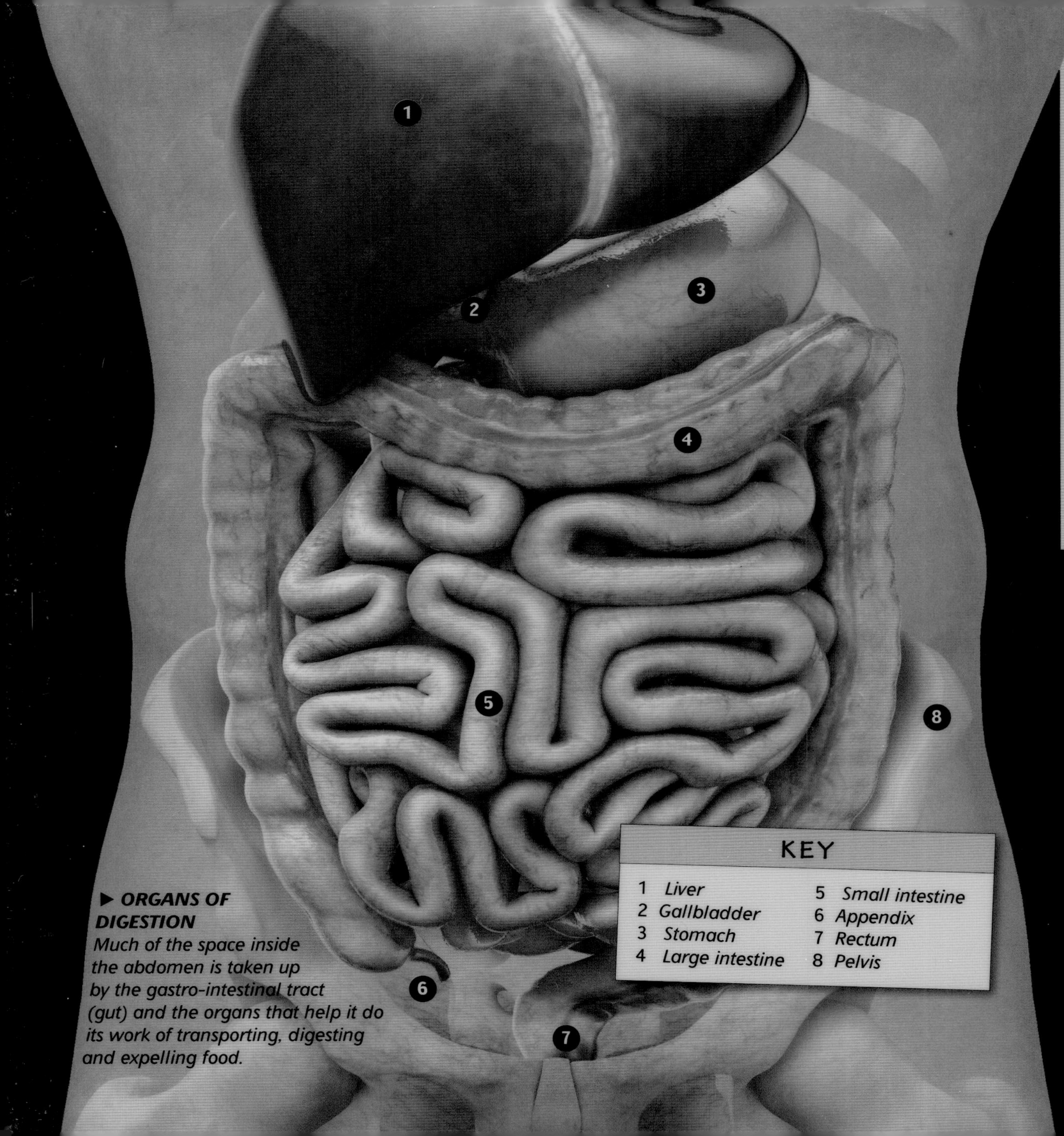
1
2
3
4
5
6
7
8
KEY
1 Liver
2 Gallbladder
3 Stomach
4 Large intestine
5 Small intestine
6 Appendix
7 Rectum
8 Pelvis

▶ ORGANS OF DIGESTION
Much of the space inside the abdomen is taken up by the gastro-intestinal tract (gut) and the organs that help it do its work of transporting, digesting and expelling food.

ABSORBING NUTRIENTS

Most of the nutrients in the food a person eats are absorbed in the small intestine. The lining of the small intestine is specially adapted to provide a huge surface area for this, with millions of tiny finger-like projections called villi. Each villus has tiny blood vessels that pick up the nutrients and carry them away into the bloodstream.

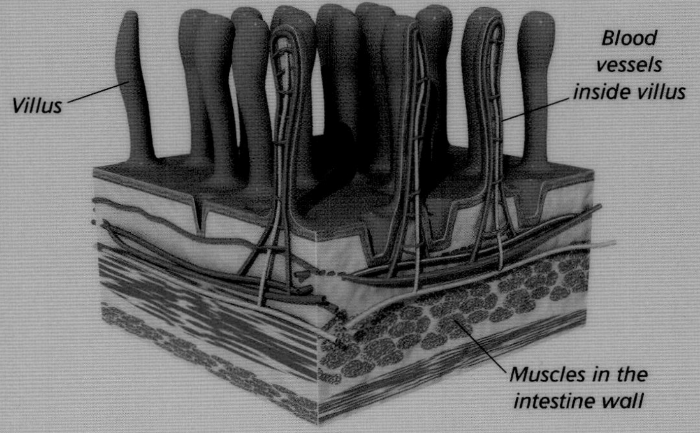
Villus
Blood vessels inside villus
Muscles in the intestine wall

APPENDICITIS

The appendix is a small worm-like tube of tissue, about 5–10 cm long, which is attached to the large intestine. It can become inflamed and infected, leading to a painful condition called appendicitis. If left untreated the appendix might burst, which can cause serious illness. If a person has appendicitis, doctors may remove the appendix in a surgical operation (appendicectomy).

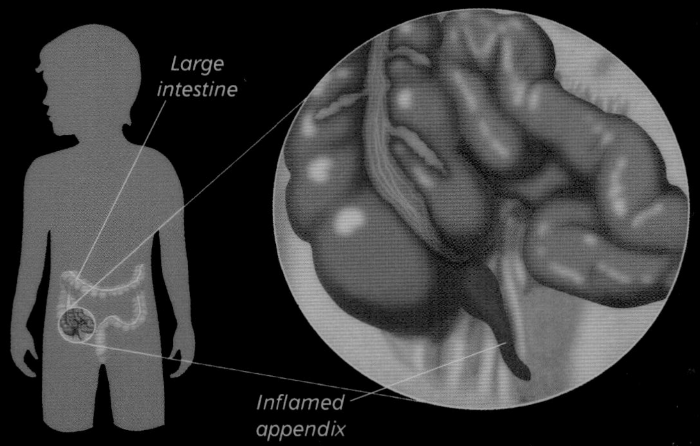
Large intestine
Inflamed appendix

ABSORBING NUTRIENTS

Most of the nutrients in the food a person eats are absorbed in the small intestine. The lining of the small intestine is specially adapted to provide a huge surface area for this, with millions of tiny finger-like projections called villi. Each villus has tiny blood vessels that pick up the nutrients and carry them away into the bloodstream.

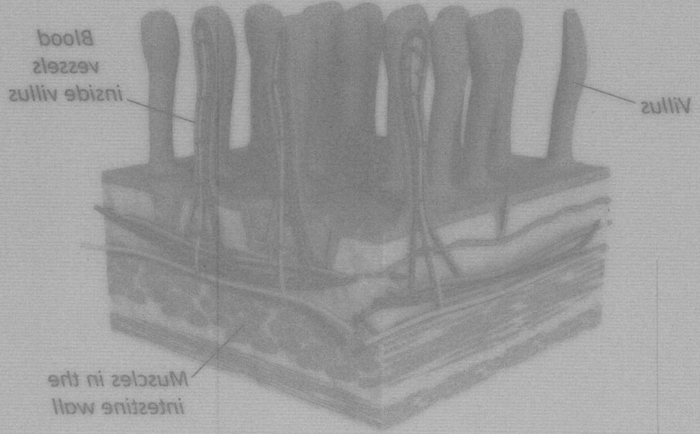

Blood vessels inside villus
Villus
Muscles in the intestine wall

APPENDICITIS

The appendix is a small worm-like tube of tissue, about 5–10 cm long, which is attached to the large intestine. It can become inflamed and infected, leading to a painful condition called appendicitis. If left untreated the appendix might burst, which can cause serious illness. If a person has appendicitis, doctors may remove the appendix in a surgical operation (appendicectomy).

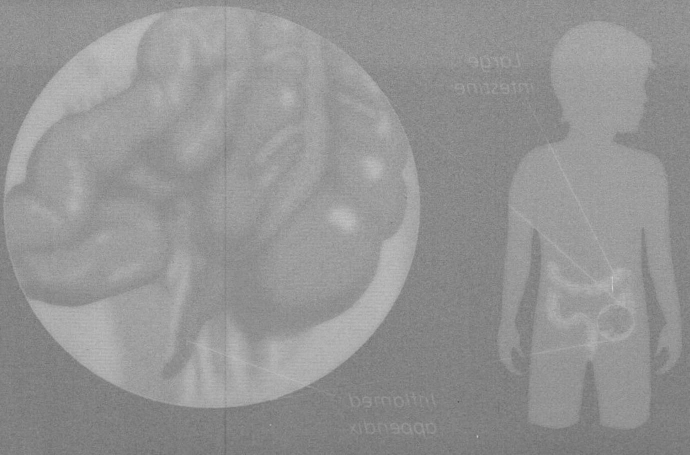

Large intestine
Inflamed appendix

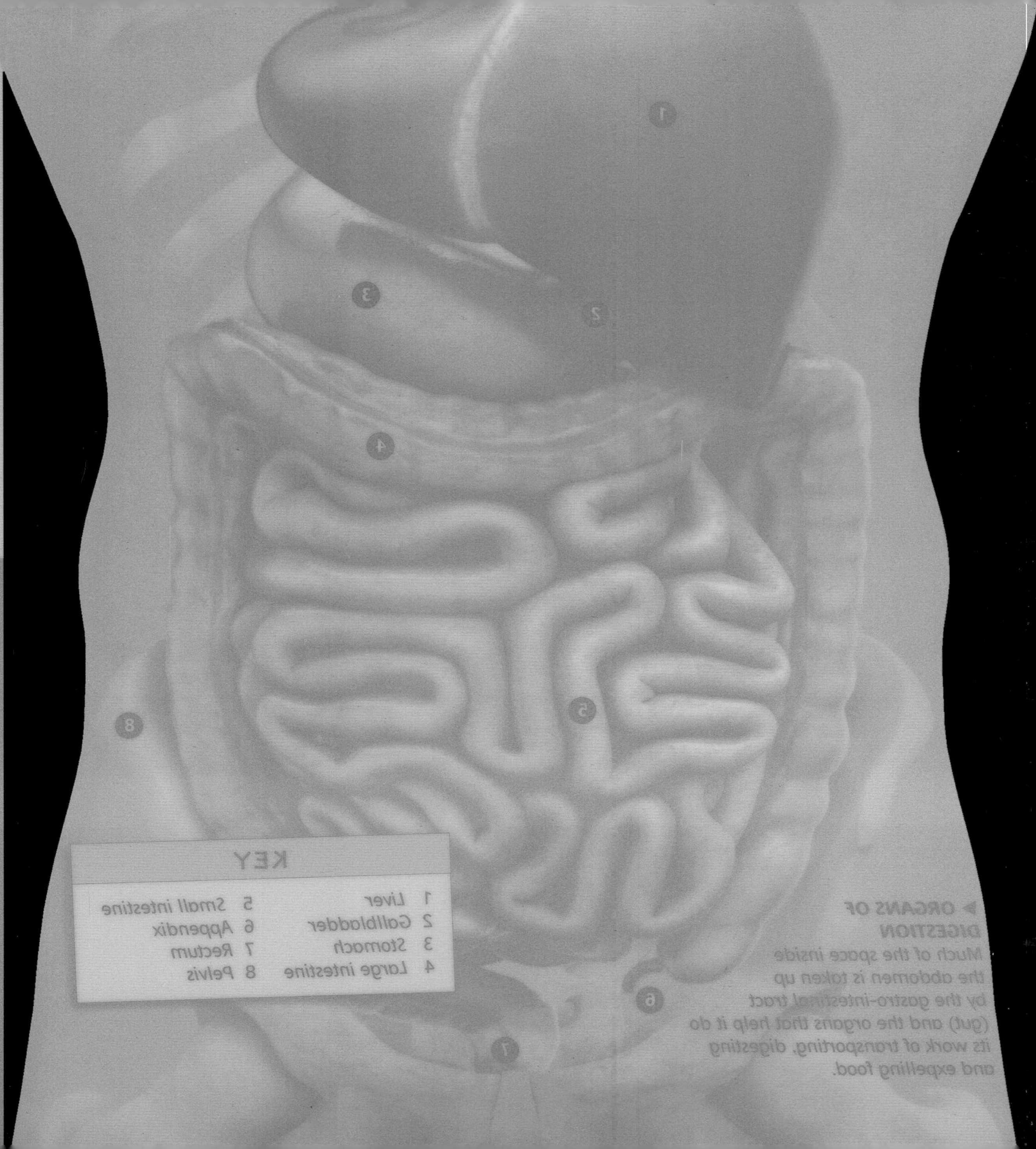

KEY
1 Liver
2 Gallbladder
3 Stomach
4 Large intestine
5 Small intestine
6 Appendix
7 Rectum
8 Pelvis

▶ **ORGANS OF DIGESTION**
Much of the space inside the abdomen is taken up by the gastro-intestinal tract (gut) and the organs that help it do its work of transporting, digesting and expelling food.

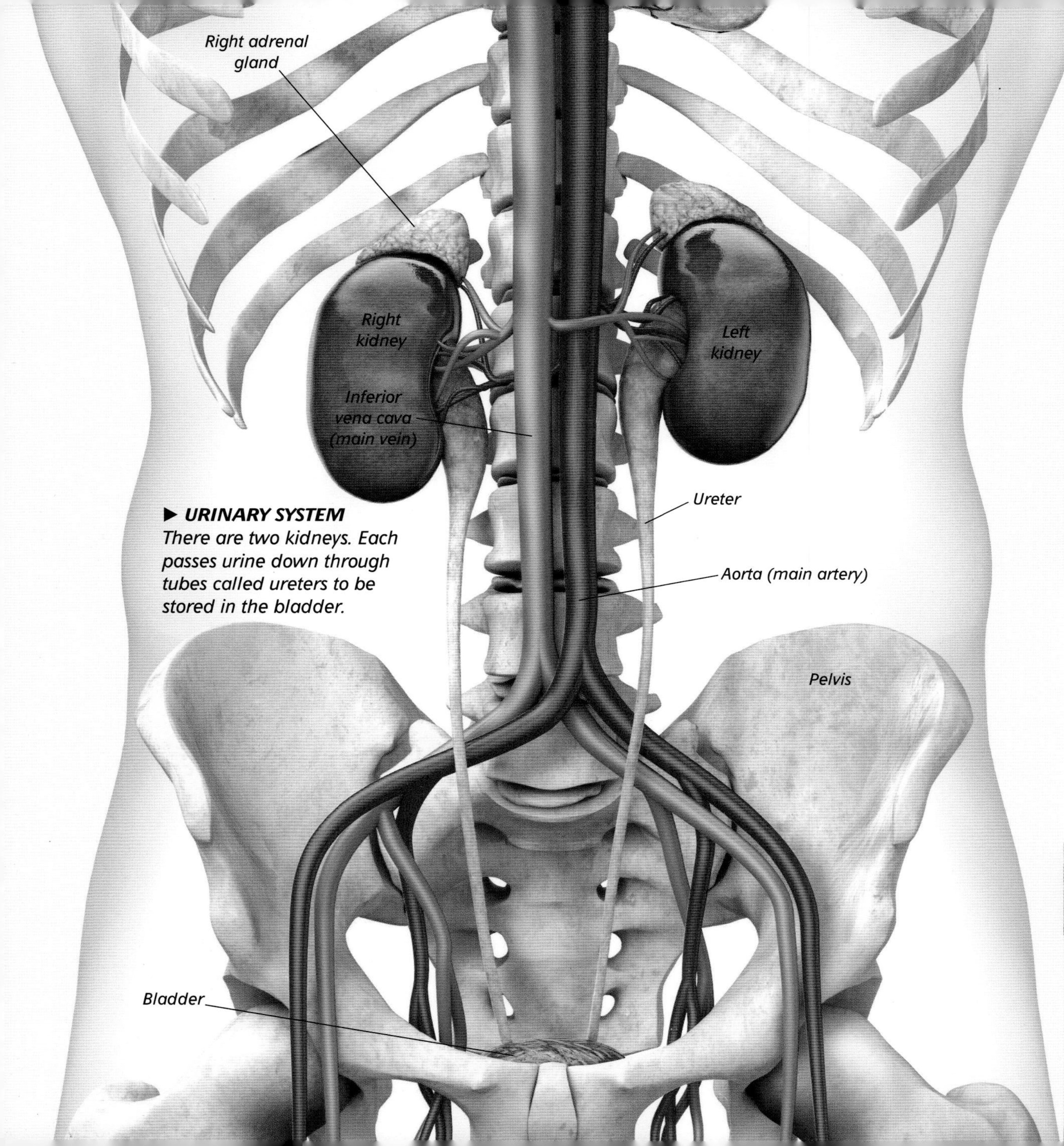
Right adrenal gland
Right kidney
Inferior vena cava (main vein)
Left kidney
Ureter
Aorta (main artery)
Pelvis
Bladder

▶ URINARY SYSTEM
There are two kidneys. Each passes urine down through tubes called ureters to be stored in the bladder.

THE KIDNEY

The kidneys filter blood and produce urine, which is made up of waste water and other substances the body wants to get rid of. To do its job each kidney needs to filter a lot of blood, and so it has a rich blood supply from the renal artery. Thousands of tiny filters, called nephrons, clean the blood and produce urine. The cleaned blood goes back to the body in the renal vein, and the waste urine travels down through special tubes (ureters) to the bladder. Urine is stored here until the time is right for a person to pass it out.

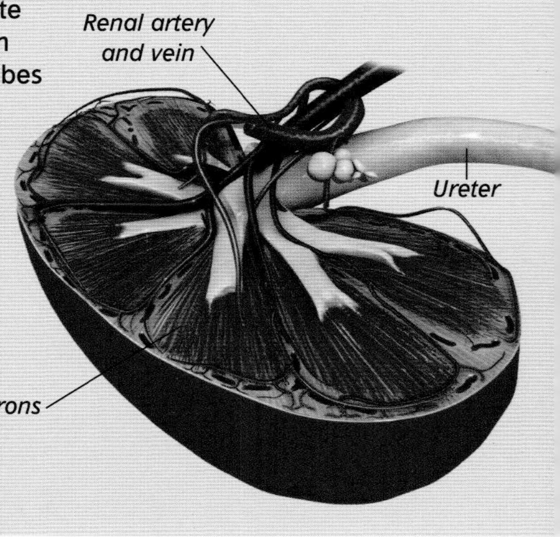
Renal artery and vein
Ureter
Kidney tissue containing nephrons (tiny filters)

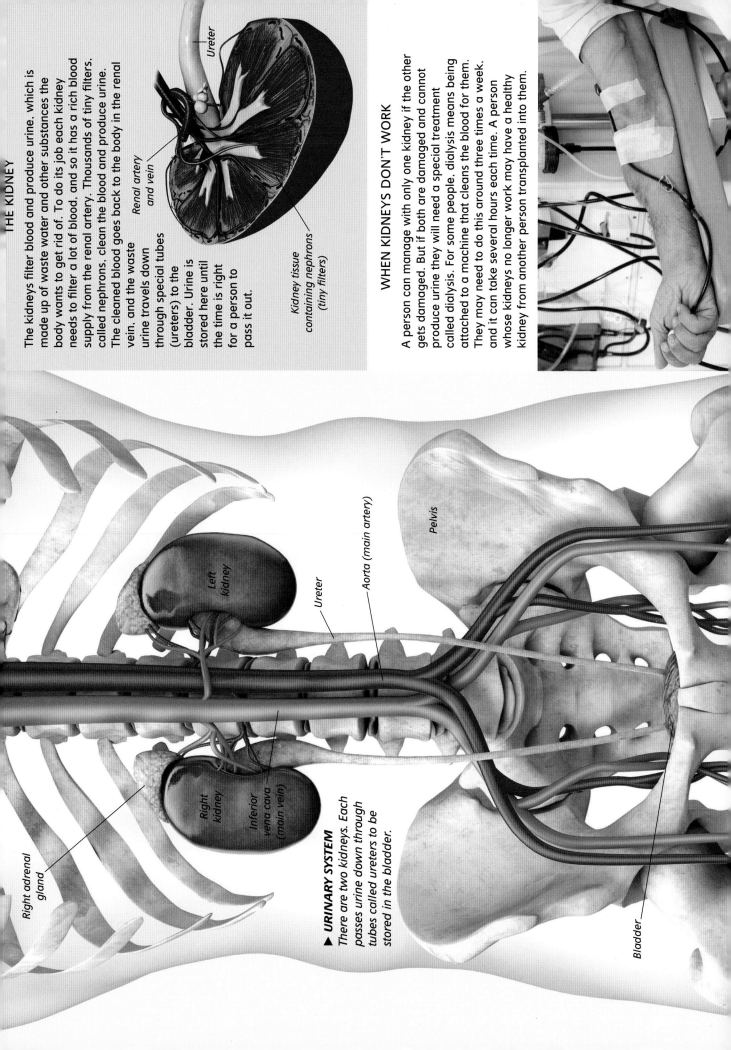

WHEN KIDNEYS DON'T WORK

A person can manage with only one kidney if the other gets damaged. But if both are damaged and cannot produce urine they will need a special treatment called dialysis. For some people, dialysis means being attached to a machine that cleans the blood for them. They may need to do this around three times a week, and it can take several hours each time. A person whose kidneys no longer work may have a healthy kidney from another person transplanted into them.

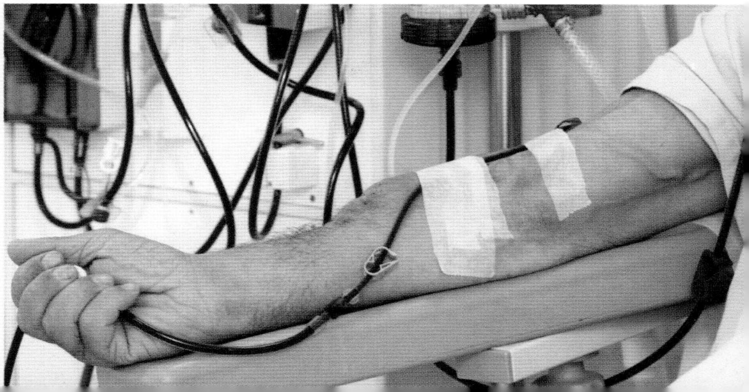

Digestion

● **Digestion** is the process by which your body breaks down the food you eat into substances that it can absorb (take in) and use.

● **The digestive tract** is basically a long, winding tube called the alimentary canal (gut). It starts at the mouth and ends at the anus.

● **If you could lay** your gut out straight, it would be nearly six times as long as you are tall.

● **The food you eat** is softened in your mouth by chewing and by chemicals in your saliva (spit).

● **When you swallow**, food travels down the oesophagus (a muscular tube) into the stomach. The stomach is a muscular-walled bag that mashes the food into a pulp, helped by chemicals called gastric juices.

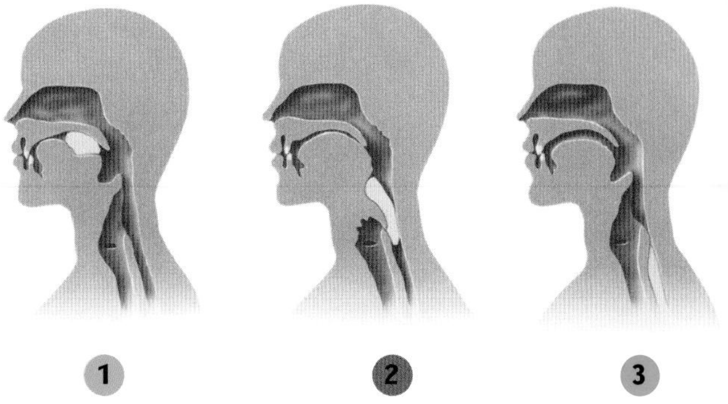
1
2
3

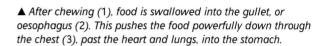

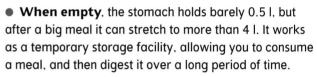

▲ *After chewing (1), food is swallowed into the gullet, or oesophagus (2). This pushes the food powerfully down through the chest (3), past the heart and lungs, into the stomach.*

● **When empty**, the stomach holds barely 0.5 l, but after a big meal it can stretch to more than 4 l. It works as a temporary storage facility, allowing you to consume a meal, and then digest it over a long period of time.

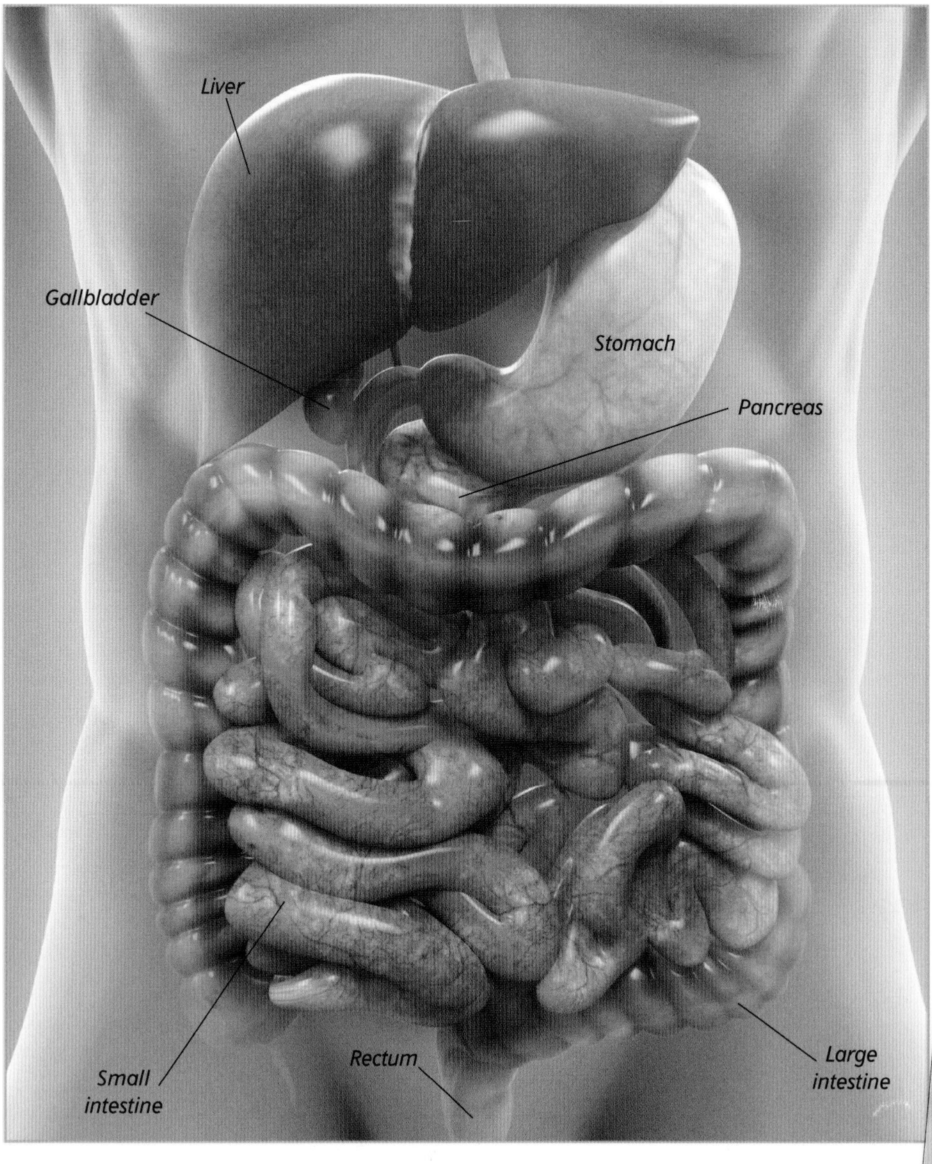
Liver
Gallbladder
Stomach
Pancreas
Small intestine
Rectum
Large intestine

▲ *The food you eat is broken down into the nutrients your body needs as it passes down your oesophagus into your stomach, and then progresses to your small intestine.*

● **The half-digested food** that leaves the stomach is called chyme. It passes into the small intestine, usually within four hours of eating a meal.

● **The small intestine** is a 6 m-long-tube where chyme is broken down further, into molecules small enough to be absorbed through the intestine wall into the blood.

● **Food that cannot be digested** in the small intestine passes into the large intestine. It is then pushed out through the anus as faeces when you go to the toilet.

● **Digestive enzymes** play a vital part in breaking food down so it can be absorbed by the body.

DID YOU KNOW?

The waves of muscular contraction along the walls of the stomach that help break food down into smaller pieces are known as peristalsis.

Diet

- **Your diet** is what you eat. A good diet includes the correct amount of proteins, carbohydrates, fats, vitamins, minerals, fibre and water.
- **Most of the food** you eat is fuel for the body, provided mostly by carbohydrates and fats.
- **Carbohydrates** are foods made from types of sugar, such as glucose and starch, and are found in foods such as bread, rice and potatoes.
- **Fats are greasy foods** that will not dissolve in water. Some, such as the fats in meat and cheese, are solid. Some, such as cooking oil, are liquid.

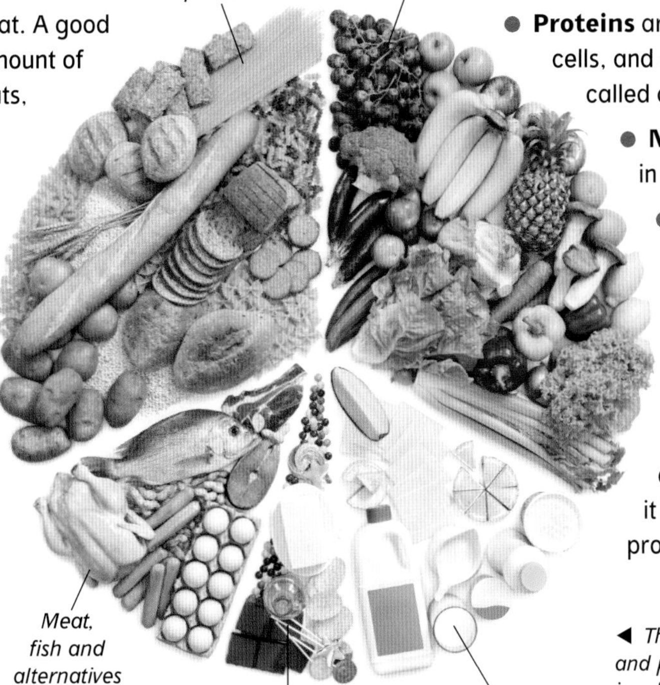
Bread, other cereals and potatoes
Fruit and vegetables
Meat, fish and alternatives
Foods that contain fat or sugar
Milk and dairy foods

◀ *This diagram shows the types and proportions of different foods in a healthy diet.*

- **Proteins** are needed to build and repair cells, and are made from chemicals called amino acids.
- **Meat and fish** are very high in protein.
- **A correctly balanced** vegetarian diet can provide all the amino acids needed for health.
- **Fibre or roughage** is supplied by cellulose from plant cell walls. Your body cannot digest fibre, but needs it to keep the bowel muscles properly exercised.

Fats

- **Fats are an important source** of energy. Together with proteins and carbohydrates, they make up your body's three main components of foods.
- **While carbohydrates** are generally used for energy immediately, your body often stores fat to use for energy in times of shortage.
- **Weight for weight**, fats contain twice as much energy as carbohydrates.
- **Fats (or lipids)** are important organic (life) substances, found in almost every living thing. They are made from substances called fatty acids and glycerol.
- **Food fats** are vegetable or animal fats that don't dissolve in water. Most vegetable fats are liquid, although some nut fats are solid. Most animal fats are solid. Milk is mainly water with some solid animal fats. Most solid fats melt when warmed.

DID YOU KNOW?

Saturated fats are linked to high levels of cholesterol in the blood and may increase certain health risks, such as heart attack.

- **Fats called triglycerides** are stored around the body as adipose tissue (body fat). These act as energy stores and also insulate the body against the cold. Fats called phospholipids are used to build body cells.
- **In your intestine**, bile from your liver and enzymes from your pancreas break fats down into fatty acids and glycerol. These are absorbed into your body's lymphatic system or enter the blood.

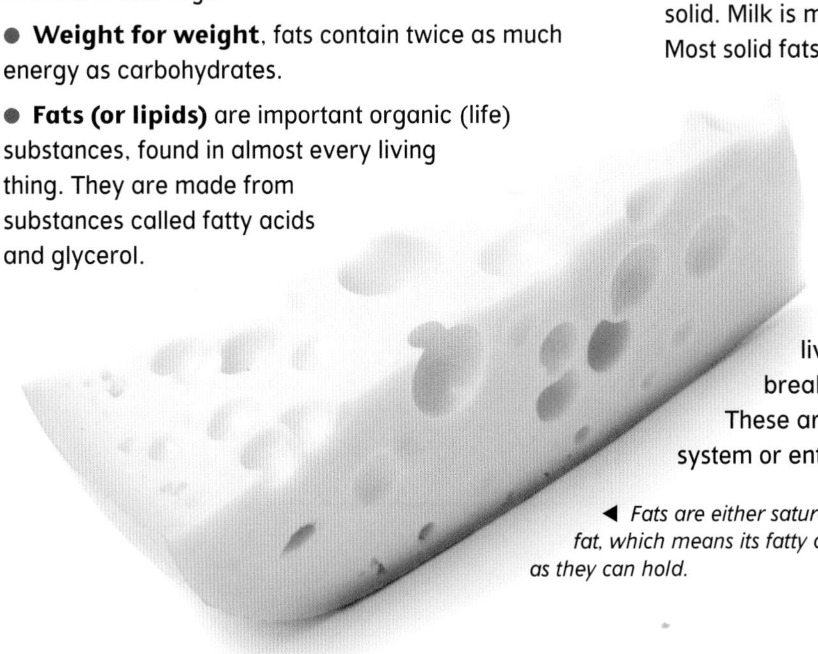

◀ *Fats are either saturated or unsaturated. Cheese is a saturated fat, which means its fatty acids are saturated with as much hydrogen as they can hold.*

Carbohydrates

- **Carbohydrates** are your body's main source of energy. They are plentiful in starchy food such as bread and cakes.
- **The body burns carbohydrates** to keep it warm and to provide energy for growth and muscle movement, as well as to maintain basic body processes.
- **Carbohydrates** are among the most common of all organic substances. Plants, for instance, make carbohydrates when they take energy from sunlight.
- **Carbohydrates are made from** chains of sugars and are classified as simple (few chains) and complex (many chains).

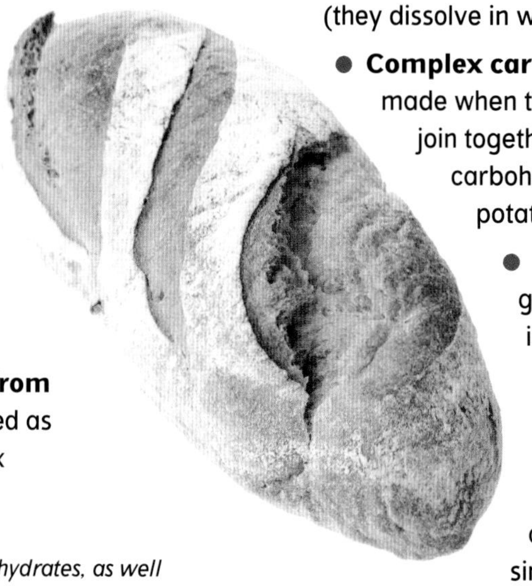

▶ *Bread is very rich in complex carbohydrates, as well as simpler ones such as glucose and sucrose.*

- **Simple carbohydrates** such as glucose, fructose (the sugar in fruit) and sucrose (table sugar) are sweet and soluble (they dissolve in water).
- **Complex carbohydrates** (polysaccharides) are made when the molecules of simple carbohydrates join together. Dietary sources of complex carbohydrates include whole cereal grains, potatoes and rice.
- **Your body** turns carbohydrates into glucose for use at once, or stores them in the liver as the sugar glycogen. More complex carbohydrates are converted into glucose more slowly.
- **Enzymes are used by the digestive system** to break complex carbohydrates such as starch into simple sugars that can be absorbed into the blood. Saliva (spit) contains the enzyme amylase that converts starch into glucose.

DID YOU KNOW?

Complex carbohydrates are a healthier source of energy in your diet than simple carbohydrates.

Glucose

- **Glucose** is the body's energy chemical, used as the fuel in all cell activity.
- **Glucose is a kind of sugar** made by plants as they take energy from sunlight.
- **The body gets its glucose** from carbohydrates in food, broken down in stages in the intestine.
- **From the intestine**, glucose travels in the blood to the liver, where excess is stored in the form of glycogen.
- **For the body to work effectively**, levels of glucose in the blood (called blood sugar) must always be correct.
- **Blood sugar levels** are controlled by two hormones, glucagon and insulin, sent out by the pancreas.
- **When blood sugar is low**, the pancreas sends glucagon to the liver to tell it to change more glycogen to glucose.
- **When blood sugar is high**, the pancreas sends insulin to the liver to tell it to store more glucose as glycogen.
- **Inside cells**, glucose may be burned for energy, stored as glycogen, or used to make triglyceride fats.

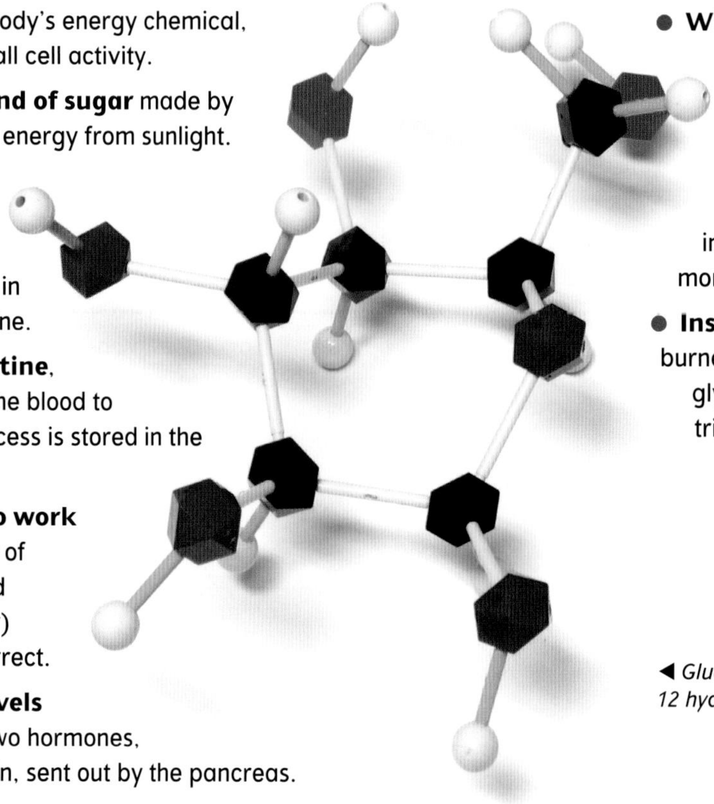

◀ *Glucose is built from six carbon, 12 hydrogen and six oxygen atoms.*

Protein

▲ *Your body is not able to store protein, so you need to eat a little every day.*

- **Proteins are essential** to the structure, function and regulation of the body.
- **Proteins are made** from strings of amino acids (molecules containing carbon, hydrogen, nitrogen, oxygen and sometimes sulphur).
- **There are 20 common types** of amino acid of which some must be eaten because they cannot be made in the body. These are called essential amino acids.
- **Protein in the diet** comes from meat, cheese, eggs, yoghurt, pulses, soya, nuts and seeds.

DID YOU KNOW?

Good sources of protein for vegetarians include nuts and seeds, pulses, cereals, eggs, milk, cheese and yoghurt.

- **Protein in the diet** is broken down in the digestive system into amino acids that can be absorbed into the blood and then made into new proteins.
- **An adult man** needs to eat about 50 to 55 g of protein a day.
- **An adult woman** needs to eat about 45 g a day.
- **Women need more protein** when they are pregnant or breast feeding.
- **Animal sources of protein** contain all essential amino acids, while most plant proteins do not.

Vitamins

- **Vitamins are special substances** the body needs to help maintain chemical processes inside cells.
- **Plants can make their own vitamins**, but humans must take most of their own from food.
- **A lack of any vitamin** in the diet can cause illness.
- **The first vitamins** discovered were given letter names such as B. Later discoveries were given chemical names.
- **Before the 18th century**, sailors on long voyages used to suffer from the disease scurvy, caused by a lack of vitamin C from fresh fruit in their diet.
- **Some vitamins** such as A, D, E and K dissolve in fat and are found in animal fats and vegetable oils. They may be stored in the body for months.

DID YOU KNOW?

Lack of vitamin A ruins night vision, because it is needed for the working of the retina.

- **Some vitamins** such as C and the Bs, dissolve in water and are found in green leaves, fruits and cereal grains. They are used by the body daily.
- **Vitamins D and K** are the only ones made in the body. Vitamin D is essential for healthy bones. It is made by the skin when exposed to sunlight – 15 minutes three times a week may be enough.

◀ *Citrus fruit, such as oranges, lemons and limes, and green vegetables are full of vitamins, which is why they are so important in our diet.*

Enzymes

- **Enzymes** are molecules – mostly protein – which alter the speed of chemical reactions in living things.
- **There are thousands of enzymes** in your body – it could not function without them.
- **Some enzymes** need an extra substance, called a coenzyme, to work. Many coenzymes are vitamins.
- **Most enzymes** have names ending in 'ase', such as lygase, protease and lipase.
- **Pacemaker enzymes** play a vital role in controlling your metabolism – the rate at which your body uses energy.
- **The activity of an enzyme** is easily destroyed by heat. This is one reason why it is important that the body temperature is kept very steadily at 37°C.
- **Many enzymes** are essential for the digestion of food, including lipase, protease, amylase and the peptidases. Most of these are made in the pancreas.
- **Lipase** is released mainly from the pancreas into the alimentary canal (gut) to help break down fat.
- **Amylase** breaks down starches such as those in bread and fruit into simple sugars. There is amylase in saliva and in the stomach.
- **In the gut**, the sugars maltose, sucrose and lactose are broken down by maltase, sucrase and lactase.

▼ Saliva contains enzymes called amylase and lipase that start to break down food as soon as it enters your mouth.

The liver

- **The liver** is the body's chemical processing centre, and the biggest internal organ. The word hepatic means 'to do with the liver'.
- **The prime task** of the liver is handling all the nutrients and substances digested from the food you eat and sending them out to your body cells when needed.
- **Carbohydrates**, the main energy-giving chemical for body cells, are turned into glucose in the liver.
- **The liver** also keeps levels of glucose in the blood steady. It releases more when levels drop, and stores it as glycogen, a type of starch, when levels rise.
- **Any excess food energy** is sent off by the liver to be stored as fat around the body.
- **Proteins are broken down** and vitamins and minerals are stored in the liver.
- **The liver produces bile**, the yellowish or greenish bitter liquid that helps dissolve fat as food is digested.
- **Old red cells** and harmful substances such as alcohol, are cleaned out of the body by the liver, and new plasma is made.
- **Thousands of hexagonal-shaped** units called lobules comprise the chemical processing units in the liver. These take in unprocessed blood on the outside and dispatch it through a collecting vein in the centre of each one.

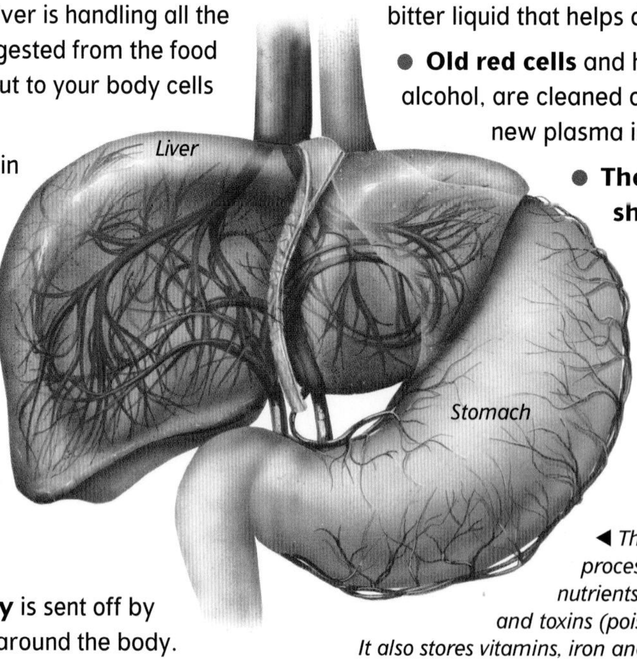
Liver
Stomach

◀ The liver is the body's cleaning and processing station for the blood, where nutrients are taken out for use by the body and toxins (poisons) are neutralized (made safe). It also stores vitamins, iron and carbohydrate.

The pancreas

- **The pancreas** is a large gland that lies just below and behind the stomach.
- **The larger end** of the pancreas is on the right, lying against the gut. The tail end is on the left, just touching the spleen.
- **The pancreas** is made from a substance called exocrine tissue, embedded with hundreds of nests of hormone glands called the islets of Langerhans.
- **The exocrine tissue** secretes (releases) pancreatic enzymes such as amylase into the intestine to help digest food.
- **Amylase** breaks down carbohydrates into simple sugars such as maltose, lactose and sucrose.
- **The pancreatic enzymes** run into the intestine via a pipe called the pancreatic duct, which joins to the bile duct. This duct also carries bile.
- **The pancreatic enzymes** only start working when they meet other kinds of enzyme in the intestine.
- **The pancreas** also secretes the body's own antacid, sodium bicarbonate, to settle an upset stomach.

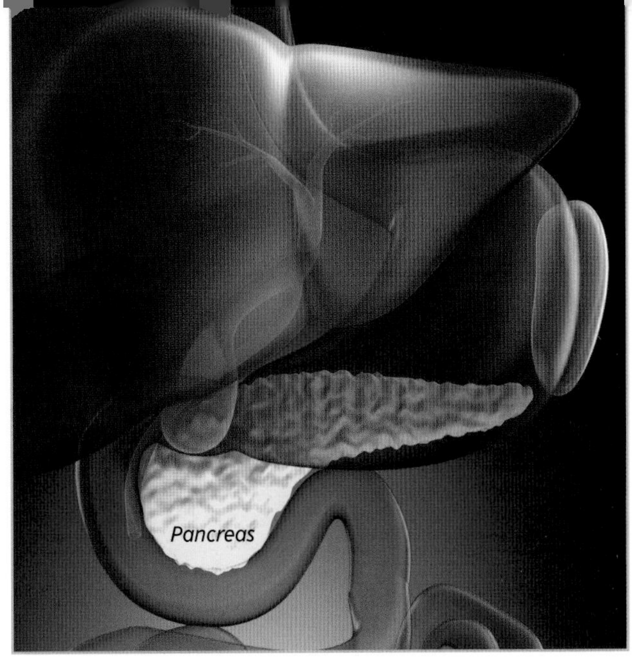
Pancreas

▲ *The pancreas is less than 20 cm long but produces one of the body's most important hormones – insulin.*

- **The islets of Langerhans** secrete two very important hormones – insulin and glucagon. These are released directly into the blood, not into the gut like the pancreatic enzymes.
- **Insulin and glucagon** regulate blood sugar levels.

Excretion

- **Digestive excretion** is the way your body gets rid of food that it cannot digest.
- **Undigested food** is prepared for excretion in the large intestine or bowel. The main part of the large intestine is the colon, which is almost as long as you are tall.
- **The colon** converts the semi-liquid 'chyme' of undigested food into solid waste by absorbing water – up to 1.5 l every day.
- **Sodium and chlorine** are absorbed, and bicarbonate and potassium are removed by the colon walls.
- **Billions of bacteria** live inside the colon and help turn the chyme into faeces. These bacteria are harmless as long as they do not spread to the rest of the body.

DID YOU KNOW?

About two-thirds of the waste we produce is water.

- **Bacteria in the colon** make vitamins K and B – as well as gases such as methane and hydrogen sulphide.
- **The muscles of the colon** break the waste food down into segments ready for excretion.
- **About a third** of all faeces is not old food but 'friendly' gut bacteria and intestinal lining.

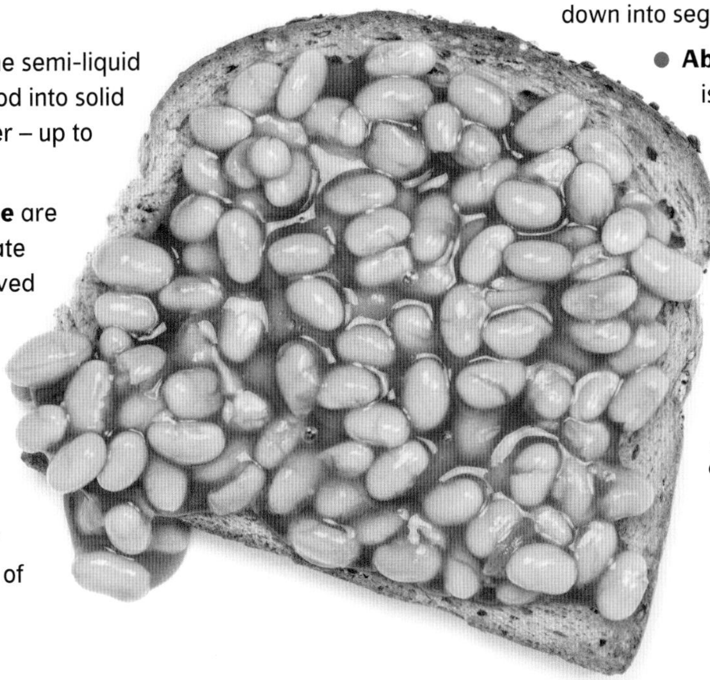

◀ *To function well, the bowel needs roughage – cellulose plant fibres found in food such as beans and wholemeal bread.*

Water

DID YOU KNOW?

Water accounts for around 60 percent of your body weight.

- **You can survive for weeks** without food, but no more than a few days without water.
- **You gain water** by drinking and eating, and as a by-product of cell activity.
- **You lose water** by sweating and breathing, and in your urine and faeces.
- **The average adult** takes in 2.2 litres of water a day – 1.4 l in drink and 0.8 l in food. Body cells add 0.3 l, bringing the total water intake to 2.5 l.
- **The average adult** loses 1.5 litres of water every day in urine, 0.5–0.6 l in sweat, 0.3–0.4 l as vapour in breath and 0.1–0.2 l in faeces.
- **The water balance** in the body is controlled mainly by the kidneys and adrenal glands.
- **The amount of water** the kidneys release as urine depends on the amount of salt in the blood.
- **If you drink lots**, the saltiness of the blood is diluted (watered down). To restore the balance, the kidneys let out water in the form of urine. If you drink little or sweat a lot, the blood becomes more salty, so the kidneys restore the balance by holding on to more water.

▶ *If you sweat a lot during heavy exercise, you need to make up for all the water you have lost by drinking. Your kidneys make sure that if you drink too much, you lose water as urine.*

Osmosis and diffusion

- **To survive**, every living cell must take in the chemicals it needs and let out the ones it does not through its thin membrane (casing). Cells do this in several ways, including osmosis, diffusion and active transport.
- **Osmosis** is the movement of water to even the balance between a weak solution and a stronger one.
- **Osmosis occurs** when the molecules of a dissolved substance are too big to slip through the cell membrane – only the water can move.
- **Osmosis is vital** to many body processes, including the workings of the kidneys and the nerves.
- **Urine gets its water** from the kidneys by osmosis.
- **Diffusion is the movement** of substances dissolved in water, or mixed in air, to even the balance.
- **In diffusion**, a substance such as oxygen moves in and out of cells, while the air or water it is mixed in stays put.
- **Diffusion is vital** to body processes such as cellular respiration, when cells take in oxygen and push out waste carbon dioxide.
- **Active transport** is the way a cell uses protein-based 'pumps' or 'gates' in its membrane to draw in and hold substances that might otherwise diffuse out. It uses energy and is how cells draw in most of their food such as glucose.

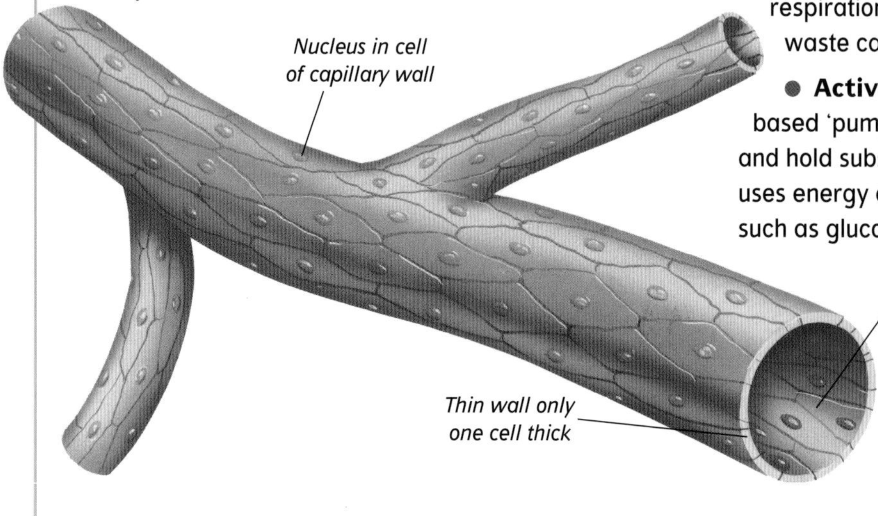
Nucleus in cell of capillary wall
Lumen (cavity)
Thin wall only one cell thick

◀ *Oxygen diffuses from the air sacs in your lungs into your blood capillaries because the concentration of oxygen is higher in the air sacs and lower in the capillary.*

Body salts

- **Body salts** are an important group of chemicals that play a vital role in your body.
- **Examples of components** in body salts include potassium, sodium, chloride and manganese.
- **Body salts are important** in maintaining the balance of water in the body, and in body cells.
- **The body's thirst centre** is the hypothalamus in the brain. It monitors salt levels in the blood and sends signals telling the kidneys to keep water or to let it go.
- **You gain salt** from the food you eat.
- **You can lose salt** if you sweat heavily. This can make muscles cramp, which is why people take salt tablets in the desert or drink a weak salt solution.

DID YOU KNOW?

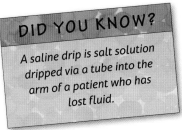

A saline drip is salt solution dripped via a tube into the arm of a patient who has lost fluid.

▲ *The body loses salt in sweat during exercise. Adequate hydration and sodium intake, either through sports drinks or food, is vitally important to keep the body going during long races.*

- **Too much salt** in food may result in high blood pressure.
- **When dissolved in water**, the chemical elements that salt is made from split into ions – atoms with either a positive or a negative electrical charge.

The kidneys

- **The kidneys** are a pair of bean-shaped organs inside the small of the back. They are the body's water control and blood-cleaning plants.
- **The kidneys are filters** that draw off water and important substances from the blood, and let unwanted water and waste substances go as urine.
- **All blood** flows through the kidneys every ten minutes, so it is filtered 150 times a day.
- **The kidneys** save nearly all the amino acids and glucose from the blood and 70 percent of the salt.
- **Blood entering each kidney** is filtered through filtration units called nephrons.
- **Each nephron** is an intricate network of pipes called convoluted tubules, wrapped around tiny capillaries. Useful blood substances are filtered into the tubules, then re-absorbed back into the blood.

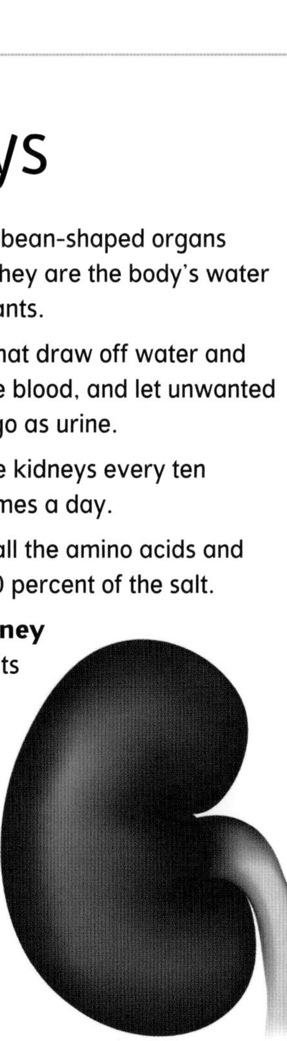

- **The production of urine** is one of the body's ways of getting rid of waste. It is produced by your kidneys, which filter it from your blood.
- **Urine runs from each kidney** down a tube called the ureter, into the bladder. When your bladder is full, you feel the need to urinate.
- **Urine is mostly water**, but there are substances dissolved in it. These include urea – a substance that is left after the breakdown of amino acids, various salts, creatinine, ammonia and blood wastes.

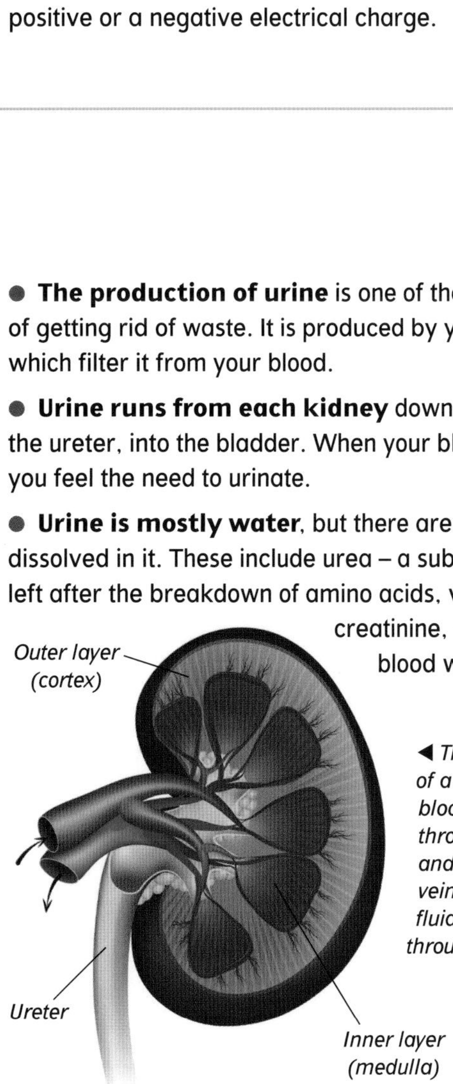
Outer layer (cortex)
Ureter
Inner layer (medulla)

◀ *This cross-section of a kidney shows blood entering through arteries (red) and leaving through veins (blue). Waste fluid drains away through the ureter.*

The endocrine system

- **Many bodily functions** are controlled by special chemicals called hormones.
- **Hormones are produced** by a number of specialized glands called endocrine glands.
- **Endocrine glands** are also called ductless glands because they release secretions directly into the blood and not into a duct (tube) like other types of gland (the salivary glands for example).
- **The endocrine glands** include the thyroid gland, the pancreas, the pituitary gland, the adrenal glands, the testes, the ovaries and the parathyroid glands.

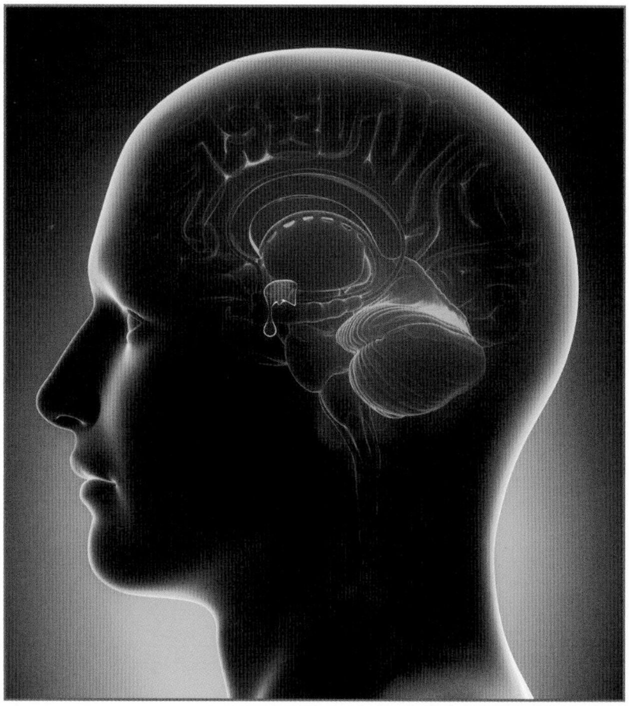

▲ *The pituitary gland releases eight different hormones, and they control major developments in the body such as growth and reproduction.*

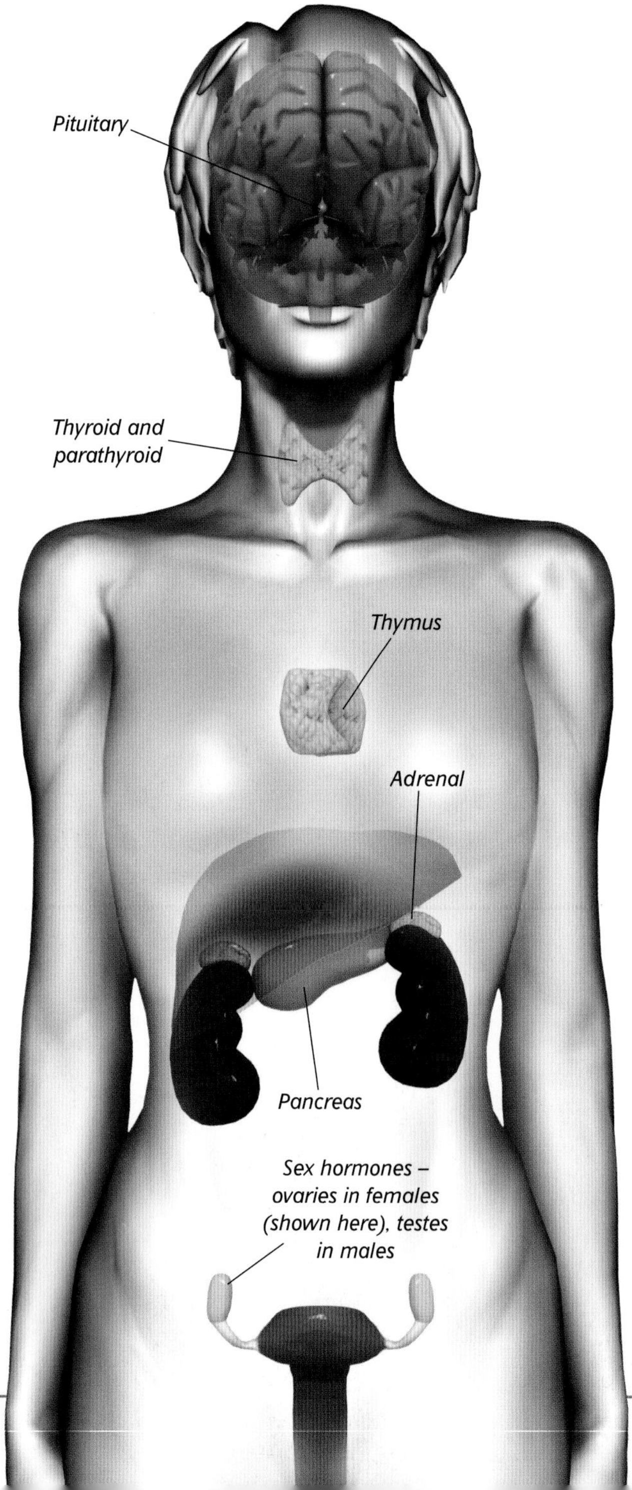
Pituitary
Thyroid and parathyroid
Thymus
Adrenal
Pancreas
Sex hormones – ovaries in females (shown here), testes in males

- **Most hormones** are proteins but some are steroids (adrenal and sex hormones).
- **The effect of the hormones** produced by the endocrine system is usually far away from the site of release.
- **The pituitary gland** is located at the base of the brain sitting in a cup-shaped depression in the skull called the sella turcica.
- **The pituitary and hypothalamus** produce the largest number of different hormones.
- **The parathyroid glands** are embedded in the back of the thyroid gland in the neck, which itself is an endocrine gland.
- **The pancreas** is unusual as it is both an endocrine gland (hormone producing) and an exocrine gland (manufactures chemicals that it secretes into a duct).
- **The thymus gland** is active only in childhood, and helps the immune system develop.

◀ *Endocrine glands are situated all over the body, and each hormone affects only certain parts, known as target organs.*

DID YOU KNOW?

The pineal gland sets your body's clock by releasing melatonin, a hormone that makes you drowsy.

The thyroid gland

- **The thyroid gland** is shaped like a bow tie and sits at the front of the neck just below the voice box (larynx).
- **The thyroid** secretes (releases) three important hormones – tri-odothyronine (T3), thyroxine (T4) and calcitonin.
- **The thyroid hormones** affect how energetic you are by controlling your metabolic rate.
- **Your metabolic rate** is the rate at which your cells use glucose and other energy substances.
- **T3 and T4** control metabolic rate by circulating into the blood and stimulating cells to convert more glucose.

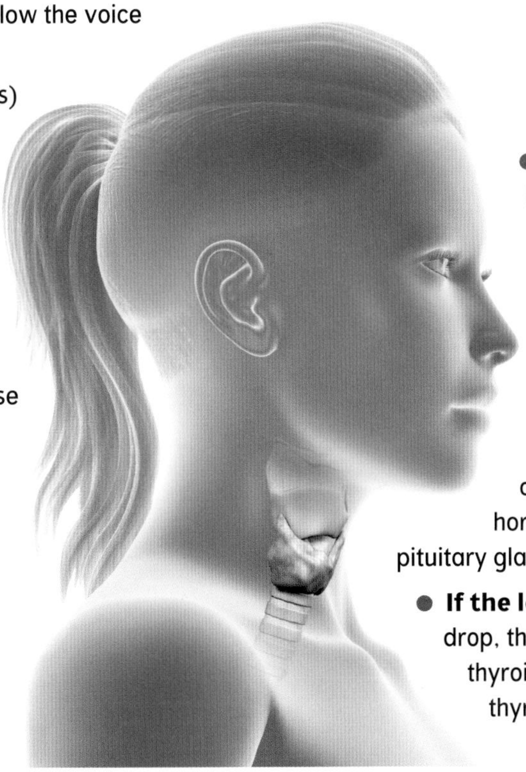

▶ *The thyroid is part of your energy control system, telling your body cells to work faster or slower in order to keep you warm or to make your muscles work harder.*

DID YOU KNOW?

Everyone has a different metabolic rate. It rises when you are afraid or if your body is working hard.

- **If the thyroid** sends out too little T3 and T4, you get cold and tired, your skin gets dry and you put on weight. If it sends out too much T3 and T4, you get nervous, sweaty and overactive, and you lose weight.
- **The amount of T3 and T4** sent out by the thyroid depends on how much thyroid-stimulating hormone is sent to it from the pituitary gland.
- **If the levels of T3 and T4** in the blood drop, the pituitary gland sends out extra thyroid-stimulating hormone to tell the thyroid to produce more.

Hormones

- **Hormones** are the body's chemical messengers. They are released from stores to trigger certain reactions in different parts of the body.
- **Most hormones** are endocrine hormones that are spread around the body in the bloodstream.
- **Hormones are controlled** by feedback systems. This means they are only released when their store gets the right trigger – which may be a chemical in the blood or another hormone.
- **Major hormone sources** include the thyroid gland, the pituitary gland, the adrenal glands, the pancreas, a woman's ovaries and a man's testes.
- **The pituitary** is the source of many important hormones, including those that control growth and metabolism.
- **Adrenalin is released** by the adrenals to ready the body for action.
- **Insulin helps** control the level of glucose (sugar) in your bloodstream.
- **Oestrogen and progesterone** are female sex hormones that control a woman's monthly cycle.
- **Testosterone** is a male sex hormone that controls the workings of a man's sex organs.

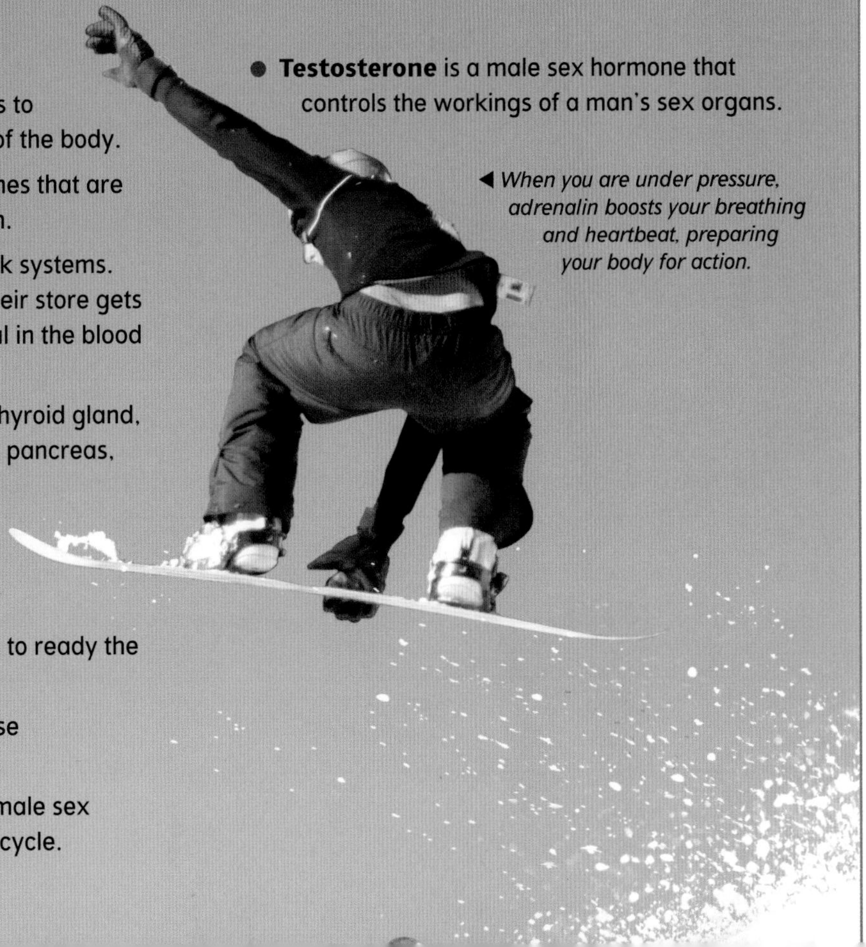

◀ *When you are under pressure, adrenalin boosts your breathing and heartbeat, preparing your body for action.*

Genes

- **Genes are the body's chemical instructions** for your entire life – for growing up, surviving and having children.
- **Individual genes** are instructions to make particular proteins, the body's building-block molecules.
- **Small sets of genes** control features such as the colour of your hair or your eyes, or create a particular body process such as digesting fat from food.
- **Each of your body cells** (apart from egg and sperm cells) carry identical sets of genes, because every one of your cells was made by other cells splitting in two, starting with the fertilized egg cell in your mother.
- **Your genes are a mixture**. Half come from your mother and half from your father, but none of your brothers or sisters will get the same combination, unless you are identical twins.
- **Genes instruct the human body** how to develop and carry out its life processes. It is our combination of genes that make us unique.
- **Genes are sections of DNA** – a microscopically tiny molecule inside each cell.

▲ *The characteristics in this family group are clear to see, and have been passed on by DNA.*

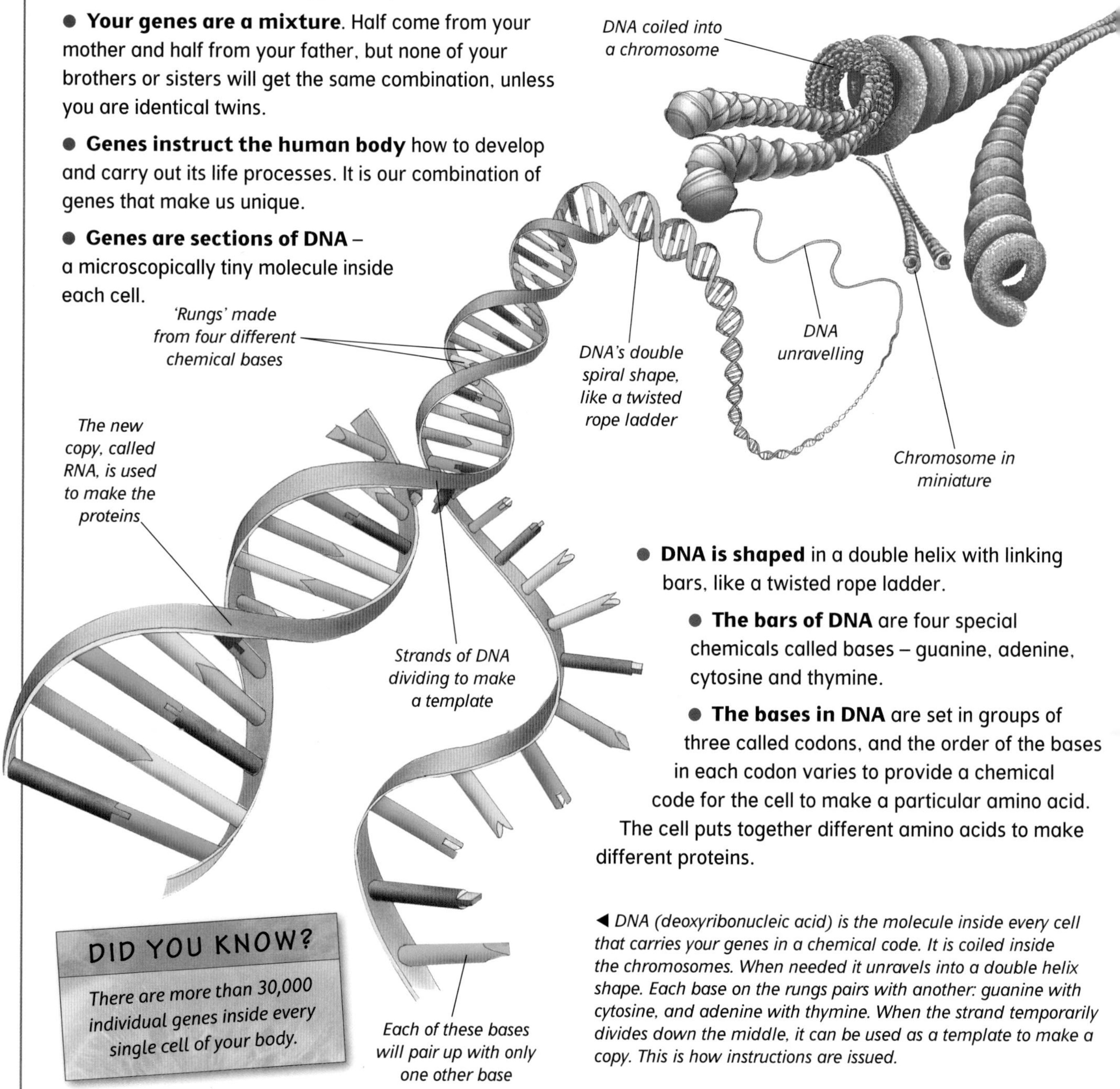
DNA coiled into a chromosome
'Rungs' made from four different chemical bases
DNA's double spiral shape, like a twisted rope ladder
DNA unravelling
Chromosome in miniature
The new copy, called RNA, is used to make the proteins
Strands of DNA dividing to make a template
Each of these bases will pair up with only one other base

- **DNA is shaped** in a double helix with linking bars, like a twisted rope ladder.
- **The bars of DNA** are four special chemicals called bases – guanine, adenine, cytosine and thymine.
- **The bases in DNA** are set in groups of three called codons, and the order of the bases in each codon varies to provide a chemical code for the cell to make a particular amino acid. The cell puts together different amino acids to make different proteins.

◀ *DNA (deoxyribonucleic acid) is the molecule inside every cell that carries your genes in a chemical code. It is coiled inside the chromosomes. When needed it unravels into a double helix shape. Each base on the rungs pairs with another: guanine with cytosine, and adenine with thymine. When the strand temporarily divides down the middle, it can be used as a template to make a copy. This is how instructions are issued.*

DID YOU KNOW?

There are more than 30,000 individual genes inside every single cell of your body.

Chromosomes

- **Chromosomes** are the tiny threads inside every cell that carry your body's life instructions in chemical form.
- **There are 46 chromosomes** (23 pairs) in each of your body cells except red blood cells, which have no nucleus, and your sex cells (ova or sperm), which have 23 chromosomes.
- **One chromosome from each pair** came from your mother and the other from your father.
- **In a girl's 23 chromosome pairs**, each half matches the other (the set from the mother is equivalent to the set from the father). Boys have 22 matching chromosome pairs, but the 23rd pair consists of two odd chromosomes.
- **The 23rd chromosome pair** decides what sex you are, and the sex chromosomes are called X and Y. Girls have two X chromosomes, but boys have an X and a Y chromosome.
- **In every matching pair**, both chromosomes give your body life instructions for the same thing.

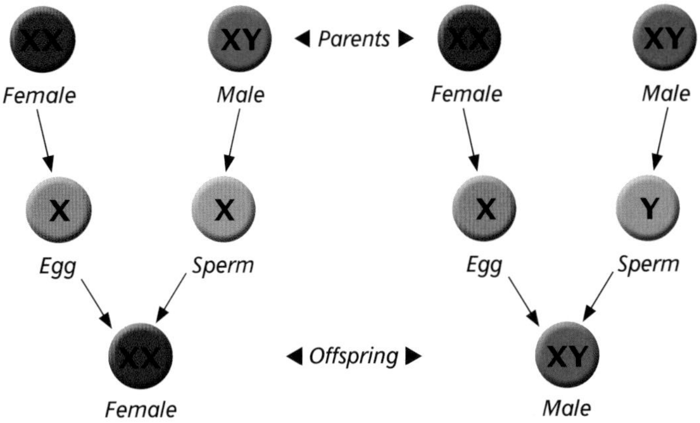
XX
XY
Parents
XX
XY
Female
Male
Female
Male
X
X
X
Y
Egg
Sperm
Egg
Sperm
XX
Offspring
XY
Female
Male

▲ *Offspring always inherit an X chromosme from their mother. If the father gives an X chromosome, the offspring will be female (XX). If the father gives a Y chromosome the offspring will be male (XY).*

- **The chemical instructions** on each chromosome come in thousands of different units called genes.
- **Genes for the same feature** appear in the same locus (place) on each matching pair of chromosomes in every human body cell. The entire pattern is called the genome.

DID YOU KNOW?

Different animals have different numbers of chromosomes. A dog has 78 and a horse has 64.

Heredity

- **Your heredity** is all the body characteristics you inherit from your parents – for example, your mother's black hair.
- **Characteristics** are passed on by the genes carried on your chromosomes.
- **The basic laws** of heredity were discovered by the Austrian monk Gregor Mendel (1822–1884) 150 years ago.
- **Your body characteristics** are a mix of two sets of instructions – one from your mother's chromosomes and the other from your father's. Which genes you have determine your characteristics such as hair colour, height, or shape of your nose.
- **Many characteristics** are determined not by a mixture of your parents' genes, but by one of the genes being stronger than the other, or 'dominant'. The dominant gene will affect your characteristic (be expressed), while the weaker 'recessive' gene won't.
- **A recessive gene** may be expressed when there is no competition – that is, when the genes from both of your parents are recessive.

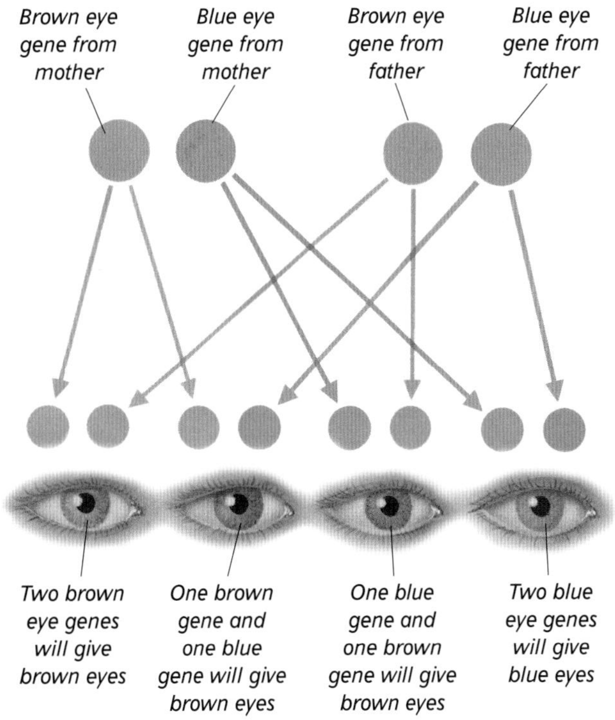
Brown eye gene from mother
Blue eye gene from mother
Brown eye gene from father
Blue eye gene from father
Two brown eye genes will give brown eyes
One brown gene and one blue gene will give brown eyes
One blue gene and one brown gene will give brown eyes
Two blue eye genes will give blue eyes

▲ *In this diagram, both parents have genes for brown and blue eyes. Brown eye genes are dominant.*

Puberty

● **Puberty is the stage** in life at which girls and boys mature sexually. The age of puberty varies, but on average it begins between 11 and 13 years.

● **Puberty begins** when two hormones – the follicle-stimulating hormone and the luteinizing hormone – are sent out by the pituitary gland.

● **Sexual development** concerns the development of primary and secondary sexual characteristics, and regulate all sex-related processes such as sperm and egg production.

● **There are three main types of sex hormones** – androgens, oestrogens and progesterones.

● **Androgens are male hormones** such as testosterone. Oestrogen is the female hormone made mainly in the ovaries. It causes a girl's sexual organs to develop and controls her menstrual cycle. Progesterone is the female hormone that prepares a girl's uterus (womb) for pregnancy every month.

● **Primary sexual characteristics** are the internal organs that indicate whether someone is male or female – the ovaries and uterus in a girl and the testes and prostate gland in a boy.

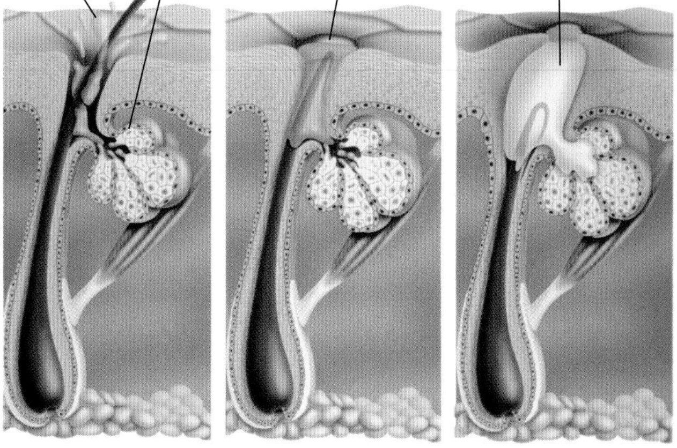
Sebum
Gland produces sebum
Pore becomes blocked
Spot forms

▲ *During puberty, glands in the skin produce extra sebum, a type of oil, that can block pores, causing spots.*

● **Secondary sexual characteristics** are the external differences that develop during puberty that indicate whether someone is male or female. A girl's breasts develop, and hair grows under her arms and around her genitals. For a boy, hair grows on his face, under his arms and around his genitals.

● **A year or so after puberty begins**, a girl has her menarche (the first menstrual period). When her periods are regular, she is able to have a baby.

Ageing

● **Most people live** for between 60 and 100 years, although a few live even longer than this.

● **The longest officially confirmed** age is that of Frenchwoman Jeanne Calment, who died in 1997, aged 122 years and 164 days.

● **Life expectancy** is how long statistics suggest you are likely to live.

● **On average in Europe**, men can expect to live about 75 years and women about 80. However, because health is improving generally, people are living longer.

● **As adults grow older**, their bodies begin to deteriorate (fail). Senses such as hearing, sight and taste weaken.

● **Hair goes grey** as pigment (colour) cells stop working.

● **Muscles weaken** as fibres die.

● **Bones become more brittle** as calcium is lost. Cartilage shrinks between joints, causing stiffness.

▶ *Changes in health standards mean that more and more people than ever before are remaining fit in old age.*

DID YOU KNOW?

In the UK, there are more people aged over 60 than there are aged under 16.

● **Skin wrinkles** as the rubbery collagen fibres that support it sag. Exposure to sunlight speeds this up, which is why the face and hands get wrinkles first.

● **With age**, circulation and breathing weaken. Blood vessels may become stiff and clogged, forcing the heart to work harder and raising blood pressure.

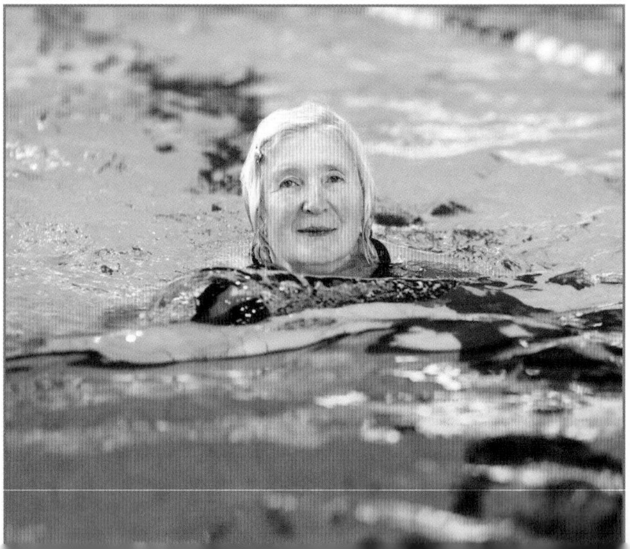

Male reproduction

- **A man's reproductive system** is where his body creates the sperm cells that combine with a female egg cell to create a new human life. Sperm cells look like tiny tadpoles, microscopic in size.
- **They are made in the testes**, inside the scrotum, which hang outside the body where it is cooler, because this improves sperm production.

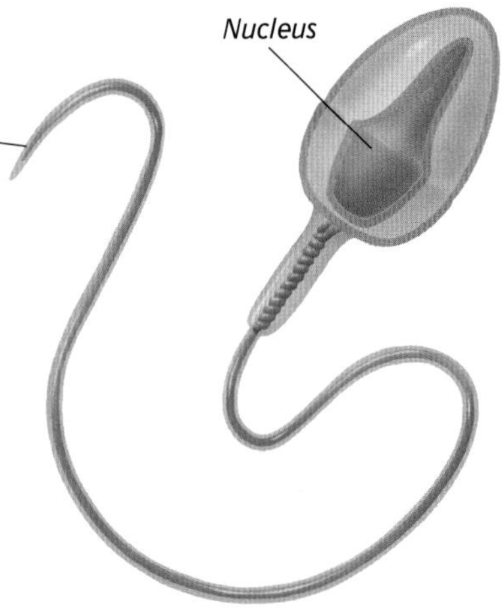
Nucleus
Tail

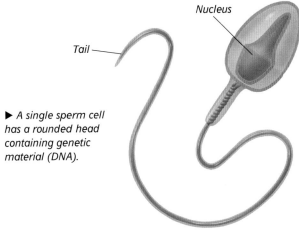

▶ *A single sperm cell has a rounded head containing genetic material (DNA).*

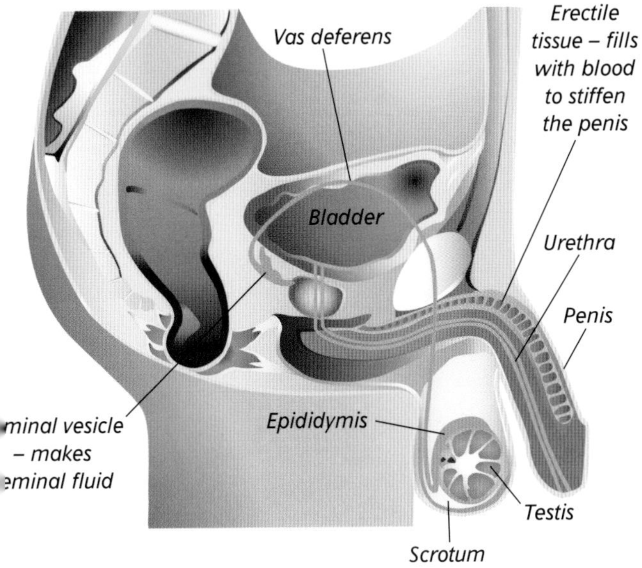
Vas deferens
Erectile tissue – fills with blood to stiffen the penis
Bladder
Urethra
Penis
minal vesicle – makes eminal fluid
Epididymis
Testis
Scrotum

- **Sperm leave** the testes via the epididymis – a thin, coiled tube. During sexual intercourse, sperm are driven into a tube called the vas deferens and mix with a liquid called seminal fluid to make semen.
- **Semen** shoots through the urethra and is ejaculated into the woman's vagina.
- **The male sex hormone testosterone** is made in the testes. Testosterone stimulates bone and muscle growth, and the development of male characteristics such as facial hair and a deeper voice.

◀ *This is a side view of the inside of a man's reproductive organs.*

Female reproduction

- **A woman's reproductive system** is where her body stores, releases and nurtures the egg cells (ova) that create a new human life when joined with a male sperm cell.
- **All the egg cells** are stored from birth in the ovaries – two glands inside the pelvic region. Each egg is stored in a tiny sac called a follicle. A monthly menstrual cycle starts when the follicle-stimulating hormone (FSH) is sent by the pituitary gland in the brain to encourage follicles to grow.
- **As follicles grow**, they release the sex hormone oestrogen. Oestrogen makes the lining of the uterus (womb) thicken.
- **When an egg (ovum) is ripe**, it is released and moves down a duct called a fallopian tube. One egg cell is released every month by one of the ovaries.
- **If a woman** has sexual intercourse at this time, sperm from the man's penis may swim up her vagina, enter her womb and fertilize the egg in the fallopian tube.

▶ *This is a side view of the inside of a female reproductive system, showing the vagina, ovaries, fallopian tubes and uterus.*

- **If the egg is fertilized**, the womb lining goes on thickening ready for pregnancy, and the egg begins to develop into an embryo.
- **If the egg is not fertilized**, it is shed with the womb lining in a flow of blood from the vagina. This shedding is called a menstrual period.

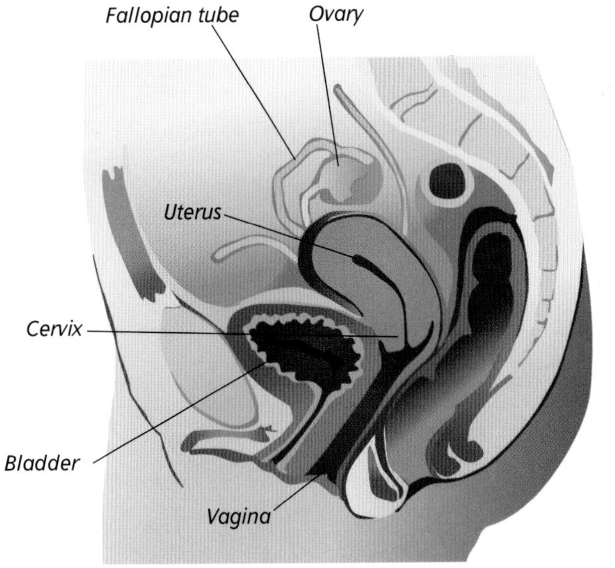
Fallopian tube
Ovary
Uterus
Cervix
Bladder
Vagina

Pregnancy begins

Pregnancy begins when an egg meets a sperm. They join together and implant in the uterus (womb) to grow into a new human being.

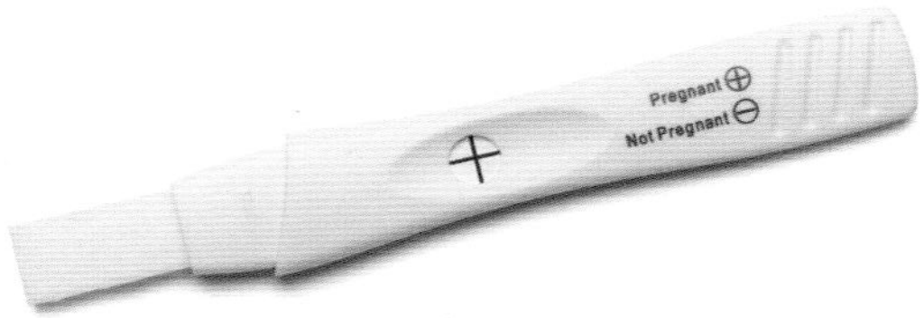
Pregnant
Not Pregnant

▲ ***PREGNANCY TESTING***
Pregnancy tests can be bought at a pharmacy and come with clear instructions. Women can often do the tests at home rather than visit the doctor.

Every month an egg is released from a woman's ovary – this is called ovulation. The egg travels down the fallopian tube (part of the uterus).

If there are sperm in the tube, following sexual intercourse, then the egg may become fertilized by one of them. This usually leads to pregnancy and a baby being born nine months later.

A woman can do a test to see if she is pregnant. It is usually done on a sample of her urine. The pregnancy test looks for a hormone called human gonadotrophin (HCG), which starts to be produced around six days after the egg is fertilized.

The new baby gets genes from both its parents. The egg and the sperm (gametes) carry half the usual number of chromosomes, so that when they merge the new baby will have the right number. The baby will have some characteristics like its mother, and some like its father.

▼ ***GENETIC MIXTURE***
The genetic make-up of a new baby is a mixture of genes (on chromosomes) from both its parents.

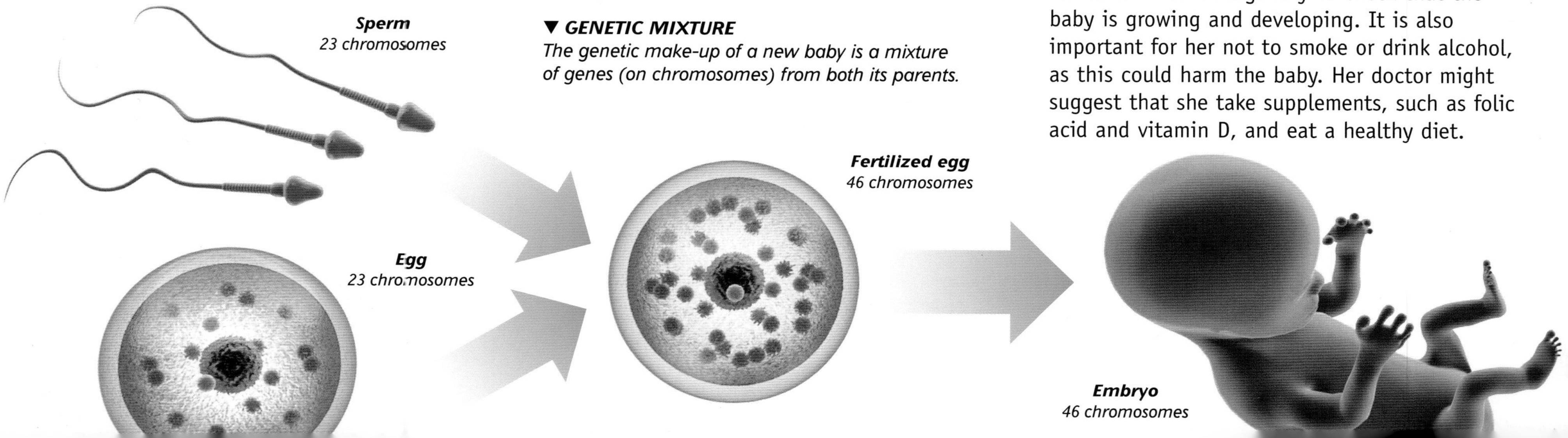
Sperm
23 chromosomes
Egg
23 chromosomes
Fertilized egg
46 chromosomes
Embryo
46 chromosomes

INFERTILITY

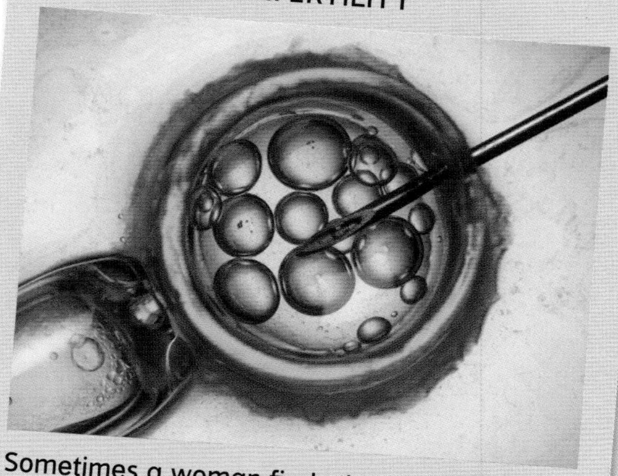

Sometimes a woman finds that she does not become pregnant. This is called infertility, and doctors can often help to treat it. One way is with IVF (in vitro fertilization) – the doctor takes an egg out of the woman and fertilizes it with sperm in a laboratory. Sometimes the sperm needs to be injected into the egg.

There are lots of ways a woman can keep herself healthy while she is pregnant. She will see a doctor or midwife regularly to check that the baby is growing and developing. It is also important for her not to smoke or drink alcohol, as this could harm the baby. Her doctor might suggest that she take supplements, such as folic acid and vitamin D, and eat a healthy diet.

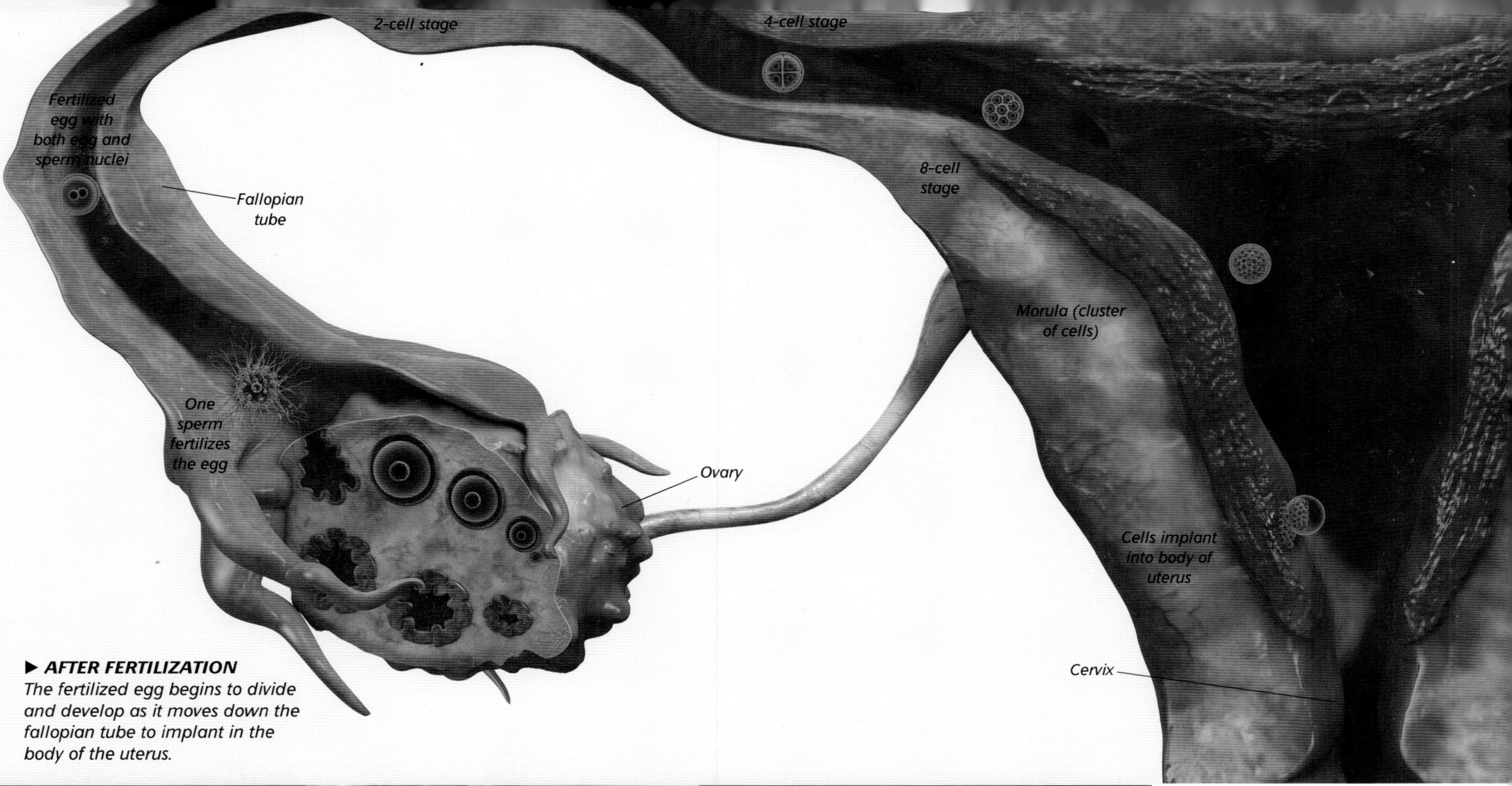
2-cell stage
4-cell stage
Fertilized egg with both egg and sperm nuclei
Fallopian tube
8-cell stage
Morula (cluster of cells)
One sperm fertilizes the egg
Ovary
Cells implant into body of uterus
Cervix

▶ AFTER FERTILIZATION
The fertilized egg begins to divide and develop as it moves down the fallopian tube to implant in the body of the uterus.

A FOETUS GROWS

The growing foetus (baby) lies safely within the womb, nourished by its mother through the umbilical cord. The time from fertilization to birth is called the gestation period. In humans this is nine months. Different animals have different gestation periods.

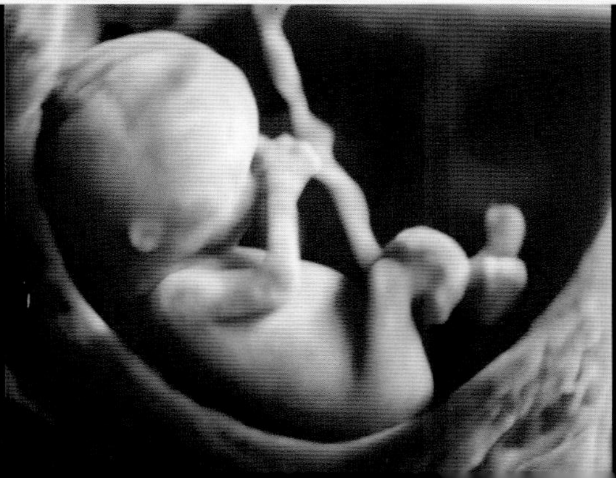

MORE THAN ONE BABY

More than one baby growing at the same time is called a multiple pregnancy. Two babies (twins) is most common, but a woman can have up to six. If the babies come from the splitting of a single fertilized egg they have the same genetic make-up so are identical – they look the same. Non-identical babies happen if more than one egg was fertilized. They are similar just like brothers or sisters.

Pregnancy

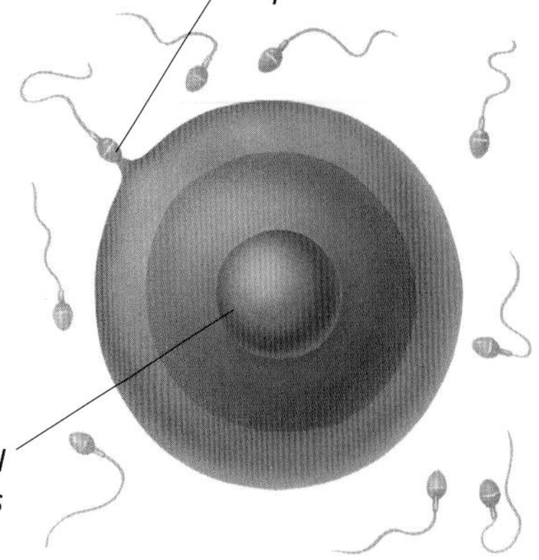
Successful sperm
Egg cell nucleus

▶ *At fertilization, tiny sperm cells swarm around the egg until one sperm manages to push its head on to the surface of the egg. The sperm head and egg membrane join, and fertilization takes place.*

● **Pregnancy begins** when a woman's ovum (egg cell) is fertilized by a man's sperm cell. Usually this happens after sexual intercourse, but it can begin in a laboratory.

● **When a woman becomes pregnant** her monthly menstrual periods stop. Tests on her urine show that she is pregnant.

● **During pregnancy**, the fertilized egg divides again and again to grow rapidly – first to an embryo (the first eight weeks), and then to a foetus (from eight weeks until birth).

● **By eight weeks** all the organs have formed in the developing baby. Pregnancy lasts nine months, and the time is divided into three trimesters (periods of about 12 weeks).

● **The foetus** lies cushioned in its mother's uterus (womb) in a bag of fluid called the amniotic sac.

● **The mother's blood** passes food and oxygen to the fetus via the placenta.

● **The umbilical cord** runs between the foetus and the placenta, carrying blood, oxygen and nutrients between them.

● **During pregnancy** a woman gains 30 percent more blood, and her heart rate goes up. Her breasts grow and develop milk glands.

DID YOU KNOW?

An ultrasound scan uses a pen-like probe moved over the skin of the abdomen to show an image of the unborn baby on a screen.

At two months the main body parts are formed

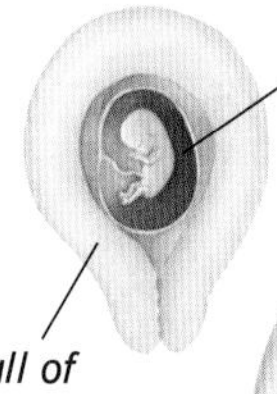
Fluid around baby
Wall of uterus

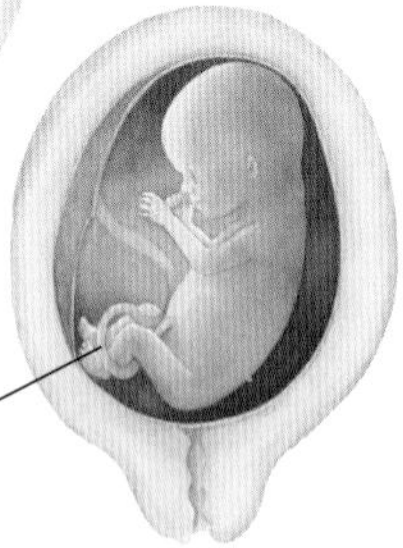
Umbilical cord

At three months the bones of the skeleton start to form

At five months the baby begins to move and kick

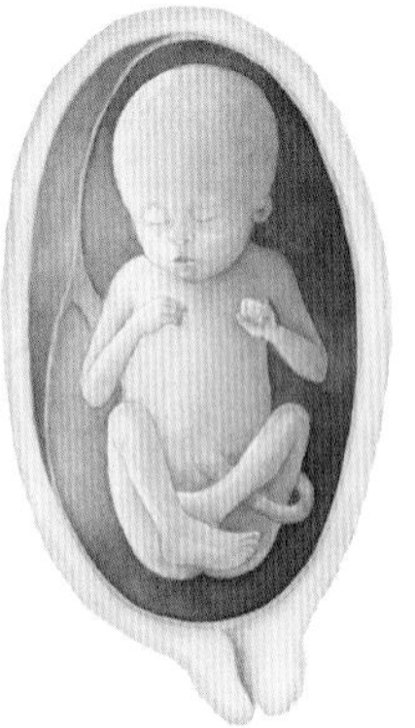

At seven months the baby can open its eyes

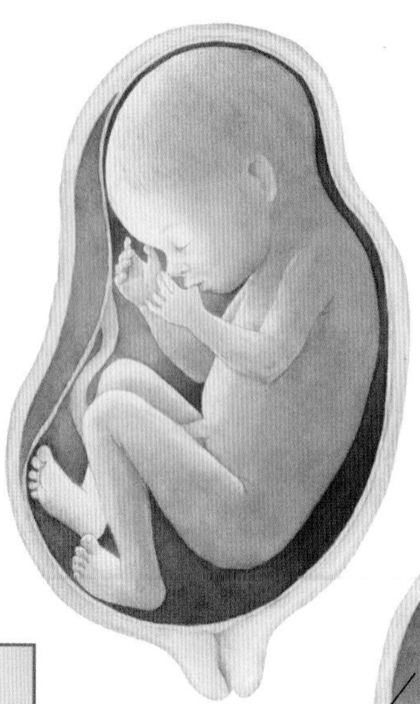

◀ *At first the tiny baby has plenty of room in the womb and can float about freely. But as it grows it becomes more cramped and has to bend its neck, back, arms and legs.*

At nine months the baby has 'turned' and is head down, ready to be born

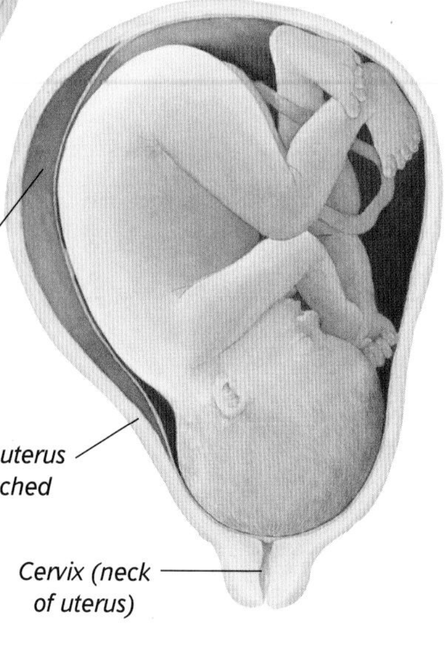
Placenta
Wall of uterus is stretched
Cervix (neck of uterus)

▼ *Being born can take an hour or two – or a whole day or two. It is very tiring for both the baby and its mother.*

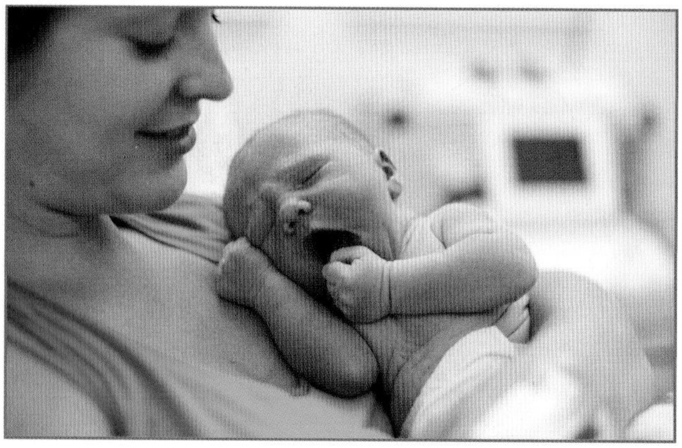

Birth

● **Babies are usually born** 38 to 42 weeks after the mother becomes pregnant.

● **Usually a few days** or weeks before a baby is born, it turns in the uterus (womb) so its head is pointing down towards the mother's birth canal (her cervix and vagina).

● **Birth begins** as the mother goes into labour – when the womb muscles begin a rhythm of contracting (tightening) and relaxing in order to push the baby out through the birth canal.

● **There are three stages** of labour. In the first, the womb muscles begin to pull on the cervix to make it thinner and the opening wider in preparation for the second stage.

● **In the second stage** of labour, the baby is pushed out through the birth canal. Then the umbilical cord – its lifeline to its mother – is cut and the baby starts to breathe on its own.

● **In the third stage** of labour, the placenta comes out through the birth canal.

● **A premature baby** is one that is born more than three weeks early. It may not be fully developed and so will need to be carefully looked after for a while in hospital.

● **A miscarriage** occurs when the developing baby is born before it is old enough to survive.

● **A Caesarian section** is an operation that is carried out when a baby can't be born through the birth canal and emerges from the womb through a cut made in the mother's belly.

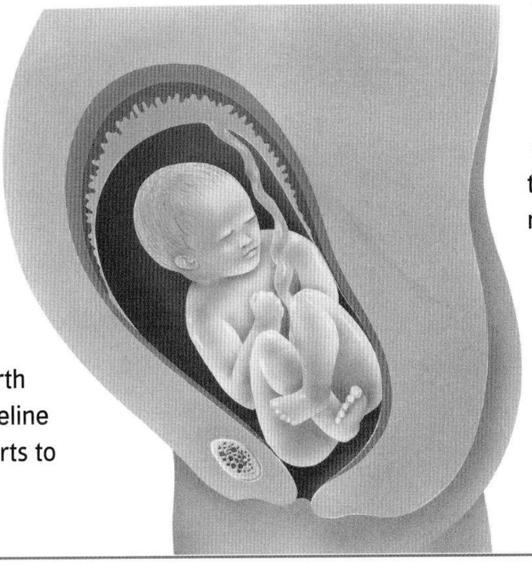

◀ *In a breech birth the baby comes out bottom first instead of head first.*

Babies

● **A baby's head** is three-quarters of the size it will be as an adult – and a quarter of its total body height.

● **The bones of a baby's skeleton** are made of cartilage when they first form and are gradually replaced by bone. The order in which the bones of the baby's body harden follows a set pattern.

● **Baby boys grow faster** than baby girls during the first seven months.

● **A baby** has a very developed sense of taste, with taste buds all over the inside of its mouth.

● **The sense of smell** is stronger in babies than adults – perhaps to help them identify their mother.

● **A baby's body weight** will usually triple in its first year.

● **Primitive reflexes** are those that we are born with, such as grasping or sucking a finger.

● **A baby seems to learn** to control its body in stages, starting first with its head, then moving on to its arms and legs.

DID YOU KNOW?

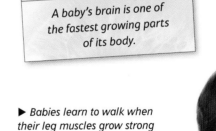

A baby's brain is one of the fastest growing parts of its body.

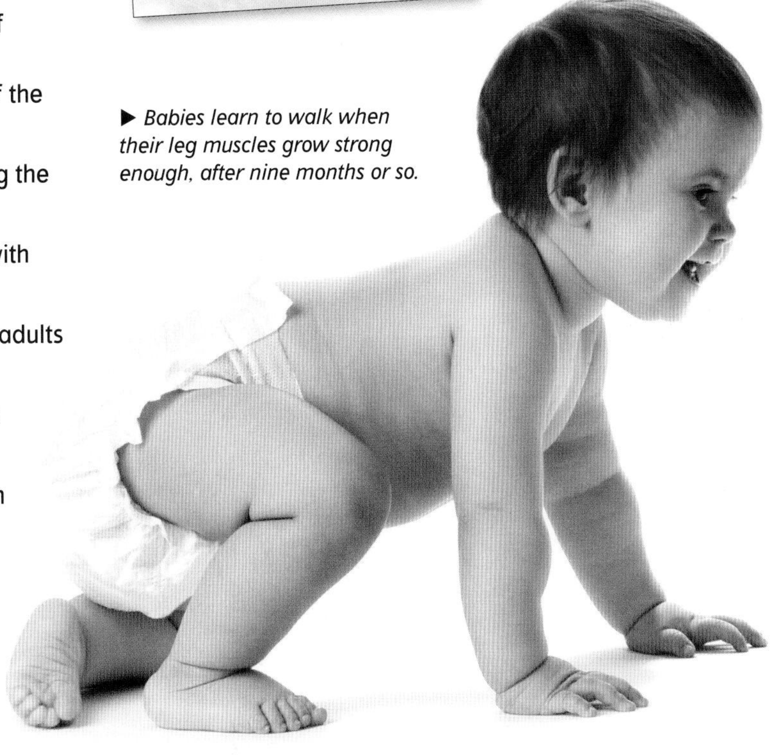

▶ *Babies learn to walk when their leg muscles grow strong enough, after nine months or so.*

The immune system

- **The immune system** is the complicated system of defences that your body uses to prevent or fight off attack from germs and other invaders.
- **Your body** has a variety of barriers, toxic chemicals and booby traps to stop germs entering it. The skin is a barrier that stops many germs getting in, as long as it is not broken.
- **Mucus is a thick, slimy fluid** that coats vulnerable internal parts of your body such as your stomach. It also acts as a lubricant (oil), making swallowing easier.
- **Mucus lines your airways and lungs** to protect them from smoke particles as well as from germs. Your airways may fill up with mucus when you have a cold, as your body tries to minimize the invasion of airborne germs.
- **Itching, sneezing, coughing** and vomiting are your body's ways of getting rid of unwelcome invaders. Small particles that get trapped in the mucus lining of your airways are wafted out by tiny hairs called cilia.
- **The body** has many specialized cells and chemicals that fight germs that get inside it.
- **Complement** is a mixture of liquid proteins in the blood that attacks bacteria.
- **Interferons** are proteins that help the body's cells to attack viruses and also stimulate killer cells.
- **Certain white blood cells** are cytotoxic, which means that they kill invaders.
- **Phagocytes** are big white blood cells that swallow up invaders and then use an enzyme to dissolve them. They are drawn to the site of an infection whenever there is inflammation.

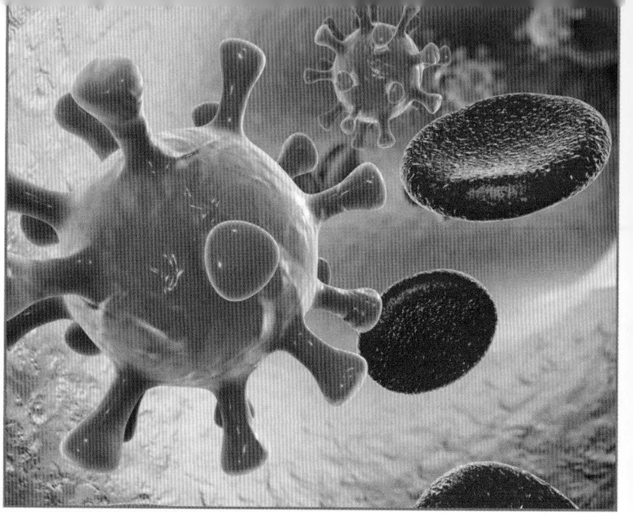

▲ HIV, the AIDS virus, attacks the body's immune cells and prevents them dealing with infections.

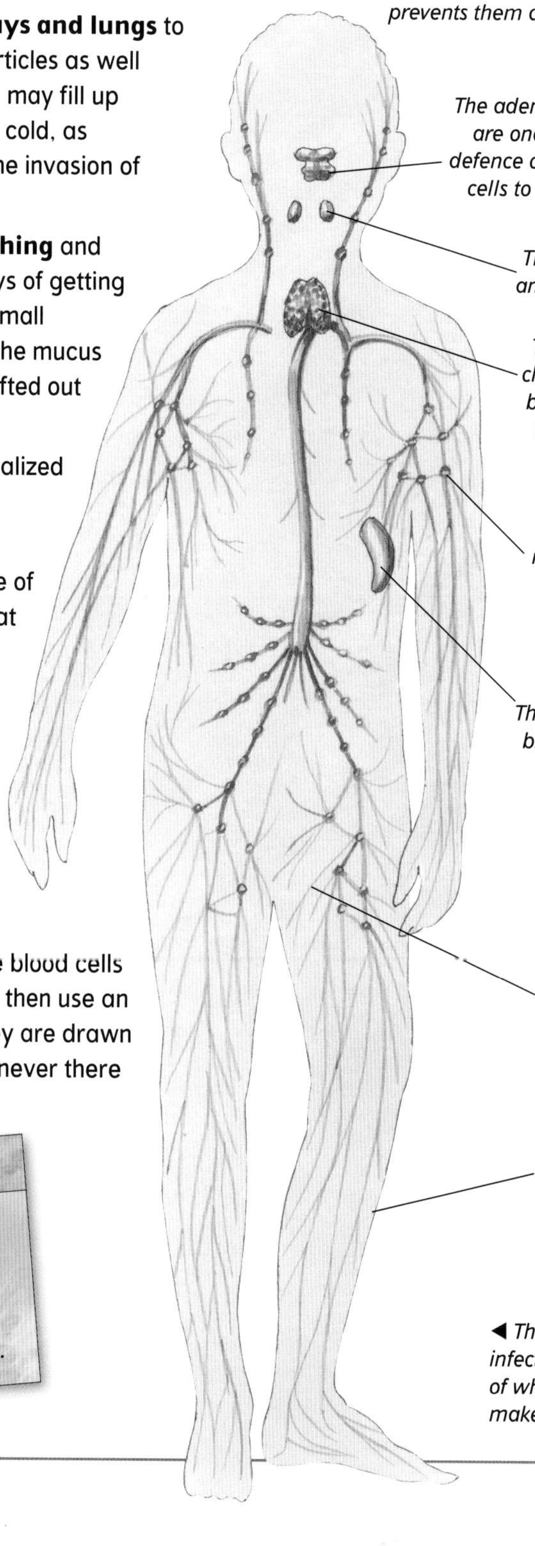
The adenoids in the nose are one of the body's defence centres, releasing cells to fight infections
The tonsils release cells to fight any infection that the throat gets
The thymus is a gland in the chest that turns ordinary white blood cells into special T-cells that fight harmful microbes
During an infection, lymph nodes may swell up with white blood cells that have swallowed up germs
The spleen not only destroys old red blood cells, but also helps to make antibodies and phagocytes
Lymph glands in the groin often swell up as the body fights an infection
Sebaceous glands in the skin ooze an oil that is poisonous to many bacteria

◀ The body's range of interior defences against infection is amazingly complex. The various kinds of white blood cells and the antibodies they make are particularly important.

DID YOU KNOW?

Your vulnerable eyes are protected by tears that wash away germs. Tears also contain an enzyme called lysozome that kills bacteria.

The lymphatic system

- **The lymphatic system** is a network of tubes that drains the fluid around the body's cells back into the bloodstream.
- **The 'pipes' of the lymphatic system** are called lymphatics or lymph vessels. They are filled with a liquid called lymph fluid that, along with bacteria and waste chemicals, drains from body tissues such as muscles.
- **The lymphatic system** has no pump to make it circulate. Instead, lymphatic fluid is circulated as a side effect of the heartbeat and muscle movement.
- **At places in the lymphatic system** there are tiny lumps called nodes. These are filters that trap germs that have got into the lymph fluid.
- **In the nodes**, armies of white blood cells called lymphocytes neutralize or destroy germs.
- **When you have a cold** or any other infection, the lymph nodes in your neck or groin, or under your arm, may swell, as lymphocytes fight germs.
- **Lymph fluid** drains back into the blood via the body's main vein, the superior vena cava.
- **The lymphatic system** is not only the lymphatics and lymph nodes, but includes the spleen, the thymus, the tonsils and the adenoids.
- **On average**, at any time about 1–2 l of lymph fluid circulates in the lymphatics and body tissues.

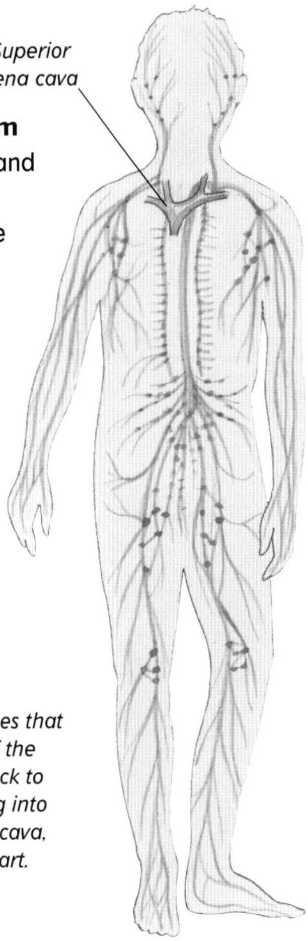
Superior vena cava

▶ The lymphatic system is a branching network of little tubes that extends to nearly every part of the body. It drains surplus fluid back to the centre of the body, running into branches of the superior vena cava, the body's main vein to the heart.

Lymphocytes

- **Lymphocytes are white blood cells** that are involved in the immune system. There are two kinds of lymphocyte – B lymphocytes (B-cells) and T lymphocytes (T-cells).
- **B-cells** develop into plasma cells that make antibodies to attack bacteria and some viruses.
- **T-cells** work against viruses and other micro-organisms that hide inside body cells, helping to identify and destroy these invaded cells or their products. They also attack certain bacteria.
- **There are two kinds of T-cell** – killers and helpers.
- **Helper T-cells** identify invaded cells and send out chemicals called lymphokines as an alarm, telling killer T-cells to multiply. Invaded cells give themselves away by abnormal proteins on their surface.
- **Killer T-cells** lock on to the cells identified by the helpers, then move in and destroy them.
- **Some B-cells**, called memory B-cells, stay for a long time, ready for a further attack by the same organism.

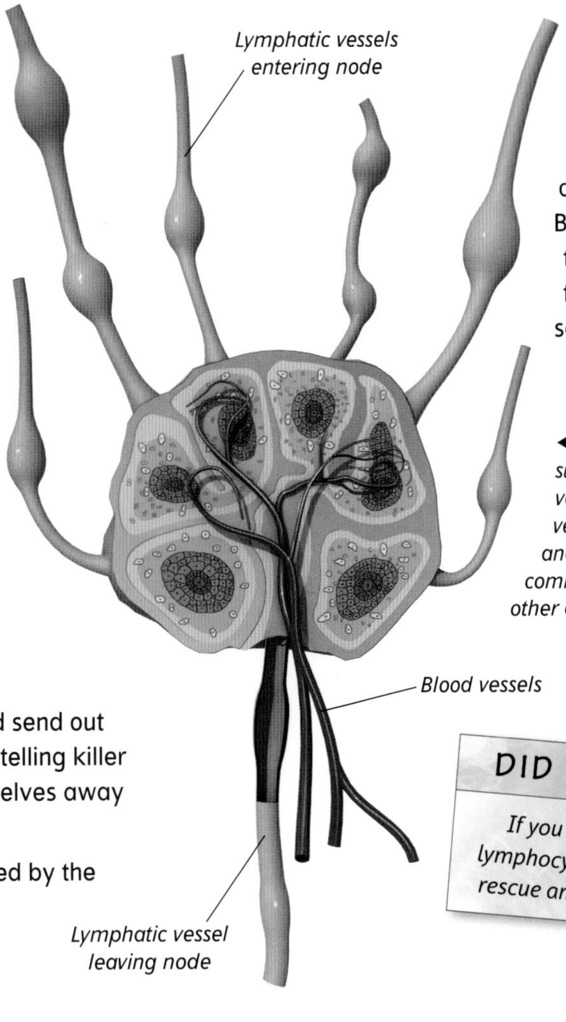
Lymphatic vessels entering node
Blood vessels
Lymphatic vessel leaving node

◀ Lymph nodes are supplied by both blood vessels and lymphatic vessels. Lymphocytes enter and leave lymph nodes, communicating with each other as they do so.

DID YOU KNOW?

If you get flu, it is your T lymphocytes that come to the rescue and fight off the virus.

Antibodies

● **Antibodies** are tiny proteins that make germs vulnerable to attack by white blood cells called phagocytes.

● **Antibodies are produced** by white blood cells derived from B lymphocytes.

● **There are thousands** of different kinds of B-cells in the blood, and each produces antibodies against a particular germ.

● **Normally, only a few B-cells** carry a particular antibody. But when an invading germ is detected, the correct B-cell multiplies rapidly to release antibodies.

● **Invaders are identified** when your body's immune system recognizes proteins on their surface as foreign. Any foreign protein is called an antigen.

● **Your body was armed** from birth with antibodies for germs it had never met. This is called innate immunity.

● **If your body** comes across a germ it has no antibodies for, it makes some and leaves behind memory cells that can be activated if the germ invades again. This is known as acquired immunity.

DID YOU KNOW?

Human beings each generate around ten billion different antibodies.

● **Acquired immunity** means you only suffer once from some infections, such as chickenpox. This is also how vaccination works.

● **Allergies are sensitivity reactions** that happen in the body when too many antibodies are produced, or when they are produced to attack harmless antigens.

● **Autoimmune diseases** are ones in which the body forms antibodies against its own tissue cells.

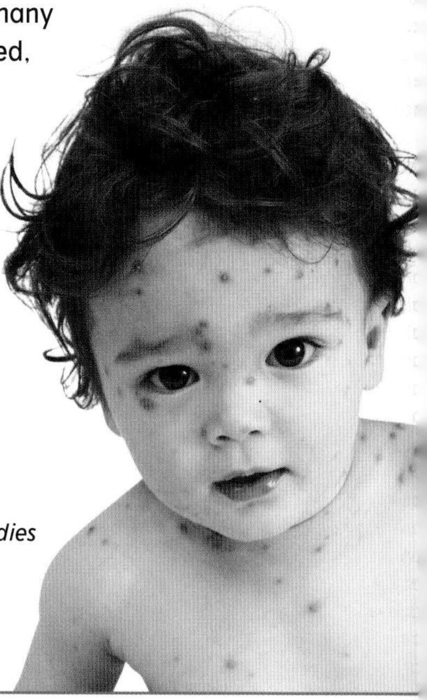

▶ *The body makes antibodies to the chickenpox virus to fight off the illness.*

Vaccination

● **Vaccination** helps protect against infectious disease by exposing you to a mild or dead version of the germ in order to make your body build up protection, in the form of antibodies.

● **Vaccination** is also called immunization, because it builds up your 'immunity' (resistance) to disease.

● **In passive immunization** you are injected with substances such as antibodies that have been made by someone exposed to the germ. This gives instant but short-term protection.

● **In active immunization** you are given a harmless version of the germ. Your body makes the antibodies itself for long-term protection.

● **Children in many countries** are given a series of vaccinations as they grow up, to protect them from serious diseases. Sometimes a number of different vaccines may be combined so that children do not have to have multiple injections.

● **If you travel abroad** you may have to have additional vaccinations against diseases that do not normally occur in your country, including yellow fever, rabies and typhoid.

● **There is a small risk** of a serious reaction against a vaccine. The risks of not being vaccinated and getting the disease are usually much greater.

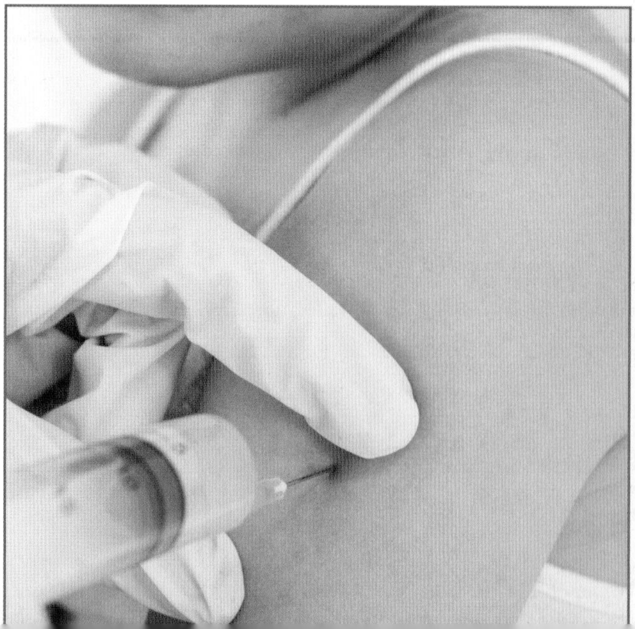

▶ *Diseases such as diphtheria and whooping cough are now rare in many countries thanks to vaccination.*

Index

ntries in **bold** refer to main
ntries; entries in *italics*
efer to illustrations.

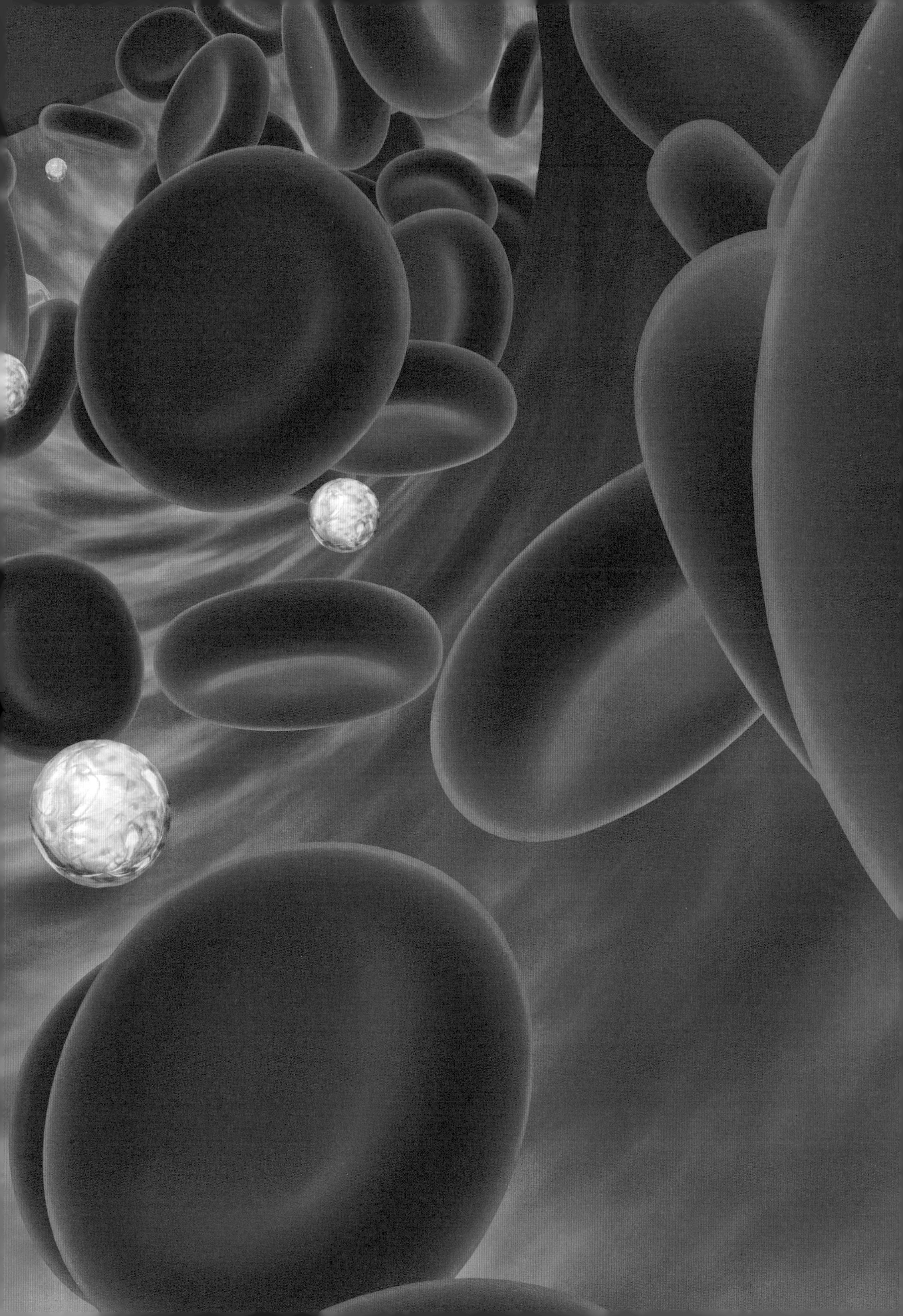

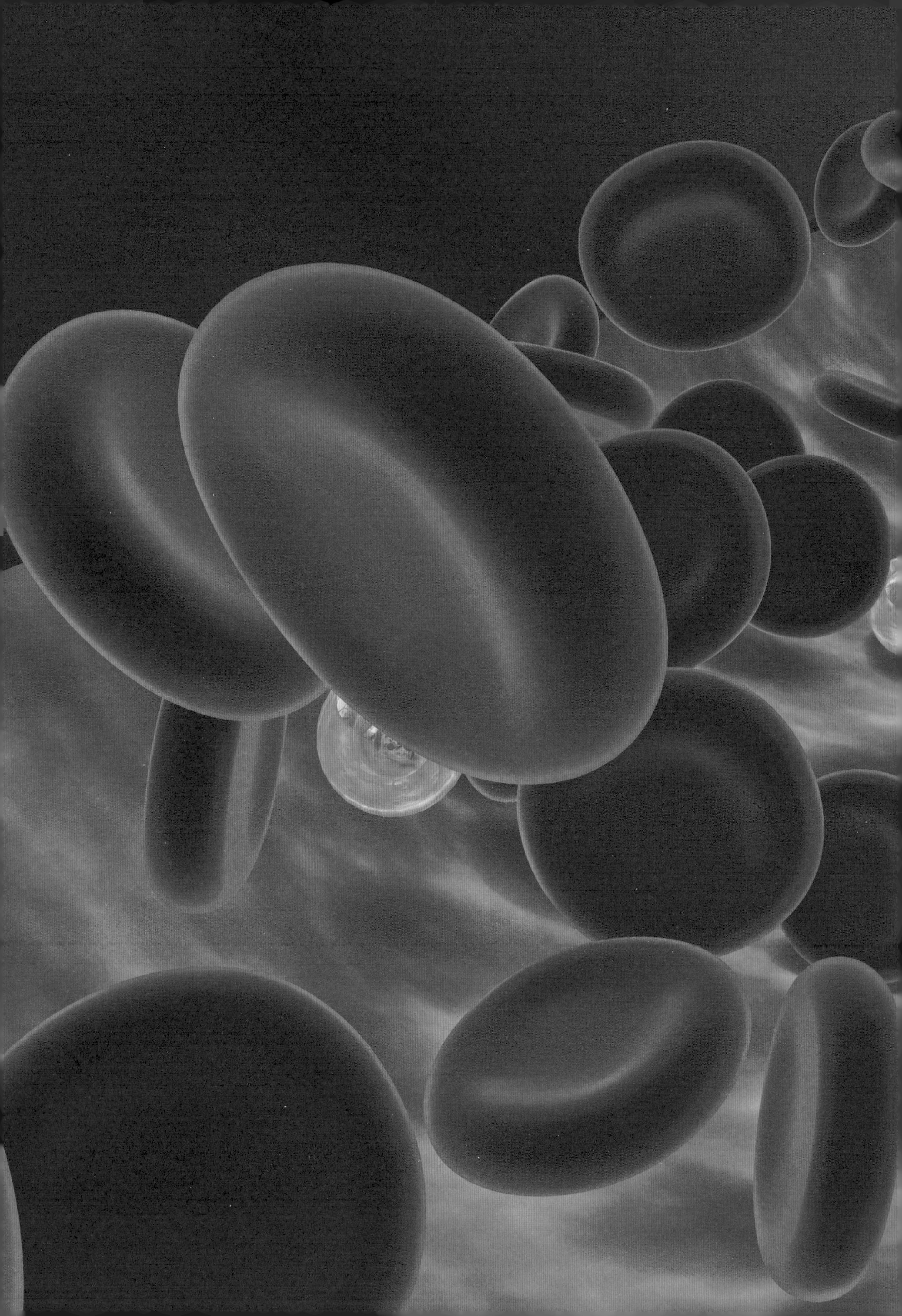